Building Modern Scotland

Building Modern Scotland

A Social and Architectural History of the New Towns, 1947–1997

ALISTAIR FAIR, LYNN ABRAMS, KAT BREEN, MILES GLENDINNING, DIANE WATTERS AND VALERIE WRIGHT

BLOOMSBURY VISUAL ARTS
LONDON · NEW YORK · OXFORD · NEW DELHI · SYDNEY

BLOOMSBURY VISUAL ARTS
Bloomsbury Publishing Plc
50 Bedford Square, London, WC1B 3DP, UK
1359 Broadway, New York, NY 10018, USA
29 Earlsfort Terrace, Dublin 2, Ireland

BLOOMSBURY, BLOOMSBURY VISUAL ARTS and the Diana logo are
trademarks of Bloomsbury Publishing Plc

First published in Great Britain 2025
This paperback edition published in 2026

Copyright © Alistair Fair, Lynn Abrams, Kat Breen, Miles Glendinning,
Diane Watters and Valerie Wright, 2026

Alistair Fair, Lynn Abrams, Kat Breen, Miles Glendinning, Diane Watters and
Valerie Wright have asserted their right under the Copyright, Designs and
Patents Act, 1988, to be identified as Authors of this work.

For legal purposes the Note on Illustrations on p. ix constitutes an
extension of this copyright page.

Cover design by Eleanor Rose | Cover image: Housing, Cumbernauld New Town,
Glasgow, Scotland, 1970 © Architectural Press Archive / RIBA Collections

This work is published open access subject to a Creative Commons Attribution-
NonCommercial-NoDerivatives 4.0 International licence (CC BY-NC-ND 4.0,
https://creativecommons.org/licenses/by-nc-nd/4.0/). You may re-use, distribute, and reproduce
this work in any medium for non-commercial purposes, provided you give attribution to the
copyright holder and the publisher and provide a link to the Creative Commons licence.

Bloomsbury Publishing Plc does not have any control over, or responsibility for, any
third-party websites referred to or in this book. All internet addresses given in this book
were correct at the time of going to press. The author and publisher regret any
inconvenience caused if addresses have changed or sites have ceased
to exist, but can accept no responsibility for any such changes.

A catalogue record for this book is available from the British Library.

A catalogue record for this book is available from Library of Congress.

ISBN:		
	HB:	978-1-3504-0170-9
	PB:	978-1-3504-0174-7
	ePDF:	978-1-3504-0171-6
	eBook:	978-1-3504-0172-3

Typeset by Integra Software Services Pvt. Ltd.
Printed and bound in Great Britain

For product safety related questions contact productsafety@bloomsbury.com

To find out more about our authors and books visit www.bloomsbury.com
and sign up for our newsletters.

Contents

Preface: Note on Authorship vi
About the Authors vii
Acknowledgements viii
Note on Illustrations ix

Introduction 1

PART ONE Architecture 23

1 East Kilbride 25
2 Glenrothes 47
3 Cumbernauld 68
4 Livingston 90
5 Irvine 111

PART TWO Life 135

6 Homes 137
7 Families 154
8 Community 170
9 Opportunity 187

Conclusion: 'Out of the Ordinary' 204

Interviewees 210
Bibliography of Published Sources 212
Index 220

Preface: Note on Authorship

In the same spirit of modernist collaboration which produced the post-war new towns, this book is credited to the whole research team to reflect the discussions which took place at our regular meetings and the extent to which team members have collaboratively developed the text.

Nonetheless, we would like to record that first drafts were produced by the team member(s) as follows, drawing on their own original research:

- Introduction and Chapter 1: **Alistair Fair**
- Chapters 2 and 5: **Kat Breen**
- Chapters 3 and 4: **Diane Watters**
- Chapters 6–9: **Lynn Abrams and Valerie Wright**
- Conclusion: **Valerie Wright**

In the cases of Chapters 3 and 4, all references to heritage issues and controversies concerning the towns, as well as specific references to Cumbernauld Town Centre, were authored by **Miles Glendinning**.

The book was co-ordinated and edited by **Alistair Fair**.

About the Authors

Lynn Abrams is Professor of Modern History at the University of Glasgow and author/co-author of numerous works on modern social and gender history, including the recent books *Feminist Lives: Women, Feelings and the Self in Post-War Britain* (2023) and *Glasgow: High-Rise Estates, Homes and Communities in the Post-War Period* (2020, with Ade Kearns, Barry Hazley and Valerie Wright).

Kat Breen, after completing a PhD at the University of Edinburgh on the post-war Scottish architects Wheeler and Sproson, was Postdoctoral Research Fellow on the Building Modern Scotland project (2021–4) at the University of Edinburgh, where she is currently a tutor in Architectural History and Heritage.

Alistair Fair is Reader in Architectural History at the University of Edinburgh. His books include studies of post-war British theatre architecture (*Modern Playhouses*, 2018) and the architects Peter Moro and Partners (2021), while recent articles have discussed the plans for the abandoned Stonehouse new town, owner-occupation in post-war Scotland, and the relationships between community, privacy and planning since 1945 in places ranging from central Scotland to Milton Keynes.

Miles Glendinning is Professor of Architectural Conservation at the University of Edinburgh, and author/co-author of books including *Hong Kong Public Housing: An Architectural and Policy History* (2025), *Mass Housing* (2021), *Scotch Baronial* (2020, with Aonghus Mackechnie), *Towers for the Welfare State* (2017, with Stefan Muthesius) and *The Conservation Movement* (2013).

Diane Watters was brought up in Cumbernauld. For more than three decades she has been researching and publishing on post-war Scottish architecture, as well as teaching and giving numerous public talks. She is the author/co-author of books including *St Peter's Cardross* (2016), *Home Builders* (2015, with Miles Glendinning) and *Little Houses* (2006, with Miles Glendinning). Her work on the present book was carried out while a Postdoctoral Research Fellow at the University of Edinburgh.

Valerie Wright from 2021 to 2023 was a Postdoctoral Research Fellow at the University of Glasgow, and is now Lecturer in Modern Scottish History at the University of Edinburgh. Her publications include several co-authored books, including *Deindustrialisation and the Moral Economy in Scotland Since 1955* (2021, with Jim Phillips and Jim Tomlinson) and *Glasgow: High-Rise Estates, Homes and Communities in the Post-War Period* (2020, with Lynn Abrams, Ade Kearns, and Barry Hazley).

Acknowledgements

This book is the principal output from a Leverhulme Trust-funded research project, 'Building a Modern Scotland: the New Towns, 1947–', undertaken between 2021 and 2024. We are extremely grateful to the Leverhulme Trust for supporting the project. We would like to thank everyone who has helped us: as interviewees, by providing access to archives, by giving permission to reproduce images and by managing the practical and financial aspects of the project.

In addition to the new oral history carried out for this project, we have drawn on interviews carried out by Barry Hazley for the earlier project 'Housing, Everyday Life and Wellbeing over the Long term: Glasgow c.1945–1975' (Leverhulme Trust, RPG 10 2014-014), and also interviews undertaken in East Kilbride in 2011 by Linda Fleming, in collaboration with East Kilbride and District Housing Association and funded by a Scottish Government First Step Award at the University of Glasgow.

We are grateful for the discussions and comments which followed conference and seminar papers in Cambridge, Dublin, Edinburgh, Glasgow, Liverpool, Nanjing and Warwick, and at Cumbernauld Doors Open Day in 2022. We were also pleased to engage with the Department for Levelling Up, Housing and Communities in the Westminster government (2022) and the All-Party Parliamentary New Towns Group (2023).

Members of the project team wish to acknowledge the assistance and support of: Grant Buttars and colleagues in the University of Edinburgh's Heritage Collections, Ewen Cameron, Rachel Collie, Luca Csepely-Knorr, Andrew Demetrius, Betony DuBock, Joss Durnan, Eve Equi, Balaji Kasirajan and colleagues at Integra, Jon Lawrence, Mindy Lynch, Colin Macilwain, Wiebke McGhee, Ros O'Cleirigh, Emma Peattie, James Thompson, David Weir and Florian Urban.

This book has been published open access thanks to the financial support of the Leverhulme Trust.

Note on Illustrations

Illustrations in almost all cases remain under copyright, as is noted in the caption to each image, and are therefore expressly exempt from the CC BY licence under which the book is published. Permission will be required from the rightsholder for any reuse.

Introduction

Between 1946 and 1973, six new towns were created in Scotland. Of those six, the development of the last – Stonehouse – was abandoned after three years, but the other five – East Kilbride, Glenrothes, Cumbernauld, Livingston and Irvine – as of 2024 together accommodate around 255,000 people, some 5 per cent of Scotland's population. Scotland's new towns were part of an international wave of planned urban construction that took place during the second half of the twentieth century.[1] Within England, Wales and Scotland, the 1946 New Towns Act inaugurated a sequence of new towns, each created by central government through a formal process known as 'designation'. The planning and construction of each new town was then overseen by an unelected public-sector body known as a 'development corporation'. Subsequent legislation built on these foundations; in 1965, the process was extended to Northern Ireland.[2] The new towns received international attention, with Cumbernauld becoming particularly prominent in the late 1960s (Figures 0.1 and 0.2).

Scotland's new towns reflected – and influenced – wider debates and practices. In particular, they shared certain conceptual and physical features (and sometimes also key personnel) with contemporaneous new towns elsewhere. Like other new towns around the world, they were planned to house, educate and employ some of the people then living in major towns and cities, thus relieving overcrowding and enabling reconstruction. Like the new towns in England and Wales, in particular, much of the housing in Scotland's new towns was designed, built and owned by the development corporations, which offered it for rent. At the same time, the Scottish new towns were the distinctive products of agendas particular to Scotland. Importantly, Scottish new towns practice was not the responsibility of London, but rather was overseen from Edinburgh by the Scottish Office, the UK government department which until devolution in 1999 had responsibility for policy affecting Scotland in areas including housing, health and education. Scotland's new towns were not only bound up with the specific need to ameliorate the very poor housing conditions found in parts of inner Glasgow but also reflected longer-rooted debates, not least about the modernization and diversification of the Scottish economy. The new towns were intended to be the places in which a new Scotland was built: architecturally, through new patterns of urban development; socially, through the provision of good housing, schools, employment and leisure opportunities; and economically, by accommodating modern jobs that would supplement or even supplant Scotland's older industries. These places were, as Guy Ortolano has argued of Milton Keynes (the largest English new town), 'the spatial dimension of the Welfare State',[3] the

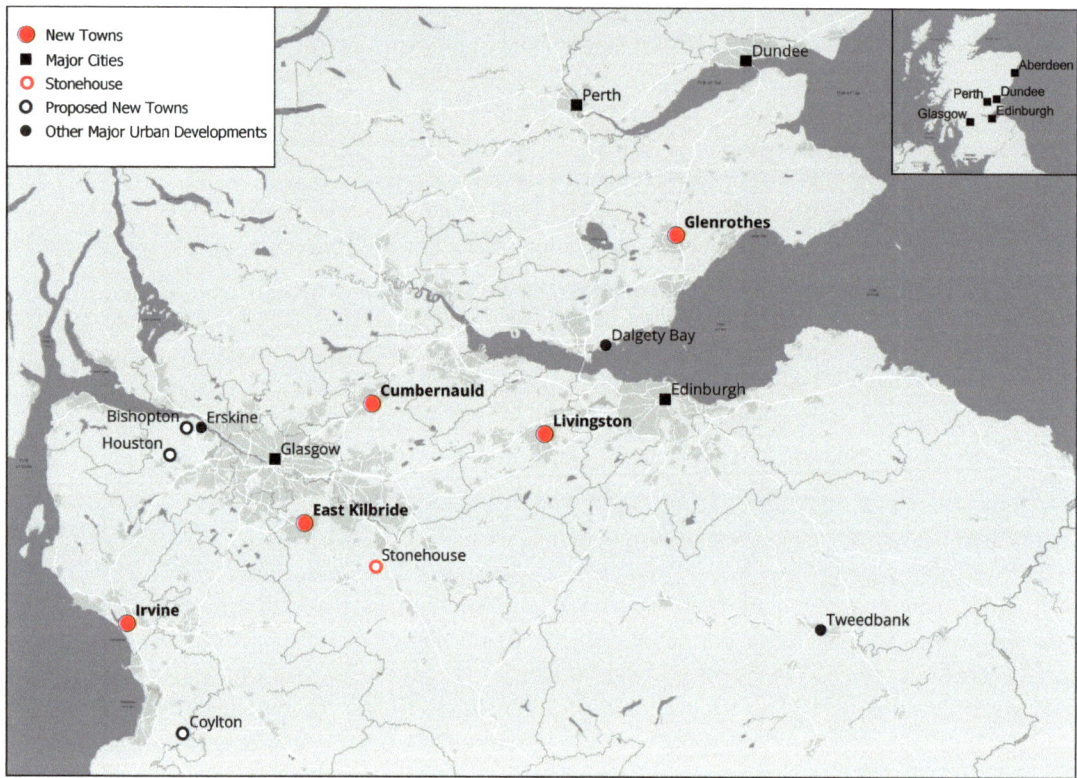

FIGURE 0.1 Scotland's new towns and other major post-war urban developments (map drawn by Kat Breen).

embodiment of the expanded public sector of the post-war decades and the representation of a belief in the power of the built environment to foster social and economic change. The new towns' transformational potential was certainly central to their appeal to early residents, who were drawn by the promise of modern housing, well-paid skilled jobs and the opportunities that their children might enjoy.[4]

The new towns attracted extensive contemporary interest from planners, architects, journalists and social scientists, were much-visited, and were featured internationally in both the specialist and the popular media.[5] They continue to attract the attention of historians. Within architectural history, Scotland's new towns loom large in surveys of post-1945 Scottish and British planning and design, and they have supplied examples for historians of diverse subjects including housing, shopping centres and churches.[6] In addition, a short but useful overview of the architecture of the Scottish new towns was published in 1997 by the planner David Cowling.[7] But it is not only historians of architecture who have studied the new towns. During the 1970s, as the new towns programme was scaled back, several more general histories appeared, in which the Scottish examples figure in a wider British context. Works by the likes of Frederick Osborn and Arnold Whittick, Hazel Evans and Frank Schaffer discuss the new towns across England, Scotland and Wales, drawing largely on published material and typically taking a positive if sometimes anecdotal view of policy and practice.[8] At the end of the 1970s, a more balanced picture was presented by Meryl Aldridge,[9]

FIGURE 0.2 Princess Margaret visits Cumbernauld (© The Scotsman Publications Ltd).

J.B. Cullingworth's substantial survey of new towns policy across Britain between the 1940s and the late 1960s represented an important early attempt to use the official archival evidence,[10] while a particularly detailed study of East Kilbride, considered from a 'policy' angle, was produced by Roger Smith.[11] A second wave of new town histories followed during the late 1980s and 1990s, coinciding with the formal winding-up of the development corporations across England and Wales, and (slightly later) Scotland.[12] These works included the *New Towns Record*, a digital compendium which brought together an unrivalled body of source material and initial analysis.[13] The last fifteen years have seen a third generation of new town histories. Alongside several surveys,[14] there have been more focused studies of examples including Skelmersdale, Runcorn, Telford and Milton Keynes, some of which explore planning themes, while others use these places' urban and social histories to consider topics such as community, deindustrialization and regional policy.[15] Among these works, Chik Collins and Ian Levitt's discussion of the impact of the new towns on Glasgow is especially relevant.[16] They have argued that the elective relocation to the new towns of skilled workers and their families represented the 'creaming off' of Glasgow's 'best tenants', leaving the city vulnerable in the present day, economically, socially, and in terms of public health.[17] Current projects-in-progress known to the authors of this book include studies of the public art of Scotland's new towns (by Andrew Demetrius), Scottish Office new towns policy and practice (by Colin Macilwain), and the planning and architecture of two of the Scottish new towns: Cumbernauld (by Diane Watters), and Irvine (by Joss Durnan).[18]

Within this context, this book innovates as an overview of the social and architectural histories of Scotland's new towns, examining the fifty years after the designation of East Kilbride in 1947 and considering these places in terms of residents' experiences as well as planners' intentions. It ends in the mid-1990s, as the Scottish development corporations were wound up, and as local government reorganization plus looming devolution changed patterns of administration across Scotland. The first part of the book comprises a topographical and architectural survey; the second engages with themes in social history. This approach allows us to address various literatures, among them the history of the British new towns programme, the history of planned post-war new towns internationally, and the architectural, social and urban histories of modern Scotland and Britain. It is our contention that the new towns should have a central place in modern Scottish history – a subject too often focused on Glasgow and Edinburgh, and on narratives of 'decline'.[19] The new towns are important for what they reveal not just about architecture and planning but also about aspirational working-class and middle-class lives, the nature of the post-war settlement as it played out in Scotland, the impact of deindustrialization, the relationship between individuals and community, the privatization of family life, changes in women's lives and social mobility. In this respect, our work engages with the arguments of scholars such as Jon Lawrence on lived community, Guy Ortolano on the welfare state, Jim Phillips et al. on deindustrialization, and Emily Robinson et al. on 'popular individualism'.[20] The Scottish new towns provide a unique context in which to explore these topics.

Questions and methods

This book asks three main questions. First, how did the new towns contribute to the project to build a modern Scotland after 1945? Although the idea of modernization was evident in the conception of new towns elsewhere, in Scotland it was allied with the growing administrative strength of the Scottish Office, and, particularly during the 1940s and 1950s, the commitment of certain officials to the new towns project. We suggest that the reimagining of the built environment was central to remaking the image and reality of Scotland in the decades following the Second World War. Scottish solutions were devised by a small group of experienced Edinburgh-based officials who remained in post for long periods, including able and committed civil servants such as J.H. McGuinness and the planner Robert Grieve, while the relative smallness of the Scottish Office, spread across just a few proximate buildings, created a tight-knit network, at least until the 1970s. The Scottish new towns became emblematic of the new Scotland being created by these technocratic elites, allied to powerful government secretaries including Tom Johnston (1941–5), Joseph Westwood (1945–7), Arthur Woodburn (1947–50) and Willie Ross (1964–70 and 1974–6) (Figure 0.3).

Our second question is: what were the ideas which underpinned the planning and design of Scotland's new towns? These places were conceived as 'a grand chance for the revival or creation of a new architecture'.[21] Their consistent visual and spatial modernity emphasized their reforming conception and was evident in contemporary housing, new public buildings, new sorts of urban space and innovative approaches to town planning which took account of rising car ownership. Architecturally, we are interested in the new towns as evidence of a 'mainstream' modernism on the one hand and more radical/theoretical ideas on the other.[22] We draw on the ideas of Sarah Williams Goldhagen, who has suggested that architectural modernism formed part of a broader discourse about what it meant to live in the modern world, being a response to modern conditions which embraced their opportunities and challenges rather than falling into revivalism.[23] Building on this argument, the decision to build new towns can be understood, in part, as a deliberate statement of intent, a comment on what Scotland was and could be. Our approach to the results understands architectural production in its wider contexts. In particular, it reflects the thinking of

FIGURE 0.3 Willie Ross (then Secretary of State for Scotland) and Sir Gordon MacMillan, Cumbernauld (© The Scotsman Publications Ltd).

historians such as Elizabeth Darling, who have productively argued for the architect to be 'de-centred' in architectural-historical analysis and have instead emphasized the creative role of a range of individuals and organizations, the importance of understanding architectural culture in a broad sense, and the lived experience of the built environment.[24] We look at the 'heroic' years of the 1950s and 1960s, but we are also interested in the ways that architecture changed during the 1970s and 1980s, as modernism was challenged and new political agendas reduced the scope of the public sector after 1979. Conceptually, our work is also shaped by recent work in the urban history of England, Scotland and Wales, in which the modern built environment is interrogated for its capacity to inform wider themes in social and political history.[25]

Third, we investigate residents' experiences of new town life and the built environment over the long term (Figure 0.4). The lives of new town residents were frequently documented by the development corporations themselves during the 1960s and 1970s, reflecting a wider context in which population relocation was a subject for the emerging social sciences. Since then, however, while contemporary housing studies research has engaged with residents' experiences in order to inform policy, there has been relatively little sustained investigation of new town life. Through oral history life narrative methodologies, we centre the experiences of those who moved to the new towns and the subsequent generations. We are interested in how people compose their narratives and the stories they tell about their lives in what were distinctive new communities, and, crucially, how these experiences changed over time.

In exploring these questions, this book has been produced collaboratively. Our approach reflects the expertise of the team members in social, urban and architectural history, and in methods including archival research, oral history and physical site survey. We have been able to use original source material not available to earlier writers; we also undertook multigenerational interviews with new town residents. As is detailed in the Preface, each chapter in this book was the work of one or two initial authors, but the drafts were then developed collaboratively. The book is accompanied by two open-access articles. One recounts, for the first time, the designation and de-designation of Scotland's last new town, Stonehouse, reflecting on what this experience reveals of the evolving character of the new towns programme.[26] It could productively be read following Chapter 5 of this book. The second article considers owner-occupation in the Scottish new towns,

FIGURE 0.4 At home in Livingston, *c.* 1970 (© West Lothian Archives and Records Centre).

offering a new interpretation not only of the new towns but also of post-war Scottish housing, and also centring the idea of the Welfare State as an enabler of opportunity.[27]

The written record of Scotland's new towns is predominantly the record of the development corporations, offering a largely top-down, policy-driven perspective. It comprises material at the National Records of Scotland, including the papers of the Scottish Development Department (SDD) and the Department of Health for Scotland (DHS). Britain-wide policy and interactions with central government in Westminster can be charted using the National Archives (London). The papers of the new town development corporations survive, though those pertaining to the former Irvine Development Corporation remain uncatalogued. These collections vary in scope but nonetheless include, in addition to official records and correspondence, publicity information, press clippings and images. Local newspapers have been especially significant not only in documenting what happened but also in capturing the views of residents through quotations and letters.

In order to interrogate the experience of residents over time we conducted life history interviews with thirty-six women and men drawn from all the new towns, spanning several generations.[28] While our interviewees represented a variety of social classes, those who responded to our call were less diverse in respect of other categories, perhaps reflecting the relative homogeneity of the new towns compared with other urban centres in Scotland. Interviews ranged across an individual's life course and were designed to gain insights into the relationship between individual experience and place or, in other words, the ways in which living and working in a new town shaped life decisions and opportunities in a rapidly changing post-war context. What is especially notable in almost all of the interviews is the ubiquity of a narrative of aspiration and opportunity – the 'new town dream' – especially in the early new towns of East Kilbride, Glenrothes and Cumbernauld. The majority of our interviewees not only recognized this overarching paradigm but deployed it to frame their memory stories. This was especially true of the first-generation residents – the pioneers – but subsequent generations also composed accounts referencing the aspiration of their parents and what we might describe as the public or official new town narrative of opportunity and modernity. This was the case despite personal stories that sometimes contradicted or challenged the new town dream. We understand that oral history accounts will often strive for composure (or coherence) and that individuals will frequently seek to align their personal experiences with public or recognizable accounts in order to narrate a life story within an externally imposed research frame.[29] Our privileging of the new town as the primary frame of reference for a diverse range of individual accounts was always likely to produce this kind of response: public versions of new town histories are rare and the new town dream narrative enables former and continuing residents to align their aspirations with a validating history, one that acknowledges their and their parents or grandparents' grasp of opportunity. And perhaps it is not surprising that this interpretive framework continues to have purchase in the present context in which new towns are no longer special and where increasingly they look and feel like any other medium-sized towns.

Running through the book are three principal arguments. The first, as already noted, relates to the close relationship between the new towns and wider goals for the modernization of Scotland – understood principally economically but also in terms of architecture and indeed image. The second is that the 'idea' of what a new town might be and do changed over time. In this respect, our suggestion is that the term 'new town' should be understood as something malleable. Our third theme is that the new towns reflect a selective, enabling state rather than one which provided universally for all. Looking at the new towns allows us to understand something of the changing characters of the post-war state and post-war society – not least by illustrating the agency of new town residents. In this way, the book highlights an aspirational, active population that hitherto has rarely figured in modern Scottish history.

Scotland's new towns: An introduction

The intellectual and philosophical roots of the post-1945 new towns are often understood to lie in the arguments of the late-nineteenth-century writer Ebenezer Howard, who called for the construction of self-sufficient 'garden cities' in co-operative ownership as a means of securing urban and social reform.[30] In Britain, Howard's ideas prompted the formation of groups such as the Town and Country Planning Association (TCPA), whose advocacy of planned urban decentralization formed an important foundation for the suite of 1940s planning legislation that included the New Towns Act. Howard's thinking also influenced Scottish examples of the early twentieth century, including the 'garden city' at Rosyth (begun 1915), the contemporaneous village built for munitions workers at Gretna and the 'garden suburb' at Westerton, north of Glasgow.[31] Yet, as Rosemary Wakeman has argued, Howard's ideas were but one influence on the new towns movement.[32] Indeed, Scotland has a long tradition of planned urbanism, taking in historical examples such as Alloa, Grantown-on-Spey, Inveraray, Ullapool and Eaglesham, as well as Edinburgh's New Town, begun in 1767. Furthermore, to see the post-1945 Scottish new towns solely in terms of Howard's ideas misses the particularities of their creation, and especially their relationship with policies intended to re-make Scotland. As Wakeman points out, urban reform was closely related to mid-twentieth-century crisis.[33]

The post-1945 new towns legislation offered a way of resolving debates which had come to the fore during the inter-war decades relating to housing, urbanism and the Scottish economy. Urban conditions in Scotland had attracted policymakers' attention since the late nineteenth century, but the key intervention came in 1917 with the Ballantyne Report, which decisively condemned the overcrowded and dilapidated housing found in parts of the country.[34] Glasgow was recognized as a particular challenge. Its population had expanded significantly during the nineteenth century, and sections of the inner city were severely overcrowded, with a preponderance of small flats lacking their own sanitary facilities. Ballantyne and contemporaries proposed new cottage-type designs, countering the Scottish urban tradition of tenement flats by advocating 'four-in-a-block' flats and semi-detached houses, arranged in low-density, 'garden suburb' layouts. The term 'house' was increasingly understood in an English sense, to refer to a type of dwelling that was not a flat, rather than its established Scottish usage for any kind of dwelling. And, as in England, Ballantyne argued that this housing should be directly built and rented out by elected local authorities, an approach to management found almost nowhere other than in Britain and which was progressively reinforced by subsequent housing acts. Glasgow Corporation, in particular, enthusiastically embraced its new role as a housing authority after 1919.[35]

The council housing programmes of the 1920s and 1930s soon prompted concern within central government, for two main reasons. First, council housing became associated with very low rents, which entrenched the power of the Labour Party in urban Scotland, and so concerned Unionist (Tory) administrations. A partial response, offsetting the dominance of council housing, was the creation by the Scottish Office in 1937 of the Scottish Special Housing Association (SSHA).[36] The SSHA's role – without parallel in England and Wales – was initially to support Scotland's post-Depression reconstruction, a task of some considerable magnitude, but the SSHA soon assumed a wider remit as a central agency, building and managing rented housing across the country. A second concern related to the design quality of recent Scottish estates, including their repetitive use of a limited range of housing types and their resulting social homogeneity. In 1935, Godfrey Collins, then Secretary of State for Scotland, told Parliament that 'drab and mean' places would never produce people with a 'bright and healthy outlook'.[37] This turn of phrase invoked wider debates about citizenship at a time when the franchise had only recently been extended. Citizenship was often understood as something active, participatory and communal – and as something which could be encouraged by the design of the built environment, the mixing of social classes and the provision of community amenities.[38] An improved urbanity was also seen as a potential element in the recovery of the nation by architects such as Robert Hurd and Alan Reiach (writing for the newly formed Saltire Society, a body dedicated to the promotion of Scottish culture).[39] In 1934, Collins created an Architectural Advisory Committee, which produced a study exploring housing design.[40] A further study commissioned by Collins examined working-class housing across Europe.[41] The DHS subsequently intervened in the choice of architect for the design of an estate at Howwood Road in the Renfrewshire town of Johnstone, seeing this project as an opportunity to set an example.[42]

In parallel with its growing interest in housing conditions and design, the Scottish Office was also adopting a more interventionist approach to the economy, partly in response to the impact of the Great Depression on Glasgow's heavy industries.[43] The 1934 Special Areas (Development and Improvement) Act led to the appointment of commissioners whose role was to promote projects that would assist in the recovery of those parts of the country which had been especially severely affected. The legislation applied across England, Scotland and Wales, but a single commissioner was responsible for Scotland, under the jurisdiction of the Scottish Office, in what was, in essence, the beginning of the Scottish Office's role in economic development.[44] Projects included new industrial estates (e.g. at Hillington in Glasgow), subsidies for industry and the construction by the nascent SSHA of housing to support economic development. In addition, new bodies were created bringing together policymakers, academics and industrialists, namely the Scottish National Development Council (1931), the Scottish Economic Council (1936) and the Scottish Council on Industry (1942); the first two merged in 1946 to create the influential Scottish Council (Development and Industry).⁴⁵ Frequently aired was the idea that unplanned industrial growth had left Scotland out-of-date and vulnerable.⁴⁶ The solution would be co-ordinated 'regional planning', an ideal which partly built on foundations laid, at the turn of the century, by Patrick Geddes, the polymath who had argued for the consideration of urban areas within their rural hinterland.

By 1939, therefore, it was well understood in Scotland that housing and industrial issues could be addressed in tandem by the state, taking advantage of the SSHA's unique position and the Scottish Office's growing strength.⁴⁷ Further attention was given to housing and industry during wartime. In particular, the Westwood Report of 1944, *Planning Our New Homes*, set out a blueprint for post-war housing design, with generous space standards (Figure 0.5).⁴⁸ Meanwhile the wartime Secretary of State, Tom Johnston, set up three regional planning committees covering the Clyde Valley, central and south-eastern Scotland, and Tayside. Johnston's aim may have been strategic, for he later claimed that he had acted to prevent the projected Ministry of Town and Country Planning (in London) from intruding into Scottish planning affairs.⁴⁹ Nonetheless, substantial and influential reports followed. That covering the Clyde Valley was co-written by a team under the DHS chief architect-planner Robert Matthew and the prominent academic Patrick Abercrombie.⁵⁰

FIGURE 0.5 Westwood Report (1944): wide-fronted terrace housing (right) in a 'mixed development' layout with flats (Crown Copyright, 1944. Contains public sector information licensed under the Open Government Licence v3.0).

Although it ultimately opted for decentralization, tenement rehabilitation within Glasgow was at least briefly considered. Planner Robert Grieve later remembered suggesting that:

> if you knocked the ends out, landscaped the back courts, and rehabilitated the better tenements, that could be an alternative [to the new towns, new estates and comprehensive redevelopment]. McGuinness's reply was that they'd talked about that already, and that the reaction of the councillors had been, 'We're no goin' to be treated like second-class citizens. We want the same thing as them down in England!'[51]

Accordingly, decentralization was advocated, as in Abercrombie's contemporaneous Greater London Plan and reflecting wider contemporary enthusiasm for new towns. The Clyde Valley Regional Plan proposed the reduction of Glasgow's population by more than 250,000 people, that is, around 25 per cent of its then total, in order to allow inner-city reconstruction for those who remained. The planners identified the villages of East Kilbride, Cumbernauld, Bishopton and Houston as places which might become new towns and thus receive some of Glasgow's so-called 'overspill' population.[52] This term – 'overspill' – was coined within planning and policy discourse in 1940s Britain to refer to the officially sponsored policy of exporting some of the population from supposedly congested cities, above all London but also Glasgow, in tandem with the imposition of green belts to curb sprawl. In this context, 'overspill' did not necessarily refer to those living in the slums, who in the case of Glasgow were often rehoused within the city's 1950s–60s Comprehensive Development Areas or on new peripherally located municipal estates (usually known as 'schemes', and typically, unlike the new towns, comprising only housing). As noted, Abercrombie's contemporaneous Greater London Plan took a similarly decentralist tone, but the Clyde Valley approach had its local advocates. In particular, Glasgow Councillor Jean Mann had set out a clear case for new towns as early as 1941, while the Scottish Office had also devoted extensive attention to the idea. Several members of the Clyde Valley planning team, indeed, were seconded from the Scottish Office, while the developed nature of their thinking on the subject explains the unusual way in which the 1946 New Towns Act covered Scotland as well as England and Wales. (More normally, given that housing policy was devolved to Edinburgh, Scotland would have been the subject of separate housing legislation.) In parallel with its proposals for population dispersal, the Clyde Valley plan was also concerned with the diversification of industry. Robert Grieve later recalled:

> It wasn't just about land use. If you took the economy first, the very strong point was made that Clydeside was so unlike those areas which were based on quickly growing modern industry – like, say, the London area, which was built upon a great mass of modern types of industry, quickly growing – whereas Glasgow was absolutely stuck in great heavy industry, which had produced the material we'd won the war with! But it was no kind of thing to be relied on after the war.[53]

The 1946 New Towns Act, passed by the post-war Labour government, thus provided a means by which the Scottish Office could apply, at ever greater scale, the ideas which it had begun to develop since the 1930s relating to housing design, planned economic development and socially mixed communities. What followed is the subject of the rest of this book, but it is worth briefly outlining the main developments here (see also Figure 0.1).

The key to the new towns was understood as 'self-containment', at least until the mid-1960s, when it was challenged by rising car ownership. The new towns would thus provide jobs, schools and shopping alongside housing, and, initially at least, residents would be required to have a job in the town to qualify for development corporation rented housing. East Kilbride, south-east of Glasgow, was quickly designated, with the DHS taking a keen interest in early developments. In July 1946, proposals were put forward for a second new town near Glasgow, based on the Renfrewshire village of Bishopton.[54] Bishopton was submitted alongside proposals for two new towns in Fife, namely Leslie-Markinch (i.e. Glenrothes) and Lochgelly-Cowdenbeath.[55] These latter proposals reflected Frank Mears's plan for central and south-east Scotland and were partly intended to support the expansion of the mining industry. However, the Treasury was unconvinced, feeling that four Scottish new towns was too great a number when understood in proportion to new town spending in England, and so, of the three proposals, only Lochgelly-Cowdenbeath was approved. It was subsequently abandoned in favour of Glenrothes, designated in 1948 (Figure 0.6). Bishopton was resubmitted at the same time, alongside proposals for a new town at Coylton in Ayrshire, but neither proceeded.[56] Although Bishopton was considered attractively sited, the opposition of the Minister of State, Hector McNeil – the MP for nearby Greenock – meant that the proposal was ultimately abandoned.[57]

At the start of the 1950s, the new towns programme was reviewed by the new Conservative government, amid a broader context which placed renewed emphasis on the potential contribution to urban development of the private sector, for ideological as well as financial reasons,[58] and which also, in England, favoured local authority-led 'town expansion' as a cheaper alternative to the new towns programme. However, the impossibility of abandoning the Scottish new towns was clear. The local authorities were financially unable to take on the new towns, and, given the strong tradition of rented housing and municipal provision in Scotland, there was little likelihood that the new towns would appeal to private enterprise in the short term. Reconstruction within Glasgow itself was now being addressed by the creation of Comprehensive Development Areas, but conditions remained more than acute enough to justify the claim that a further new town was necessary.[59] And while Glasgow had previously adopted a hostile attitude to the principle of new town construction, by the early 1950s its attitude was softening in the face of practical reality: there were simply insufficient sites within the city to provide enough new housing at appropriate

FIGURE 0.6 Early proposal by Anthony Wheeler for Glenrothes civic centre, *c.* 1949, and very much in the style of Tecton or the Festival of Britain (© Courtesy of HES, reproduced with permission from the RIAS and Fife Cultural Trust/OnFife.)

densities.⁶⁰ The designation of Cumbernauld – the only 1950s new town anywhere in Britain – was felt to be the only real option, and proposals were submitted in April 1955. Encouraged by the DHS (and in tune with wider planning fashions), a more high-density planning approach was envisaged than had been adopted at East Kilbride or Glenrothes, rejecting the separate neighbourhood units of those earlier towns for a tighter development of housing clustered around a single centre. As early as December 1955, Cumbernauld was being referred to as a 'Mark 2' new town for this very reason.⁶¹

Despite the start of work on Cumbernauld (and despite increases in East Kilbride's population target), the problem of Glasgow overspill remained pressing. Alongside the designation of Cumbernauld, the Housing & Town Development (Scotland) Act 1957 echoed English legislation of 1952 by introducing extensive subsidies for 'town expansion' schemes to accommodate further Glasgow overspill. Payments would be made between Glasgow Corporation, as the so-called 'exporting' authority, and 'receiving' authorities across Scotland who would take people from the city's housing waiting list.⁶² These 'expanded towns' lie outwith the scope of this book, but one of the most successful was in Haddington, East Lothian, masterminded from 1960 by County Planner Frank Tindall. The mainstream new towns programme, too, would soon also step up another gear. After consideration of sites in Ayrshire, attention turned to the Lothians. Livingston – set between Edinburgh and Glasgow – was designated in 1962. It was conceived as a regional centre in which thoughts of 'self-containment' were less significant in an era of growing mobility. Its plan reflected new agendas including flexibility, which generated a gridded plan, plus a desire to improve the deindustrializing landscape. There was also a new focus on facilitating owner-occupation, either through house sales or through dedicated new construction. In this respect, a target of 25 per cent owner-occupation was set for all the Scottish new towns in the mid-1960s.⁶³ This figure was half the target applied in England, reflecting the stronger Scottish tradition of renting among all social classes. At the same time, a practice known as 'social development' assumed growing significance (Figure 0.7). Reflecting the transformative ambitions which had lain at the core of the new towns

FIGURE 0.7 Community exhibition in Livingston (© West Lothian Archives and Records Centre).

programme since the early days, social development sought not only to encourage the formation of new communities but also to enable individuals to pursue their own interests.[64]

Irvine on the Ayrshire coast came next. A town which was already growing, designation in 1966 was a way to formalize and catalyse existing developments, and the plan took a fashionably polycentric approach, with a chain of new residential units strung to the east of the historic town. By this time, the Scottish new town development corporations were increasingly acting in what might be considered an 'entrepreneurial' fashion, actively courting potential employers while also maintaining a London office and producing vigorous publicity campaigns that often included vibrant promotional films (Figure 0.8). There were some conspicuous successes, and it is worth noting that, in addition to the new designations of Livingston and Irvine, the 1960s saw sustained growth in the earlier new towns, East Kilbride in particular. Yet at the same time, the expense of the new towns programme was prompting growing concern in government, by now Labour once again, and in some ways the new emphasis on owner-occupation and the increased involvement of the private sector in building the new towns, especially the town centres, were ways to reduce their cost.

The two 1960s Scottish new towns came into being alongside contemporaneous designations in England, Wales and Northern Ireland. The 1960s generation of new towns involved plans of increasing complexity and scale and, in some cases, took in towns of considerable pre-existing size. Nonetheless, this period also saw important contrasts between the Scottish new towns programme and its English and Welsh equivalent, in three key ways. First, in legislative and organizational terms, the Commission for New Towns (CNT) was created at the end of the 1950s to assume responsibility for new town assets when the local development corporation was wound up. However, the CNT's remit never extended to Scotland. Second, there was an important conceptual difference between the Scottish new towns and those in southern England, in particular, which during the 1960s were tasked mainly with providing housing and employment away from London for a rapidly growing population.[65] The difference lay in the economic function intended

FIGURE 0.8 Livingston promotional display (© West Lothian Archives and Records Centre).

for the Scottish new towns. Though economic modernization had been emphasized in Scotland from the 1940s onwards, it assumed especially distinctive significance for Scottish policymakers during the 1960s.[66] The course was set in 1961, when the Scottish Council (Development and Industry) published a well-received report on the Scottish economy, produced by a committee under Sir John Toothill.[67] Toothill proposed that priority should be given to encouraging the growth of 'industrial complexes and centres' in specific areas, chosen for their growth potential rather than their depressed status. This report not only informed the creation in 1962 of the Scottish Development Department (SDD) as a central agency for regional planning, but was subsequently taken up in Westminster, which during the early 1970s sought to apply the 'growth point' model in England and Wales.[68] A third factor specific to Scotland by the 1960s was a desire to stem the flow of out-migration to England and beyond, a flow which was not balanced by incomers.[69] The new towns were thought to be essential not only in providing skilled jobs but also desirable, modern housing. This housing, and the well-designed settings in which it and other amenities would be provided, would attract residents, potentially keeping them in Scotland, and would also encourage international businesses to invest in Scotland at a time when the image of Glasgow was felt to be off-putting and much of its housing stock was thought to be unappealing.[70] In particular,

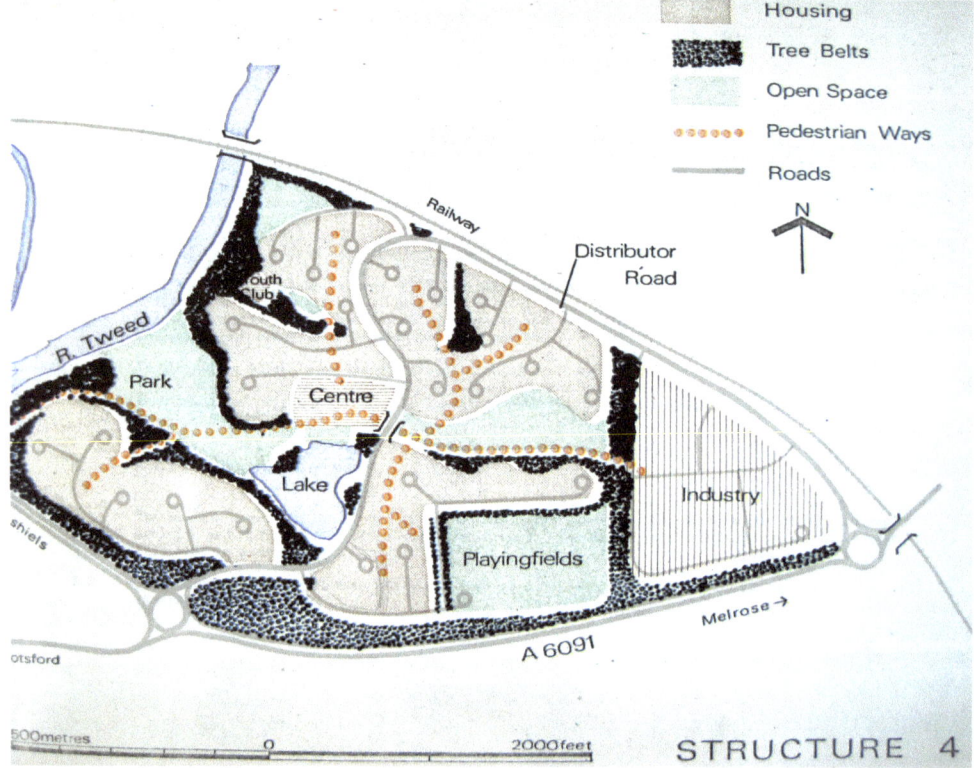

FIGURE 0.9 Tweedbank masterplan, 1969 (Scottish Borders Archive (GB1097) Ref No: SBA1210/33/6, Report prepared on behalf of the Tweedbank Working Party by the Scottish Special Housing Association, June 1969).

there was a notable lack of recently built middle-market housing; the new towns could plug this gap by offering quality rented housing (i.e. perceived as superior to other forms of public-sector design), as well as homes for sale.[71] Tenement flats – even the better specified types in middle-class areas – were perhaps also thought not to appeal to people from England or North America who were more used to individual houses, as well as those Scots tired of the communality of the shared staircase. With the entry of the UK into the European Economic Community in 1973, policymakers were acutely aware that Scotland was now competing for investment not only with England, Wales and Northern Ireland, but also other European nations.[72]

New town designations were not the only way in which new communities were brought into being in post-war Scotland. There were extensive developments for owner-occupation just beyond Glasgow's city boundary, for example in the suburbs of Newton Mearns and Bearsden, while

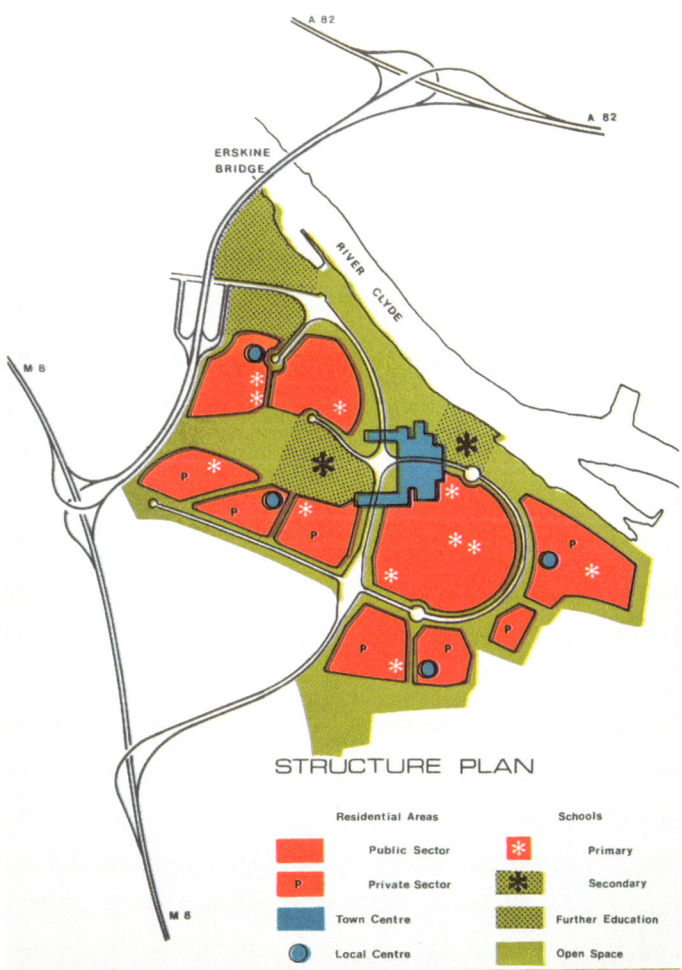

FIGURE 0.10 Erskine Structure Plan, 1970. © OneRen, the trading name of Renfrewshire Leisure Limited, managing museums' collections on behalf of Renfrewshire Council.

Dalgety Bay in Fife was essentially a mini-new town developed by the private sector.[73] There were also public-sector urban developments beyond the formal new towns programme. In addition to the 'expansion' of such places as Haddington, we might note the state-led development of the Highlands, not least as a centre for hydroelectric and nuclear power, which saw Thurso grow significantly.[74] Meanwhile, the SSHA remained a major provider of rented housing across Scotland, in developments of often considerable design and landscape quality. In particular, it became involved in two large projects in the late 1960s.[75] The first comprised 1,000 homes plus new industrial units at Tweedbank, between Galashiels and Melrose, which was approved in principle in 1967 (Figure 0.9).[76] The SSHA's second major project, Erskine in Renfrewshire, was bigger. Erskine – described as a 'new community' to differentiate it from the officially designated new towns – was planned with neighbourhood units focused on a town centre initially conceived in megastructural terms, with shops set above a dual carriageway, akin to a mini-Cumbernauld or Irvine; there was less emphasis on providing employment than in the mainstream new towns (Figure 0.10).[77] The SSHA was also involved in proposals for Maryculter, an unbuilt new village conceived in the 1960s by Kincardineshire County Council and taken forward after 1971 by the Salvesen company. David Gosling, who had led the planning of Irvine in the late 1960s, worked with Gordon Cullen to produce a layout which stressed visual experience and landscape character.[78] The proposed pedestrianized centre would have been a miniature open-air cousin of Gosling's contemporaneous shopping mall at Irvine.

The village of Stonehouse, south-east of Glasgow, was first considered in the mid-1960s for a potential local-authority/SSHA development on similar lines to Erskine, but after the 1970 election was reconceived as a new town 'proper'.[79] Designated in 1973, the last formal new town designation to date anywhere in the UK, it was to be realized by East Kilbride Development Corporation (briefly renamed East Kilbride and Stonehouse Development Corporation), though with substantially greater private-sector involvement than the earlier new towns. In a novel move which demonstrates the flexibility of the new town process and what Ortolano has termed the 'dynamic social democracy' of the 1970s,[80] as well as, perhaps, continued concern about the cost of major public-sector projects, the development corporation was understood as much as a co-ordinator as a provider, and owner-occupation was emphasized. The proposals were revised several times, with, for example, the projected size of the new town varying dramatically. The purpose of the town was also debated, with the initial justification of providing for Glasgow overspill soon being challenged by downwards revisions in population growth projections and the discovery that Glasgow's overspill needs were not so great as had earlier been imagined. Stonehouse was thus reimagined as an economic 'growth point' of the kind advocated by Toothill, and ambitious claims were made regarding employers who might locate in the town, including the Japanese car maker Nissan/Datsun. The masterplan, developed during 1974–5, was relatively straightforward, eschewing the compactness of Cumbernauld, the grid of Livingston or the polycentric form of Irvine. It located housing to the west of the M74 motorway and industry largely to the east; there were echoes of the neighbourhood unit principle, albeit in less clearly defined form. Plans for the town centre remained hazy, but there was talk of building a hypermarket (Figure 0.11).

The de-designation of Stonehouse in 1976 was not inevitable, nor was it centrally mandated.[81] Rather, following the reorganization of Scottish local government in 1975 and the introduction of a two-tier system of regions and districts, the newly created Strathclyde Regional Council under

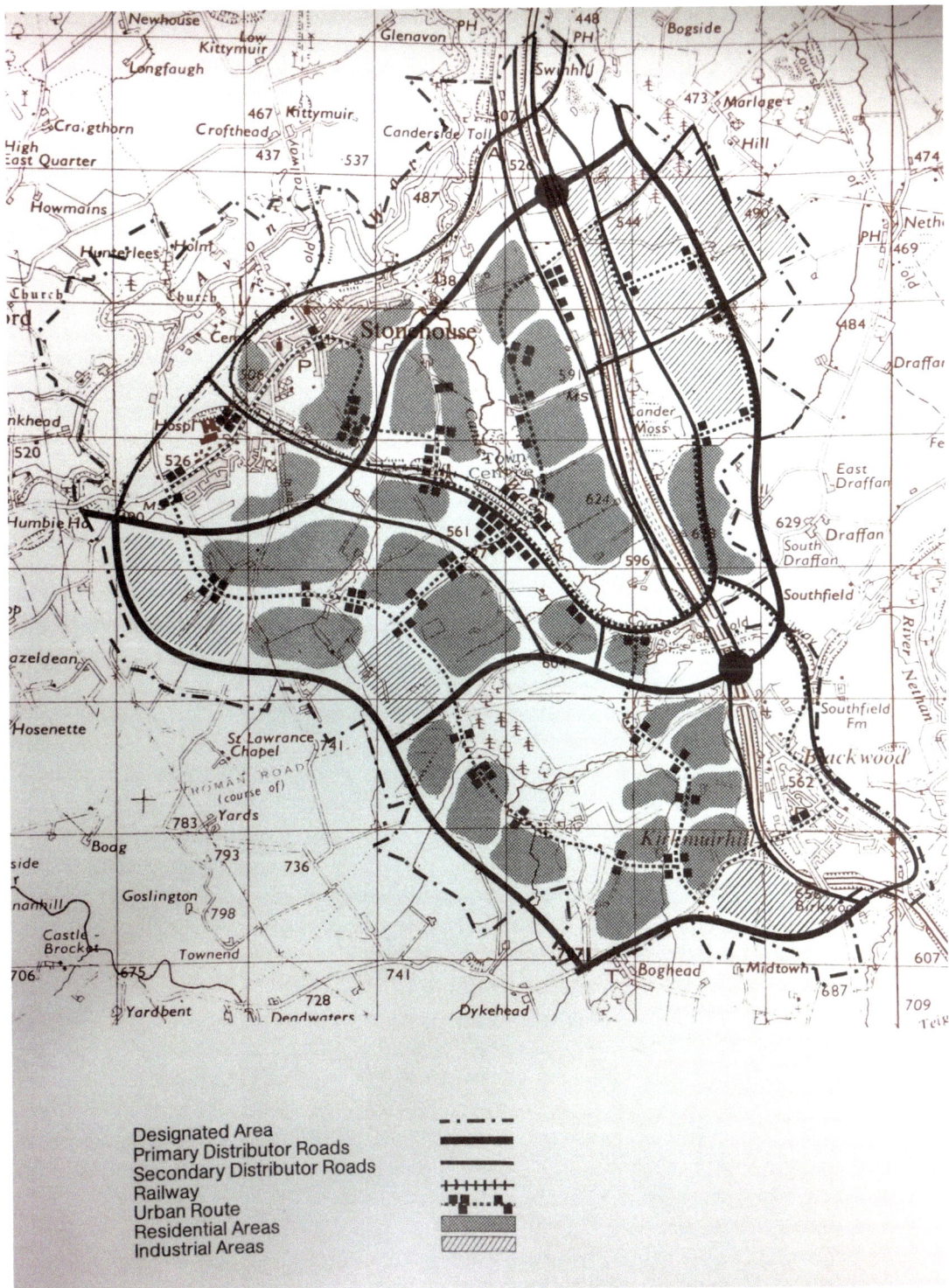

FIGURE 0.11 Stonehouse 'Basic Plan', 1975. Courtesy of South Lanarkshire Archives, and National Records of Scotland.

Councillor Geoff Shaw argued that, at a time of limited economic resources, it was better to focus on Glasgow's regeneration.[82] Strathclyde was a force to be reckoned with, taking in a swathe of west-central Scotland. Its refusal to co-operate was significant, as it controlled the provision of necessary major infrastructure (such as sewerage). The hand of the Scottish Office was forced in a way that perhaps would not have been possible with the previous, smaller units of local government. Days after the first families arrived in Stonehouse, it was announced that no further building would take place. It is perhaps ironic that the formation of Strathclyde and the other regional councils in 1975 was inspired by the same theories of regional planning which had earlier informed the creation of the new towns.

Stonehouse's de-designation marks a turning point in the new towns programme, bringing to an end the 'pioneer' days of optimistic growth. It heralded a broader retrenchment in urban policy across England, Scotland and Wales, and a new focus on inner-city regeneration at a time of economic recession. Yet while Stonehouse was dropped, the other Scottish new towns did continue – something which is often overlooked. Here the Scottish story is distinctive. Many of the English new town development corporations were wound up during the 1980s, with housing transferring to elected local government and commercial assets either folded into the CNT or sold. However, the bodies responsible for East Kilbride, Glenrothes, Cumbernauld, Livingston and Irvine all remained in place until 1996. This period was one of change. The development corporations' remit in terms of 'general needs' housing was reduced, the private sector took on greater responsibility for house construction, and 'Right to Buy' saw a growing number of homes sold to their tenants. The corporations nonetheless retained a key role in planning and building infrastructure for employment as well as housing for special groups such as the elderly. Architecturally, the results were often notable, suggesting the vitality of the social-democratic project as well as the continued quality of public-sector design. However, a further phase in the history of the new towns began in 1996 with the winding-up of the Scottish development corporations, accompanied by the abolition of the regional and district councils and the introduction of new unitary local authorities; these changes decisively removed the new towns' previous privileged status.

Scotland's new towns are at a pivotal moment. The original housing stock is ageing and its tenure has become fragmented; its design, furthermore, was based on particular assumptions relating to patterns of living and levels of car ownership. Town centres have suffered from the rise of online shopping, and there are currently proposals to reconstruct sections of central Cumbernauld and East Kilbride. Key employers have left. In these circumstances, a rounded, research-led understanding of the new towns' history might usefully inform present-day decision-making. The long-term history of the new towns could also usefully contribute to contemporary planning debates. While Scotland's current planning framework, 'NPF4', seems set against further major urban extensions or new towns, a number of projects conceived under earlier frameworks remain on site, including Tornagrain near Inverness, Blindwells in East Lothian and, more than seventy years after the site was first identified for potential development, Bishopton in Renfrewshire. Meanwhile in England there are as of spring 2024 proposals for a 'development corporation' to expand Cambridge on a scale akin to several of the 1960s new towns, while the Labour Party has called for the construction of at least two new towns.[83] The legacy of the new towns programme is thus a matter of live debate. In that context, this book offers a broad perspective, considering vision and lived experience.

Notes

1. Rosemary Wakeman, *Practicing Utopia: An Intellectual History of the New Town Movement* (Chicago: Chicago University Press, 2016).
2. 'An Overview of New Towns in Northern Ireland', *New Towns Record* (Planning Exchange CD-ROM set, 1996).
3. Guy Ortolano, *Thatcher's Progress: From Social Democracy to Market Liberalism through an English New Town* (Cambridge: Cambridge University Press, 2019), 3.
4. Valerie A. Karn, *East Kilbride Housing Survey: A Study of a New Town* (Birmingham: Centre for Urban and Regional Studies, 1970), 14.
5. To take just one example: South Lanarkshire Archives, EK9/1/11, undated German magazine clippings entitled 'Neue Städte entstehen aus den Nichts' and 'Aus den Slums hinaus ins Gründe'.
6. Surveys: Miles Glendinning, Ranald Macinnes and Aonghus Mackechnie, *A History of Scottish Architecture, from the Renaissance to the Present Day* (Edinburgh: Edinburgh University Press, 1997), 458–62 (Cumbernauld Town Centre); *Rebuilding Scotland: The Postwar Vision*, ed. Miles Glendinning (East Linton: Tuckwell, 1997); John R. Gold, *The Practice of Modernism: Modern Architects and Urban Transformation, 1954–1972* (Abingdon: Routledge, 2007), 146–64; Rob Close, John Gifford and Frank Arneil Walker, *Lanarkshire and Renfrewshire* (New Haven and London: Yale University Press, 2016), 277–99 (East Kilbride) and 232–62 (Cumbernauld, by Miles Glendinning and Diane Watters). More focused works: Miles Glendinning, 'Cluster Homes: Planning and Housing in Cumbernauld New Town', *Twentieth Century Architecture* 9: *Housing the Twentieth Century Nation* (2008): 131–46; Janina Gosseye, '"Uneasy Bedfellows" Conceiving Urban Megastructures: Precarious Public–Private Partnerships in Post-War British New Towns', *Planning Perspectives* 34, no. 6 (2019): 937–57; Diane Watters, 'St Columba's, Glenrothes: A Post-War Design Laboratory for Reformed Worship', *Architectural Heritage* 12 (2001): 66–87. See also examples from the new towns in e.g. Robert Proctor, *Building the Modern Church: Roman Catholic Architecture in Britain, 1955 to 1975* (Farnham: Ashgate, 2014).
7. David Cowling, *An Essay for Today: The Scottish New Towns, 1947 to 1997* (Edinburgh: Rutland Press, 1997).
8. Frederick J. Osborn and Arnold Whittick, *New Towns: Their Origins, Achievements and Progress* (London: Leonard Hill, 1977); *New Towns: The British Experience*, ed. Hazel Evans (New York: Wiley, 1972); Frank Schaffer, *The New Towns Story* (London: Paladin, 1972).
9. Meryl Aldridge, *The British New Towns: A Programme without a Policy* (London: Routledge, 1979).
10. J.B. Cullingworth, *Environmental Planning Volume III: New Towns Policy* (London: HMSO, 1979).
11. Roger Smith, *East Kilbride: The Biography of a Scottish New Town, 1947–73* (London: HMSO, 1979).
12. E.g. Philip Riden, *Rebuilding a Valley* (Cwmbran: Cwmbran Development Corporation, 1988).
13. *New Towns Record* (Planning Exchange CD-ROM set, 1996). The files are coded for Windows 3.1 and 95, which can make access challenging in the 2020s. See also Mark Clapson, *Invincible Green Suburbs, Brave New Towns: Social Change and Urban Dispersal in Postwar England* (Manchester: Manchester University Press, 1998).
14. Wakeman, *Practicing Utopia*; Anthony Alexander, *Britain's New Towns: Garden Cities to Sustainable Communities* (Abingdon: Routledge, 2009); Katy Lock and Hugh Ellis, *New Towns: The Rise, Fall and Rebirth* (London: RIBA, 2020).
15. Jessica Taylor, 'Cumbernauld: The Conception, Development and Realisation of a Post-War British New Town', PhD dissertation, University of Edinburgh, 2010; Ortolano, *Thatcher's Progress*; Lauren Pikò, *Milton Keynes in British Culture: Imagining England* (Abingdon: Routledge, 2019); Thomas

Szydlowski, 'Skelmersdale: Design and Implementation of a British New Town, 1961–1985', *Planning Perspectives* 37, no. 2 (2022): 341–68; Salvatore Dellaria, 'A New Town and a Numbers Game: Runcorn, Merseyside and Liverpool', *Planning Perspectives* 37, no. 2 (2022): 243–65; Otto Saumarez Smith, 'Landscapes of Hope and Crisis: Dereliction, Environment and Leisure in Britain During the Long 1970s', *Journal of British Studies* 62, no. 4 (2023): 988–1010; Alistair Fair, '"The Needs of New Communities": Social Development, the New Towns, and the Case of Milton Keynes, c. 1962–87', *Modern British History* 35, no. 4 (2024): 261–77.

16 Chik Collins and Ian Levitt, 'The Policy Discourses that Shaped the "Transformation" of Glasgow in the Later 20th Century: "Overspill", "Redeployment" and the "Culture of Enterprise"', in *Transforming Glasgow: Beyond the Post-Industrial City*, ed. K. Kintrea and R. Madgin (Bristol: Bristol University Press, 2019), 21–38. Also see Chik Collins and Ian Levitt, 'The "Modernisation" of Scotland and Its Impact on Glasgow, 1955–1979: "Unwanted Side Effects and Vulnerabilities"', *Scottish Affairs* 25, no. 3 (2016): 294–316, especially 299–300; Ian Levitt, 'New Towns, New Scotland, New Ideology, 1937–57', *Scottish Historical Review* 76, no. 2 (1997): 222–38.

17 This argument was made at the time. See 'Minister Hits at Divisive Housing Policies', *Glasgow Herald*, 11 October 1974. The Minister was of the Church of Scotland.

18 In addition, a UK-wide study of the new towns by the late Elain Harwood is understood to be forthcoming.

19 Though note e.g. Linda M. Ross, 'Dounreay: Creating the Nuclear North', *Scottish Historical Review* 100, no. 1 (2021): 82–108; Ewen Cameron, 'The Scottish Highlands as a Special Policy Area, 1886–1965', *Rural History* 8 (1997): 195–216.

20 Jon Lawrence, *Me, Me, Me: The Search for Community in Post-War England* (Oxford: Oxford University Press, 2019); Jim Phillips, Valerie Wright and Jim Tomlinson, *Deindustrialisation and the Moral Economy in Scotland since 1955* (Edinburgh: Edinburgh University Press, 2021); Emily Robinson, Camilla Schofield, Florence Sutcliffe-Braithwaite and Nathalie Thomlinson, 'Telling Stories about Post-War Britain: Popular Individualism and the "Crisis" of the 1970s', *Twentieth Century British History* 28, no. 2 (2017): 268–304.

21 Scottish Moving Image Archive, 1826, *New Towns*, 1969.

22 'Mainstream modernism': e.g. Alistair Fair, *Modern Playhouses: An Architectural History of Britain's New Theatres, 1945–1985* (Oxford: Oxford University Press, 2018), 4–5.

23 Sarah Williams Goldhagen, 'Something to Talk About: Modernism, Discourse, Style', *JSAH* 64, no. 2 (2005): 144–67.

24 Elizabeth Darling, 'Towards Narratives of Modernity *after* Reconstruction', in *Reconstruction: Architecture, Society and the Aftermath of the First World War*, ed. Neal Shasore and Jessica Kelly (London: Bloomsbury, 2022), xviii–xxv.

25 E.g. Otto Saumarez Smith, *Boom Cities: Architect-Planners and the Politics of Radical Urban Renewal in 1960s Britain* (Oxford: Oxford University Press, 2019); Alistair Kefford, *The Life and Death of the Shopping City: Public Planning and Private Redevelopment in Britain since 1945* (Cambridge: Cambridge University Press, 2022); Ortolano, *Thatcher's Progress*.

26 Alistair Fair, 'Stonehouse: Scotland's Last New Town, c. 1967–76', *Urban History* 50, no. 4 (2023): 818–39. Available via: https://doi.org/10.1017/S0963926822000281.

27 Valerie Wright and Alistair Fair, 'The Opportunity and Desire to Buy: Owner-Occupation in Scotland's New Towns, c. 1950–80', *Contemporary British History* 38, no. 2 (2024): 219–44. Available via: https://doi.org/10.1080/13619462.2023.2294972.

28 The material will be archived within the UK Data Archive.

29 Penny Summerfield, 'Culture and Composure: Creating Narratives of the Gendered Self in Oral History Interviews', *Cultural and Social History* 1, no. 1 (2004): 65–93; Lynn Abrams, *Oral History Theory* (London: Routledge, 2016), 66–70.

30 Wakeman, *Practicing Utopia*, 20.

31 Lou Rosenburg, *Scotland's Homes Fit for Heroes: Garden City Influences on the Development of Scottish Working-Class Housing, 1900 to 1939* (Edinburgh: Word Bank, 2016).
32 Wakeman, *Practicing Utopia*, 20–46.
33 Ibid., 20.
34 Glendinning et al., *History of Scottish Architecture*, 386.
35 Miles Horsey, *Tenements and Towers: Glasgow Working-Class Housing 1890–1990* (Edinburgh: RCAHMS, 1990), 11–25.
36 Tom Begg, *Fifty Special Years: A Study in Scottish Housing* (London: Henry Melland, 1987), 43–60.
37 *Hansard*, HC Deb 21 February 1935 vol. 298 c. 561.
38 A fuller discussion of this idea is found in Alistair Fair, 'Community Centre: New Housing Estates in Scotland', in *Reconstruction: Architecture, the Built Environment and the Aftermath of the First World War*, ed. Neal Shasore and Jessica Kelly (London: Bloomsbury, 2023), 119–42.
39 Alan Reiach and Robert Hurd, *Building Scotland: A Cautionary Guide* (Edinburgh: Saltire Society, 1941).
40 DHS, 'Report of the Scottish Advisory Committee on the Incorporation of Architectural Quality and Amenity in the Lay-Out, Planning and External Appearance of Houses for the Working Classes' (Edinburgh: HMSO, 1935), 3.
41 DHS, 'Working-Class Housing on the Continent' (Edinburgh: HMSO, 1935).
42 Renfrewshire Archives, Paisley: Johnstone Town Council Special Meeting, 10 February 1936. See also Fair, 'Community Centre' 134–40.
43 Jim Tomlinson and Ewan Gibbs, 'Planning the New Industrial Nation: Scotland 1931 to 1979', *Contemporary British History* 30, no. 4 (2016): 584–606 (p. 588).
44 Tom Begg, *50 Special Years: A Study in Scottish Housing* (London: Henry Melland, 1987), 57.
45 Tomlinson and Gibbs, 'Planning the New Industrial Nation', 588.
46 Ibid.
47 Ibid., 590.
48 Scottish Housing Advisory Committee [SHAC], *Planning Our New Homes* (Edinburgh: HMSO, 1944).
49 Smith, *East Kilbride*, 15.
50 Miles Glendinning, *Modern Architect: The Life and Times of Robert Matthew* (London: RIBA, 2008), 68–73.
51 Robert Grieve, interviewed by Miles Glendinning, 1987.
52 For the 62 per cent reduction in the population of the Gorbals area – which had a population density of 459 persons per acre before reconstruction in the 1960s – see Gold, *Practice of Modernism*, 178.
53 Robert Grieve interviewed by Kirsteen Borland, 1993; transcript by Miles Glendinning.
54 Cullingworth, *Environmental Planning*, 33, 39, 56.
55 Ibid., 57.
56 Ibid., 86.
57 Ibid., 56, 89.
58 Alistair Kefford, 'Global Rise of the British Property Development Sector, 1945–1975', *Past and Present* 264, no. 1 (2024): 199–235.
59 Cullingworth, *Environmental Planning*, 149–51.
60 The National Archives (London) [TNA], T227/412, 'Cabinet Economic Policy Committee – Glasgow Housing' [1955].
61 *Glasgow Herald*, 19 December 1955.

62 1957 Act: https://www.legislation.gov.uk/ukpga/Eliz2/5-6/38/contents (accessed on 30 March 2024); Miles Glendinning and Stefan Muthesius, *Tower Block: Modern Public Housing in England, Scotland, Wales and Northern Ireland* (New Haven and London: Yale University Press, 1994), 159–61.

63 For more on owner-occupation: Wright and Fair, 'Opportunity and Desire'.

64 For more on social development, albeit in an English context: Fair, 'The Needs of New Communities'.

65 Ministry of Housing and Local Government, *The South East Study: 1961–1981* (London: HMSO, 1964).

66 Tomlinson and Gibbs, 'Planning the New Industrial Nation', 594.

67 Cullingworth, *Environmental Planning*, 178–9.

68 TNA, HLG116/334, 'Growth Point Argument', November 1969 [Central Lancashire New Town]. For the SDD: Ian Levitt, 'The Origins of the Scottish Development Department, 1943–62', *Scottish Affairs* 14 (1996): 42–63.

69 'Eight Growth Areas', *Scotsman*, 15 November 1963.

70 'New Towns Launch Counter-Attack', *Scotsman*, 29 January 1974.

71 NRS, DD6/2382, First Draft Report; Second Draft Report.

72 'New Towns Launch Counter-Attack'.

73 Miles Glendinning and Diane Watters, *Home Builders: Mactaggart and Mickel and the Scottish Housebuilding Industry* (Edinburgh: RCAHMS, 2015).

74 Ross, 'Nuclear North'; Ian Levitt, 'The Creation of the Highlands and Islands Development Board', *Northern Scotland* 19 (1999): 85–105.

75 Begg, *50 Special Years*, 220–3.

76 Scottish Borders Archive, SBA1210/33/6, Report prepared on behalf of the Tweedbank Working Party by the Scottish Special Housing Association, June 1969.

77 Renfrewshire Archives, 914.1441 ER PC13865 PAM, 'Erskine New Community'; 941.41 ER, Town Centre Concept Drawing, 1973.

78 'Maryculter: A New Community Near Aberdeen. Final Report November 1974' [copy in the possession of Alistair Fair]; David Gosling, *Gordon Cullen: Visions of Urban Design* (London: Academy Editions, 1996), 101–9.

79 For a full account of the conception, planning and de-designation of Stonehouse, see Fair, 'Stonehouse', which the next two paragraphs summarize. See also Scottish Moving Image Archive, 0949, *Stonehouse: Centre for Success*, 1974.

80 Ortolano, *Thatcher's Progress*, 17.

81 Alexander, *Britain's New Towns*, 50, attributes de-designation to Peter Shore, then Secretary of State for the Environment in Westminster, but his remit did not extend to Scotland.

82 See Fair, 'Stonehouse', for the detail of this argument. The Wheatley Report of 1969 – which set out the basis of the reorganized system of Scottish local government – in fact proposed that the new towns could be transferred to the new regional authorities. This, however, did not happen. Stonehouse's de-designation followed the recommendation of the West Central Scotland Plan team that it be paused: see West Central Scotland Plan Team. *West Central Scotland – A Programme for Action* (Glasgow: WCS Plan Team, 1974).

83 'No Jet Packs or Monorails', *Guardian*, 14 October 2023, online at https://www.theguardian.com/commentisfree/2023/oct/14/no-jetpacks-or-monorails-new-towns-just-need-to-be-places-people-want-to-live (accessed on 26 October 2023).

PART ONE

Architecture

1

East Kilbride

East Kilbride offered an early post-war response to the question of what 'modern Scotland' might be: architecturally, socially and economically. In terms of the built environment, at least, the answer was modest and pragmatic. For Magnus Magnusson, writing in 1964 (and perhaps comparing the town with the avant-garde plans for Cumbernauld, then under development), East Kilbride's architecture was 'indecisive';[1] for the authors of the *Buildings of Scotland* some fifty years later, it was 'undemanding'.[2] David Cowling, however, took a more nuanced position in 1997:

> Public-sector housing in East Kilbride has never been significantly different from the architecture, design and layout that was contemporary with it. Housing in the town has generally not been about innovation but, at its best, simply being better done than other contemporary housing.[3]

While East Kilbride's low-density housing and dispersed, neighbourhood-based plan have much in common with contemporaneous 'Mark 1' new towns in England and Wales, the drive to be exemplary was significant. It casts the conception and realization of East Kilbride in a distinctive and hitherto unappreciated light, situating it within broader, reformist contexts relating to planning and architecture that go beyond its status as Scotland's first post-war new town. Designated in 1947, East Kilbride reflected particularly clearly the hope of the Scottish Office not only for a more considered approach to housing and industry but also for an improved standard of urban design and architecture – one which critiqued local-authority efforts and reflected wider battles over political authority. Indeed, it literally embodied this idea, because the Department of Health for Scotland (DHS) took a leading role in the initial plan, and senior DHS civil servant J.H. McGuinness worked closely with the development corporation. The resulting 'mixed development' of East Kilbride's neighbourhood units contrasted with Glasgow's Victorian tenement flats as well as its inter-war cottage estates; the early new town's flats and (especially) its houses, typically laid out in terraces with generous landscaping, suggested and accommodated new ways of living. This was a positive, mainstream modernism which, along with the other opportunities offered by the new town, would attract many new residents: the modern people who would forge modern Scotland.

Designation and plan

As we saw in the Introduction, the Scottish Office during the 1930s became increasingly critical of municipal and suburban housing provision in Scotland. This critique was elaborated in the likes of the Patrick Abercrombie and Robert Matthew-led Clyde Valley Regional Plan – the substantial wartime planning report which proposed East Kilbride as one of four Clydeside new towns. Post-war, the Scottish Office continued to take a sceptical view of municipal efforts; Glasgow's low-rent policies remained a bone of contention. The new towns thus offered an opportunity for reform: of rent levels, housing design and neighbourhood layout.

That East Kilbride was a critique of earlier efforts was made especially plain in the formal Designation Order, which criticized Glasgow's inter-war estates for doing little more than providing homogenous housing of apparently undistinguished design: '[an] unco-ordinated mass [...] equivalent to a new town of the size proposed for East Kilbride, predominantly of one social class, with no civic identity, practically no independent social facilities and no industry'.[4] In contrast, J.H. McGuinness hoped that East Kilbride would be 'a model for the rest of Scotland', on account of its planning and facilities, and as a socially mixed community.[5] Reference was made in the Designation Order to 'the best possible standards in such matters as industrial estate layout, the provision of houses at appropriate densities, and planned open space for recreation and amenity [...] and other community facilities'.[6] Elsewhere, inadequate facilities and commuting were thought to mean that 'individuals begin to live anything but a full life [...] their usefulness as citizens is impaired'.[7] In this respect, East Kilbride, like other new towns, embodied broader ideas about democratic citizenship, understood in participatory and communal terms, and as something which might be fostered by bodies including the state.[8]

The Scottish Office's desire to seize the initiative is also evident in the speed with which East Kilbride was begun. Work on the plan began during spring 1946, in advance of the publication in October that year of the Designation Order.[9] This early start reflected Secretary of State Joseph Westwood's enthusiasm for the new towns, as well as the close relationship between the Clyde Valley planning team and the Scottish Office.[10] McGuinness visited the site with Abercrombie and Matthew in mid-1946, while a new towns section was set up in the DHS under F.R. Stevenson, including F.J. Connell, A.B. Wylie and Maurice Brown. They took early responsibility for the plan for East Kilbride, before East Kilbride Development Corporation (EKDC) came into being.[11] DHS planner Robert Grieve walked the area and determined some working rules early on: 'No trees should be cut down. No hedges should be cut down. No woman will have to cross a main road with a pram. Houses will be set back two hundred yards from main roads.'[12]

An initial layout was published in late 1946.[13] It featured distinct, holistically conceived neighbourhood units. Neighbourhood-based planning had appeared in the late 1930s (e.g. in the MARS Group's proposals for the reconstruction of London) and was then given quasi-official sanction in Scotland, as in England and Wales, by wartime planning documents, such as the Westwood Report of 1944, *Planning Our New Homes*.[14] In East Kilbride, the total population of 40,000 was to be divided between four identifiable areas (i.e. 'neighbourhood units') of *c.* 10,000 people each, wrapped around the town centre. Each neighbourhood in turn was divided into two sub-units. Although contemporaries often invoked the idea that neighbourhood units could encourage community formation and local identities, in East Kilbride they were presented in practical terms. Echoing the recommendations of the London policeman Alker Tripp on routing through traffic away from residential areas, the neighbourhoods were to be 'precincts', divided by the town's major roads.[15] Their size was also related to school provision, with each having a non-denominational secondary school and two primary schools; further provision was made for Roman Catholic education. Local shops were to be provided, while a network of footpaths and cycleways would offer links to the town centre.

The Designation Order was subject to a public inquiry in May 1947.[16] There were objections to the loss of agricultural land, while Glasgow Corporation strongly opposed the entire idea of Scottish Office-led decentralization.[17] The inquiry nonetheless confirmed the new town designation, albeit with modifications. The built-up area was moved slightly to the south; there was also a slight increase in population density. The DHS planners accordingly revised their proposals.[18] The town centre was relocated away from the existing village and railway station, as had previously been proposed, but there were still to be four neighbourhoods (later named Mains, Westwood, Calderwood and The Murray), plus three industrial areas on the edge of the town. The DHS plan was subsequently elaborated in-house by the development corporation's team under D.P. Reay; the noted landscape architect Brenda Colvin was also involved and set out fundamental principles relating to open space and tree planting.[19] The proposals appeared in *Town Planning Review* in May 1949 before being formalized into a masterplan document (Figure 1.1).[20] In 1951, the ambition that

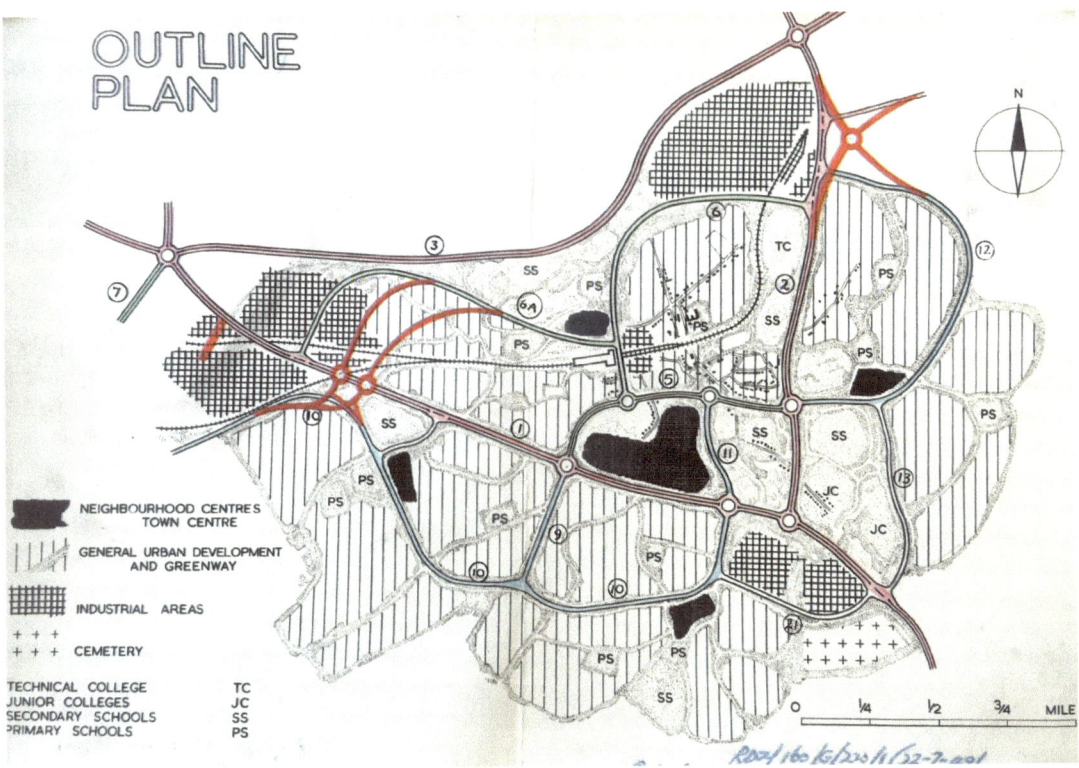

FIGURE 1.1 East Kilbride masterplan, working document of 1949. Compared with the initial layout proposed during 1946–7 by the DHS, the town centre is shown in its actual location, well south of the railway line rather than straddling it. (National Records of Scotland, DD4/2547)

East Kilbride might be exemplary was confirmed when a model of the proposals was exhibited in London at the Festival of Britain, with 'the particular function of demonstrating efficient road patterns, layout and construction'.[21]

Early neighbourhoods

Within early 1950s Scotland, the distinctiveness of East Kilbride lay not simply in its neighbourhood-based planning but also in the kind of housing that was provided. It largely comprised houses, rather than the flats typical of pre-1919 urban Scotland. These houses were laid out in 'urban' terraced arrangements, and in this respect they also contrasted with the semi-detached ('suburban') cottages of the inter-war municipal estates (Figure 1.2). The masterplan allocated around 1000 acres to housing, that is, a third of the designated area. The initial target of thirty people per acre was increased to forty following the public inquiry, in order to preserve agricultural land, though the masterplan suggested that the latter figure was 'more suitable to Scotland where closer building gives protection from the winds and where gardens cannot be used so continuously as in the South of England'.[22] The desirability of houses had been emphasized in 1944 by the Westwood committee, whose report sought to legitimize the terraced layout, as opposed to the semi-detached house or 'four-in-a-block' flat, by relating it to Scottish traditions of urban enclosure.[23] Furthermore, houses were the preference of the development corporation's first Chairman, Patrick Dollan, the ex-Lord Provost of Glasgow who had been closely involved with the city's largest estate of the 1920s, Knightswood.[24] In addition, incoming residents displayed a strong preference for houses with gardens.[25]

Despite national cuts affecting public expenditure in the late 1940s, building work began in May 1948, when development corporation board member (and long-time advocate of 'garden city' principles) Elizabeth Mitchell drove a peg into the ground.[26] The first contract, at Whitemoss in the old village, comprised sixty-eight houses to the designs of Lockhart Hudson of Hamilton.[27] Contracts were also placed for some 150 houses of 'non-traditional' construction, including Blackburn aluminium-framed houses and Weir steel houses – types chosen in the interests of speed and in recognition of post-war materials shortages.[28] Detailed designs for more conventional buildings were soon in hand for The Murray, parts of Westwood and the Nerston industrial area.[29] A pattern was established in which housing was divided into groups of 200–300 dwellings, each group comprising a range of house types plus low-rise flats.[30] This approach, typically called 'mixed development', was thought to have social value.[31] It accommodated a variety of household types, and so contrasted with the more homogenous provision of many 1920s–1930s estates.[32] It also created a more visually varied townscape than was typical of inter-war developments. Visual matters were certainly significant.[33] 'Some blocks [...] have been placed on the hillsides to break the roof lines of the smaller houses',[34] reported East Kilbride's masterplan, in a turn of phrase which echoed wider discussions at this time of the application to urban planning of picturesque landscape theories.[35] To add to the visual variety, some areas were designed in-house by the development corporation, while others were given to private architects.

Among the key early developments was a small group in East Kilbride village by Alan Reiach and Ralph Cowan, comprising flats and shops, including an octagonal bank building (Figure 1.3).[36] It embodied the kind of rational, sensitive modern design advocated by Reiach and Robert Hurd

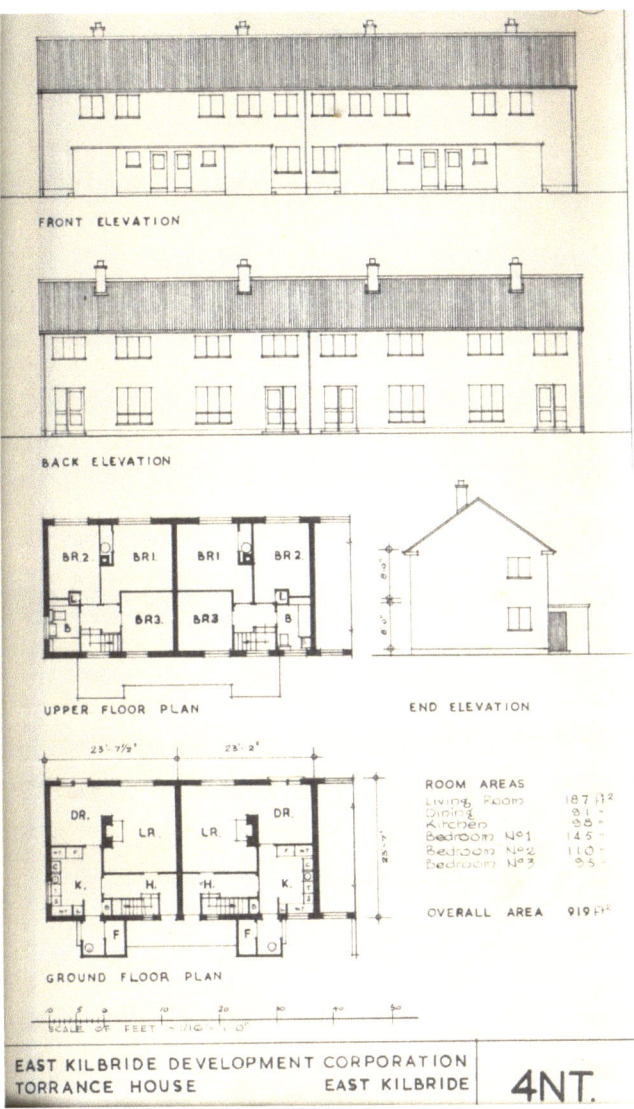

FIGURE 1.2 Wide-fronted terrace housing design, 1955, with main living rooms to rear for privacy and garden access (© South Lanarkshire Council).

in the Saltire Society's 1941 booklet *Building Scotland*. Similar thinking was evident in the first major development, the northern part of The Murray. Its layout followed the recommendations of the Westwood Report, as did the design of the houses themselves. The Murray also echoes a wartime pilot scheme for the Leven valley, designed by Reiach (who had also contributed to the Westwood committee) and illustrated in the Clyde Valley Regional Plan. The area was conceived as an integrated whole, with a sinuous arrangement of feeder roads and small culs-de-sac, and a mixture of houses, low-rise flats, shops and schools. Houses were arranged in terraces and groups, sometimes staggered in plan or set at angles to the street, suggesting an 'urban' sensibility that promised enclosure and definition to the street without denying each house its own private

FIGURE 1.3 East Kilbride village scheme by Alan Reiach and Ralph Cowan (© Crown Copyright: Historic Environment Scotland).

FIGURE 1.4 The Murray – first development (© Crown Copyright: Historic Environment Scotland).

outdoor space (Figure 1.4). A contemporaneous layout at Stuarton Park, Limekilns, demonstrates a similar approach. The two-storey houses are arranged gable-end to the street, but read as a single entity because they are connected by one-storey projections formed of stores, garages and screen walls. This was a quiet modern architecture, softened by planting and visually varied. The *Scotsman* was positive, concluding that 'modern materials and methods, allied with aesthetic sense, can have excellent results' and suggesting that the use of a range of colours on doors and rendering gave East Kilbride a Mediterranean quality.[37] The *Hamilton Advertiser* described 'a housewives' dream' with built-in wardrobes, pram stores, heated towel rail, kitchen with gas boiler and built-in cupboards. Space was certainly generous. Functions were separated, in contrast to the undifferentiated kitchen-living rooms and curtained bed recesses of older Glasgow flats. Back gardens offered space for leisure and horticulture; such was the degree of development corporation oversight that approved designs for garden sheds and fences were circulated.[38] The hope that East Kilbride might set new standards for post-war Scottish housing appeared to be well-placed. The Saltire Society in 1952 commended the design of houses at Telford Terrace in the Murray, while a 1953 award recognized nearby Freeland Lane, by Gillespie Kidd and Coia.[39]

Housing output increased significantly after 1953, especially once the corporation moved to a system of 'several works' contracting, in which a single contract was placed for each development, thus attracting larger building firms.[40] More than 1000 houses were completed in each of 1953–4, 1954–5 and 1955–6. However, although there were further awards (e.g. Stuarton Park in 1956),[41] reductions in funding posed challenges. The 1956 Annual Report noted

> the reduction or elimination of features such as porches, door canopies and so on. The use of varying roughcasts and colour wash has also been reduced. The Corporation's architects are finding it difficult to provide the interest, variety and freshness which should be apparent in a New Town.[42]

Visual interest was nonetheless not entirely lost:

> A few new house types are, however, under construction […] a 4-apartment or 3 bedroom terraced type which consists of blocks of two houses connected by a recessed link which contains for each house a general store, fuel store and access passage to the back of the house. The upper floor of the link contains the third bedroom. An alternative arrangement of the same plan places the recessed link between individual houses, giving in elevation a series of connected gables which give variety to the street picture.[43]

The pace of completions picked up again in the mid-1960s, with 1345 houses ready in 1964–5 and 1486 in 1967.[44] In 1968, the corporation reported that its 1433 completions was the highest number of any of Britain's new towns, for the fourth year running.[45]

As befitted their holistic conception, each neighbourhood was intended to have shopping facilities. In Mains the spreading form of the neighbourhood led to the construction of several small clusters of shops, while in Calderwood a central precinct, located in a natural valley, was to be complemented by a minor group of shops on the northern fringe of the neighbourhood. The Murray's centre was the first to be completed (in two phases, 1954 and 1959), with flats above shops (Figure 1.5).[46] Later centres, in neighbourhoods further from the town centre, were yet more comprehensive. Calderwood, for example, offered seventeen shops, a surgery, library, rent

FIGURE 1.5 Murray Neighbourhood Centre (© South Lanarkshire Council).

office, optician, photographer and watch repair shop,[47] while Westwood's 'more sophisticated' centre was planned in 1964 as a pedestrian precinct including offices, a church, hall and pub.[48]

Other focal points were provided by schools, which were designed in many cases by private-sector architects, notably Basil Spence's practice in the case of Duncanrig High School (Figure 1.6). Community centres were slower to arrive, on account of tight budgets and the need for local-authority co-operation; the first purpose-built centre opened in the mid-1960s in The Murray.[49] Churches, too, formed visual landmarks as well as being important social centres. By 1957, ten were in use; other religious groups met in halls and meeting rooms.[50] Further churches followed, keeping pace with the expansion of the town; among the most recent Church of Scotland examples are Mossneuk (1991) and Westwood (1993).[51] The most prominent (and celebrated) of the early churches was St Bride's, built between 1960 and 1963 for a Roman Catholic congregation to the designs of Gillespie Kidd and Coia. A chunky, apparently windowless box of rough red brick, originally complemented by a campanile, it quickly attracted critical acclaim – as well as local attention, being dubbed 'Fort Apache' on account of its inscrutable character (Figure 1.7).[52] Architect Jack Coia quipped in response that he remembered Fort Apache 'from the Shirley Temple film' as a strong, well-built structure.[53]

FIGURE 1.6 Duncanrig High School (© Courtesy of HES (Spence Glover and Ferguson Collection)).

FIGURE 1.7 St Bride's Church. The tower (left) was demolished in the early 1980s (© Crown Copyright: Historic Environment Scotland).

Later neighbourhoods

The masterplan for East Kilbride was not conceived in terms of flexibility in the way that would characterize later new town plans, such as Livingston. However, it proved adaptable. The population target was increased several times and by 1960 stood at 70,000.[54] By this date, formal 'overspill' agreements with Glasgow had been signed, using the subsidy provisions of the 1957 Housing and Town Development (Scotland) Act. Although much of East Kilbride's population could be understood as Glasgow overspill, the latter city would now take a more formal role in encouraging migration among those on its housing list.[55] The planners' response was to add further neighbourhood units. An initial extension area was identified east of the town, potentially housing around 23,000 people.[56] Developed after 1963 and named St Leonards, it included low-density areas intended for higher-rent housing/owner-occupation (including one-off designs) as well as housing at rent levels similar to the earlier neighbourhoods. The neighbourhood centre, begun after 1969, innovated by being a single building, with its shops (provided by the private sector) all located under one roof.[57] New emphasis was placed on pedestrian/vehicle segregation. Accordingly, 'Radburn' layouts were favoured, with housing accessed from the front via a footpath, while traffic routes, parking and garaging were placed to the rear. This approach was increasingly applied elsewhere in the town.[58] It accorded with the recommendations of the recent government report *Traffic in Towns* (the Buchanan report), and recognized the rapidly increasing number of cars on the road. Indeed, particular attention was, by the mid-1960s, being given in East Kilbride to parking and garaging, although it was anticipated in 1965 that the number of garages might in future be reduced, as, somewhat optimistically, it was hoped that modern cars were less likely to corrode than their predecessors.[59]

Design-wise East Kilbride's 1960s housing was not unlike that of the 1950s (Figure 1.8). Nonetheless, specifications were updated with, for example, the widespread installation of

FIGURE 1.8 Housing at St Leonards, *c.* 1970 (© South Lanarkshire Council).

central heating, while timber cladding plus flat and monopitch roofs added visual variety. The key innovation was in multi-storey housing, with a first tower block of 'executive' flats (featuring full central heating, double glazing and coloured bathroom suites) opening in 1967. With more than 1000 potential tenants showing interest,[60] further blocks followed. The provision of these flats reflected the long-held goal to achieve a 'balanced community'. Earlier attempts to build what was often described as 'managerial' housing had faltered due to the high rates that were chargeable,[61] but by the 1960s lower-density, higher-rent housing was being constructed in several of the neighbourhoods.

In 1966, to accommodate further overspill as well as growing demand for housing from the children of first-generation residents, a study was commissioned from the Jack Holmes Partnership by the Burgh Council, which was then expecting to take over planning the town during the 1970s, when it was projected that the development corporation's work would be complete.[62] A seven-phase scheme for expansion to the south was prepared, accommodating up to 25,000 people.[63] It was, however, the corporation rather than the council which implemented these plans, building the Greenhills neighbourhood after 1970, as well as a further industrial area, named Kelvin. The corporation – which had started to lose staff in the late 1960s in anticipation of wind-up – had in effect been granted a reprieve by the decision in 1970 that its staff would also plan the then-projected Stonehouse new town.[64] In its layout, Greenhills reprised the precinctal approach of the earlier neighbourhoods, though densities were higher and full Radburn planning was abandoned in favour of a more intricate layout of courts and culs-de-sac. The site was exposed to moorland winds and had poor ground conditions, so housing was clustered into groups sheltered by natural undulations, with small gardens. The neighbourhood centre – at the intersection of various pedestrian routes, reached via a dramatic timber bridge – was developed by the corporation and included a supermarket as well as smaller shops and a library.[65] Similar principles shaped later 1970s layouts at Whitehills and Newlandsmuir, by which time East Kilbride was following other new towns by incorporating art and sculpture throughout its new estates and at major junctions, with work by designers including Stan Bonnar and Wendy Taylor.

Owner-occupation was encouraged from the late 1950s, as post-war austerity eased, private-sector housebuilding numbers increased more generally, rates reform made it more advantageous, and the 'never had it so good' consumer boom developed.[66] Sites for the construction of one-off owner-occupied houses were made available across the town, not least in Thorntonhall, where the grounds of a large house falling within the designated area (but detached from the new town proper) were developed as a village of executive housing; half the plots had been sold by 1962.[67] In addition, owner-occupier developments were begun. Wimpey, for example, was building at Birniehill and Calderwood by the end of the 1950s, though the development corporation – used to strict control of its own estates – was sometimes critical of the standard of their designs.[68] Opportunities were provided for tenants to buy their homes, well in advance of the 'Right to Buy' of the 1980s, while during the 1960s homes falling vacant in certain areas were sold rather than re-let.[69] While the vast majority of houses remained rented, East Kilbride's early encouragement of owner-occupation is notable, suggesting an interpretation of the public sector as an enabler rather than simply a 'provider' – a role which it would subsequently embrace in the changed political and architectural context of the 1980s. Residents, meanwhile, might be understood in this reading as 'consumers' as much as citizens, both in making the choice to move to the new town and then, for those who bought, also in their house purchase. In this respect, East Kilbride presents an early example of the 'consumer citizenship' seen by the historian Alistair Kefford in the Parker Morris report on housing design in England and Wales of 1961.[70]

The nationwide moratorium after 1980 on the construction by the public sector of 'general needs' housing meant that the baton was passed to private-sector builders. The 1985 Annual Report noted new owner-occupied developments at Newlandsmuir (McLean Homes), Whitehills VI (Whelmar), Brancumhall (Laing), Gardenhall (Wimpey) and Mount Cameron Drive (Bellway).[71] Although some 'general needs' rented developments did follow later in the decade,[72] the corporation's enabling role was now well-established, as the example of the Northern Extension Area (Stewartfield) makes clear:

> This unique venture in public authority-private developer co-operation will mean in physical terms the development of a community the size of Lanark, a substantial expansion to what is already the sixth largest town or city in Scotland, and in social terms will create a well-rounded community offering an even wider range of housing opportunities to our second generation and incoming families.[73]

Visually, houses of the 1980s and 1990s were increasingly eclectic in style, with red brick coming to dominate and more overtly 'historicist' motifs appearing, in common with developments across central Scotland (Figure 1.9).[74] It is nonetheless notable that the 'neighbourhood' idea persisted as a practical planning device, albeit in transformed fashion: Stewartfield's centre is a large supermarket. The completion of Stewartfield meant that by 1996 more than 29,000 houses had been built, 23,500 of them by the development corporation. After a gradual increase in sales to tenants during the 1970s (reaching 21 per cent by 1979), sales picked up following the 1980 'Right to Buy', with nearly 70 per cent of homes being owner-occupied in 1996.[75]

FIGURE 1.9 Owner-occupied housing, late 1980s (© James Gardner).

Town centre

Construction of the town centre did not begin until the mid-1950s, but the design of this area was an early focus. Like the neighbourhoods, the town centre was to be a new kind of urban space, derived from international best practice and offering a new model for post-war Scotland. Initial newspaper reports were illustrated with a drawing of a lively pedestrianized street with shops and flats, 'a comprehensive civic centre' with a 'recreational centre [...] based on one in Copenhagen'.[76] In the earliest plans, the projected town centre was located to the north of its eventual site. In the same way as the neighbourhoods brought together a planned mix of functions, it was conceived in integrated terms. Early drawings show a shopping precinct laid out on symmetrical, formal Beaux-Arts lines, akin to the wartime proposals for central Coventry and Plymouth, with a nearby 'social and recreational area'; there would also be offices, a large cultural centre and a health centre.[77] This integrated approach reflected wider debates. In the years around the Second World War, the term 'centre' was often understood, on the one hand, as an individual, multi-functional building dedicated either to the physical, social or cultural reform of the individual (e.g. health centres, community centres, arts centres) or to efficient urban governance (the civic centre).[78] At an urban scale, meanwhile, the town centre (or core) was conceived as a rationally planned district, efficiently combining civic and commercial functions. The individual would become an active, informed member of democratic society through visiting and using the centre (at both scales). East Kilbride's town 'centre' was thus to be made up of buildings called 'centres', each of which had a specific and important role. Similar thinking is evident in a later version of the plan, more informal in character, which was illustrated by *Town Planning Review* in spring 1949 (Figure 1.10). Next to an L-shaped grouping of shops and a market hall were to be a church, arts centre, community centre and health centre.

Further plans were prepared during 1950–1; there is a tantalizing drawing of 1952 by Basil Spence which shows a colonnaded, multi-level structure with cheerful striped awnings.[79] However, as in the new towns in England (and as was typical of town-centre redevelopment across Britain), the practical and financial challenges of keeping this sort of project within the public sector soon became apparent, and so, with the 1950s Conservative government keen to encourage private enterprise, a commercial developer was appointed.[80] A revised design of 1955 comprised thirty shops, with space being left for a town hall, central library, cinema and hotel (Figure 1.11). Two blocks were begun in 1956, with Harold Macmillan opening the scheme in May 1959.[81] Initially, the shops were arranged along a conventional street – Princes Street, its name perhaps evoking Edinburgh's eighteenth-century New Town – but very quickly this area was remodelled as a pedestrian precinct, leading to Princes Square, where shops were set below an office tower. Although reflecting the pattern of developments in such places as Coventry and Stevenage, which pioneered pedestrian planning in England, the tendency to compare East Kilbride to more far-flung examples persisted, with the press referring in 1963 to Scandinavian and American precedents.[82]

The town centre quickly proved a commercial success, attracting not only residents but also shoppers from further afield (Figure 1.12).[83] The development corporation noted that some shopkeepers had reported significant increases in their takings since moving to the centre, and some had leased space in preference to 'congested and expensive sites in Glasgow'.[84] Rising levels of car ownership meant that East Kilbride town centre could be understood as a wholly

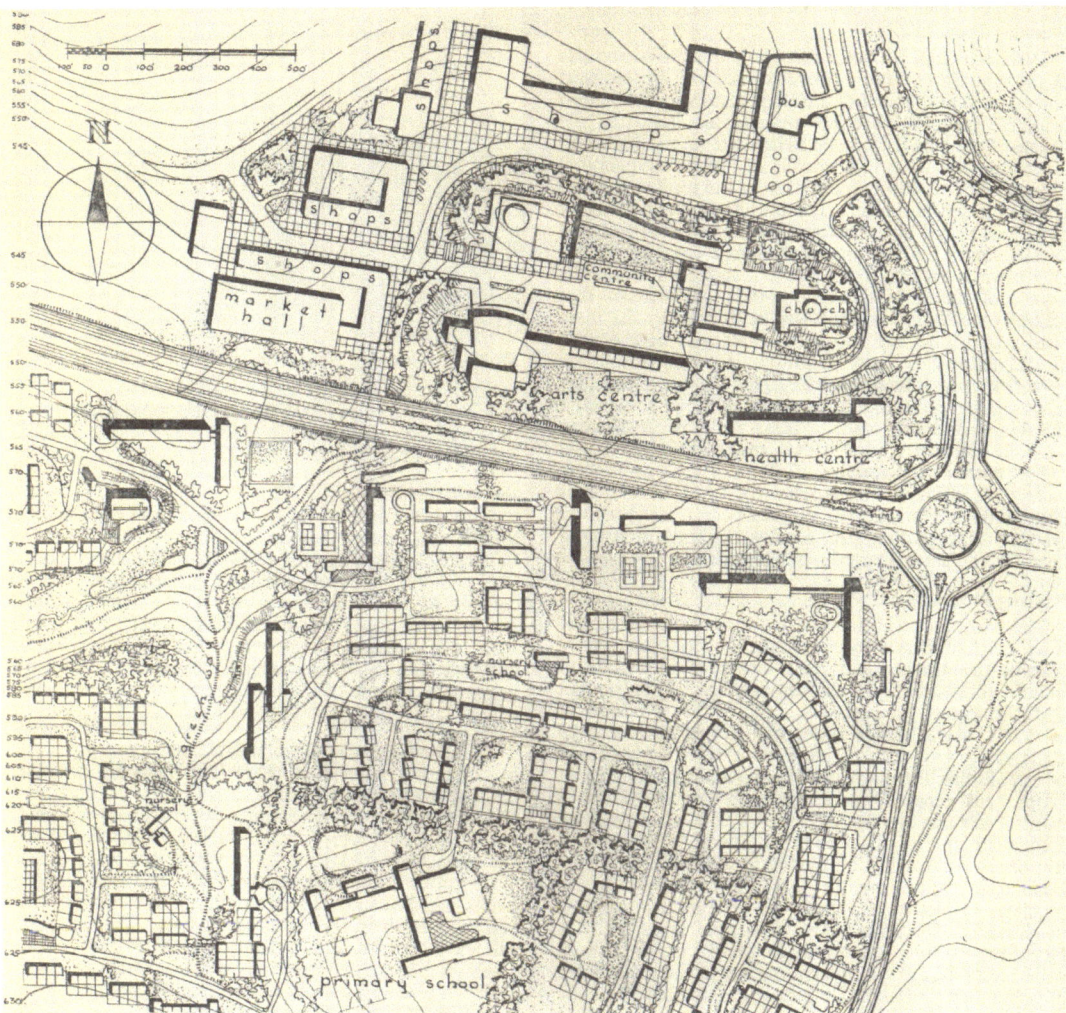

FIGURE 1.10 The 1949 layout for the town centre, with a collection of 'centre' buildings. To the south, the housing is varied in type and laid out in clusters, rather than following the street pattern (Authors' collection).

new kind of urban environment, 'based as it is on the modern American concept of an out-of-town shopping centre with vast car parks and vehicle-free pedestrian precincts'.[85] Similarly transatlantic thinking – and continued evidence of a search to re-fashion urban space – was certainly clear in the next phase of expansion. Reportedly modelled on Yorkdale Plaza in Toronto, planned from 1965 and opened in 1973–4, the Plaza Centre provided more than 7000 square metres of under-cover, air-conditioned shopping as well as an office tower and multi-storey car park.[86] Evidently this kind of indoor shopping was a hit, because by the end of the decade proposals were being developed to enclose Princes Street,[87] with the always ebullient development corporation claiming in 1981 that East Kilbride would be the 'only town in Britain with a totally covered and temperature-controlled

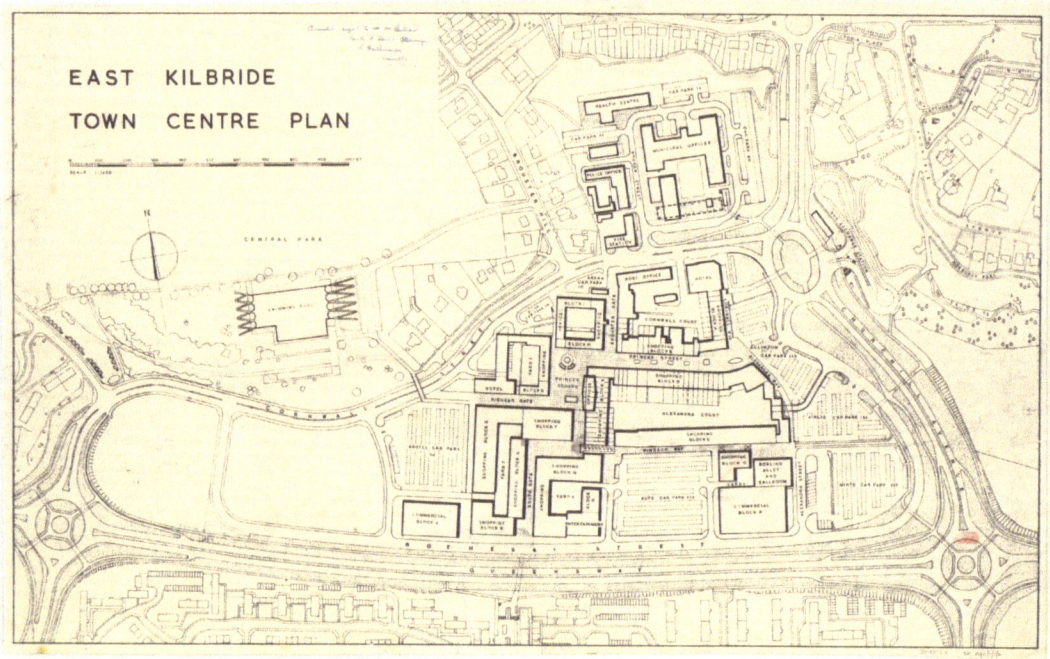

FIGURE 1.11 Town centre layout c. 1965 (© HES, Alexander Buchanan Campbell and Partners Collection).

FIGURE 1.12 East Kilbride town centre, late 1960s (Collection of Miles Glendinning).

town centre complex of this size'.[88] By then, proposals were also being prepared for a further phase of construction, including an ice rink, cinema and library: 'the aim was to project an image for East Kilbride as a thrusting and vigorous community.'[89] Official approval came in August 1981, and in 1983 Corporation members toured facilities in the United States.[90] Subsequently named the Olympia, after the town's former bowling alley and disco, the new centre was completed in 1990, receiving the Premier Award of the International Council of Shopping Centres (Figure 1.13).[91] At the start of the twenty-first century, a further phase ('Centre West') delivered yet more shops, while the out-of-town Kingsgate retail park offered alternative facilities.

FIGURE 1.13 Olympia Shopping Centre, c. 1990 (© South Lanarkshire Council).

As with the masterplan as a whole, the town centre demonstrated an ad hoc, evolutionary approach. Princes Street – architecturally modern but initially conventional in planning terms – gave way first to a pedestrian precinct and then to various styles of enclosed mall. Though novel as urban spaces, there is a pragmatism which contrasts with the later attempts in Cumbernauld or Irvine to re-think the town centre as a multi-functional megastructure. Yet ambition was hardly absent. The development corporation's boosterism was to be expected, but international parallels, aspiration and novelty permeated contemporary discussions. In the mid-1960s, for example, Reo Stakis' Norfolk Restaurant offered a cocktail bar, Ercol chairs and bold colours; a 'new-style licensed grocer' emphasized its delicatessen rather than general groceries; the Queensway pub had a Spanish theme and welcomed women in all its bars; the Bruce Hotel was conceived as a luxury venue.[92] Safeway – breathlessly described as 'an American company' – was reportedly interested in East Kilbride town centre for one of its first Scottish sites.[93] The new types of urban space offered by central East Kilbride evidently offered new possibilities.

While retail dominated, the growing population also needed public buildings: the Post Office (by the Ministry of Works) in 1958–60, the Fire Station (1959–61) and the Police Station (1963–4). The civic centre of 1968, by F.C. Scott, was intended in its concrete cladding and bold forms to convey the gravitas appropriate to local government, distinct from the commercial structures that surrounded it. The designers suggested the aim was a 'strength of character which would lift it above the glass-fronted commercial premises which abound today and have a certain anonymity', possessing 'an authority appropriate to a building of government'.[94]

East Kilbride's most significant town-centre public building, the Dollan Baths of 1968, reflects a similar search for a new image of public architecture, as well as a new emphasis on leisure (Figure 1.14). Initial provision for recreation had been patchy. The development corporation had only limited powers, while the elected local authorities, which could fund community buildings, were occupied with the construction of schools and were averse to providing community rooms in these buildings owing to the difficulties of management as well as the demand for school places.[95] And while Patrick Dollan in 1955 reported that 'East Kilbride is very much alive socially', noting more than fifty clubs and societies and high levels of library membership,[96] he had earlier commented that many residents appeared content to stay at home.[97] The lack of provision meant that there were complaints of 'malaise'; questions were asked in the House of Commons at the end of 1958.[98]

FIGURE 1.14 Dollan Baths (© HES, Alexander Buchanan Campbell and Partners Collection).

The promotion of East Kilbride to burgh status in 1963 (and large burgh in 1968) was significant, especially because housing – typically a key function of local government in twentieth-century Scotland – was largely the responsibility of the development corporation, allowing the local authority to focus its attentions elsewhere. In 1959, Councillor Matt McDonald called for 'one central building which will knit the town [...] the best swimming pool in Scotland'.[99] His comments prefigured the Dollan Baths. Its elevated site – next to the town centre – and its dramatic concrete arches – designed by Alexander Buchanan Campbell – made a highly visible statement of the place of leisure in the new town. The official brochure issued at the opening of the baths highlighted its ambitious conception, referring to the desire for 'a building of distinction' and noting that it had been inspired by continental European models, including the work of Pier Luigi Nervi: 'the fact that a lead was taken from European architect, both structurally and from the point of view of environment, could only be described as a reaction against the traditional methods of designing swimming pools in this country.'[100] Next door was the Key Youth Centre, also by Campbell. Judith Hart, the local MP, echoed earlier reformers in suggesting in 1963 that 'the young person needs to establish relationships outside the home within a congenial and good environment', in so doing dovetailing personal development and 'improving' space.[101] The Youth Centre was to be a home for the town's youth organizations as well as a place for socializing, being planned to be 'gay and welcoming, and sophisticated in the modern idiom' – a turn of phrase that perhaps could have been applied to the town as a whole.[102]

Employment

The provision of employment – not least in engineering and light industry – was core to the purpose of the new town. East Kilbride was conspicuously successful from the outset. Early arrivals included ICI, Schweppes, and Standard Telephones and Cables. Rolls Royce, which already had plants in Glasgow and Blantyre, built a large factory for aero engines, while the government's Mechanical Engineering Research Laboratory was drawn initially by space at Thorntonhall, which would be available until a purpose-built facility could be constructed near Birniehill.[103] By the mid-1950s, Rolls Royce employed more than 3000 people, over one-third of the town's total labour force at that date.[104] These initial successes led to a rapid take-off, prompting concerns that the provision of housing was not keeping pace with the creation of jobs – an important consideration, given that housing was offered to those with employment in the town.[105] The development corporation innovated with the provision of 'nest' factories for small firms, built in advance of known demand, with similar 'advance' provision made for larger enterprises.[106]

Though often architecturally unremarkable, the new factories were clearly distinct from their Victorian forebears in Glasgow in their contemporary appearance and improved facilities, offering a new type of working environment, and new types of work for women and men. The initial industrial areas at College Milton and Nerston were followed by a further estate begun in the late 1960s at Kelvin, on the south-eastern edge of the town, where Motorola opened a major electronics plant at the start of the 1970s, creating 2000 jobs.[107] Just as a 'balanced community' was desired in housing, so too did the corporation aim to attract a range of jobs. The Inland Revenue centralized its Income Tax processing for Scotland in East Kilbride in the mid-1960s, providing employment for 1000 office workers in a move which, it was suggested, would help change the image of central Scotland.[108] By 1975, East Kilbride had a higher proportion of white-collar workers than any other town in Scotland, a proportion which increased further at the end of the decade when the Ministry of Overseas Development announced that it was to build new offices at Hairmyres.[109] Designed by the development corporation, the building opened in 1981.[110]

East Kilbride's 1960s expansion reflected the 'economic growth point' theories set out by policymakers at the start of the decade, notably in the Toothill report, in which the new towns were to be a particular focus for investment.[111] This idea soon lost its force, but the development corporation continued to display an entrepreneurial attitude when it came to 'selling' the town to employers. A 1965 brochure asserted that 'East Kilbride is Open for Business', offering a unique blend of 'prosperity, markets and labour supply', a 'rapidly growing consumer market', high standards of living and the chance to 'make leisure hours happy hours'.[112] The pace of salesmanship ramped up after 1969, when George Young became the managing director. Young, previously chief executive of the Scottish Council (Development and Industry), undertook numerous international tours, while advertisements were regularly placed in the press, with evident success.[113] In 1984, for example, it was reported that more industry had been attracted into East Kilbride during the previous twelve months than in any year since designation.[114]

During the early 1980s, with the design and delivery of new 'general needs' housing having been suspended, the construction of industrial premises assumed particular prominence, emphasized by the appointment in 1983 of James Barrie as Head of Architecture; his expertise in the design of industrial estates was noted.[115] New emphasis was placed on design quality, moving away from the more functional approach of earlier industrial buildings. A key project from 1981 onwards was the 'hi-tec [sic] campus' at Peel Park, described as 'a totally new concept in industrial design' whose well-designed buildings would be located within a high-quality parkland landscape in order to attract (and reflect) a new generation of high technology employers with a strong image of efficient modernity (Figure 1.15).[116] Peel Park – along with similar 'prestige' developments at Kelvin Park and Nerston Park – reprised aspects of the development corporation's unbuilt proposals for Stonehouse new town, which had included well-landscaped employment areas (see Figure 10.1), and placed East Kilbride at the vanguard when it came to the construction of 'business parks'. Similar thinking was evident in 1995 when the Inland Revenue vacated the town centre for a

FIGURE 1.15 Peel Park, *c.* 1994, with sculpture by Wendy Taylor of 1987 (© South Lanarkshire Council).

well-received new building (by Building Design Partnership) on the western edge of the town.[117] A low-rise complex, faced in brick, naturally ventilated and organized around an atrium, the new 'Centre One' reflected emerging interest in low-energy design. In this respect, it (and Peel Park) appealed to the well-established idea that East Kilbride could be both a pragmatic example of best practice and a glimpse of the future.

Conclusion

As it looked towards wind-up, the development corporation's 1990 Annual Report trumpeted its achievements, referring to its 'ability to deliver economic and social objectives and at the same time match the commercial objectives of the business world'.[118] This tone was to be expected, a defiant response to impending dissolution as well as an appeal to the Thatcherite emphasis on the private sector. Yet others came to similar conclusions. The *New Towns Record* in 1995 catalogued East Kilbride's economic and social successes, noting that it was sought after by Glasgow commuters: the antithesis of 'self-containment', but evidence of its desirability.[119] That desirability extended to business, too: the corporation's 1969 Annual Report referred to 'the fastest growth point in Scotland'.[120] Later, East Kilbride was distinctive among British new towns in routinely generating a financial surplus.[121]

The development corporation's choice of words in 1990 also shows how the conception of East Kilbride had fundamentally changed. It had been conceived as something essentially paternalistic, a critique of local-authority provision married to ideas of improved design, reformed citizenship and the redistribution of population and industry. By the 1990s, it was a dynamic force, its target now the private sector, which it was able to match (or even outpace) in delivering an environment that compared well with national and international precedents. Its modernism, at least until the 1980s, embedded it within the wider project of modernization. MP Judith Hart in 1963 dubbed East Kilbride 'a product of the new age of science and technology [...] a fine example of modern economic and architectural planning'.[122] In this context, the corporation was an enabler, providing new opportunities for individuals and families, businesses and industry, and Scotland as a whole. Its story – and the built environment it enabled – reveals how the new town 'idea' changed.

Notes

1. Quoted in Maurice Brown, 'The Planning of East Kilbride, 1946–1951', unpublished MS in the possession of Miles Glendinning.
2. Rob Close, John Gifford and Frank Arneil Walker, *Lanarkshire and Renfrewshire* (New Haven and London: Yale University Press, 2016), 288.
3. David Cowling, *An Essay for Today: The Scottish New Towns, 1947 to 1997* (Edinburgh: Rutland Press, 1997), 24.
4. Department of Health for Scotland [DHS], *New Town at East Kilbride* (Edinburgh: HMSO, 1947), 2.
5. National Records of Scotland [NRS], SEP15/75, J.H. McGuinness to H.T. MacCalman, 16 November 1946.
6. DHS, *New Town*, 12.
7. East Kilbride Development Corporation (EKDC), Annual Report 1947–48 [South Lanarkshire Archives, EK1/5].
8. E.g. Elizabeth Darling and Alistair Fair, '"The Core": The Centre as a Concept in Twentieth-Century British Planning and Architecture. Part One: The Emergence of the Idea', *Planning Perspectives* 38, no. 1 (2022): 69–98.
9. Roger Smith, *East Kilbride: The Biography of a Scottish New Town, 1947–1973* (London: HMSO, 1979), 27.
10. Ibid., 19; Elizabeth Mitchell, *The Plan That Pleased* (London: Town and Country Planning Association, 1967), 27–8.
11. Brown, 'East Kilbride', 6.
12. Robert Grieve, interviewed by Miles Glendinning, 1995.
13. *Hamilton Advertiser*, 16 November 1946.
14. Scottish Housing Advisory Committee [SHAC], *Planning Our New Homes* (Edinburgh: HMSO, 1944).
15. Alker Tripp, *Town Planning and Road Traffic* (London: Edward Arnold and Co., 1942).
16. Smith, *East Kilbride*, 19–22.
17. Andrew Gibb, 'Policy and Politics in Scottish Housing since 1945', in *Scottish Housing in the Twentieth Century*, ed. Richard Rodger (Leicester: Leicester University Press, 1989), 155–83 (pp. 159–61); Mitchell, *Plan That Pleased*, 27–8.
18. Smith, *East Kilbride*, 27.
19. EKDC, Annual Report 1950; Mitchell, *Plan That Pleased*, 33, 38. Colvin's engagement was, however, short-lived, and many of her ideas were not fully enacted.
20. 'The New Towns: No. 4, East Kilbride', *Town Planning Review* 35, no. 5 (May 1949): 158–60; NRS, DD4/2547, 'The Master Plan – Explanation of Proposals'.
21. EKDC, Annual Report 1951.
22. 'East Kilbride', *New Towns Record* (Planning Exchange CD-ROM set, 1996) [*NTR*].
23. SHAC, *Planning our New Homes*, 57, 86.
24. Brown, *East Kilbride*, 53.
25. EKDC, Annual Report 1954.
26. Mitchell, *Plan That Pleased*, 33.
27. EKDC, *East Kilbride: A Story of Success*, 31 [uncat. report of 1987 at East Kilbride Library].

28 EKDC, Annual Report 1949; Scottish Moving Image Archive, 6844, 'Town of Tomorrow', dir. Stanley Russell, 1954.
29 EKDC, Annual Report 1949.
30 NRS, DD4/2547, 'The Master Plan – Explanation of Proposals'.
31 Nicholas Bullock, *Building the Post-War World: Modern Architecture and Reconstruction in Britain* (London: Routledge, 2002), 164.
32 Smith, *East Kilbride*, 35.
33 Mitchell, *Plan That Pleased*, 38.
34 NRS, DD4/2547, 'The Master Plan – Explanation of Proposals', para 64.
35 E.g. Thomas Sharp, *Oxford Replanned* (London: Architectural Press, 1948).
36 'Shops and Flats', *Architects' Journal* 116, no. 2992 (3 July 1952): 16–20.
37 'New Town Types: Social Groupings Emerge at East Kilbride', *Scotsman*, 10 May 1955.
38 See Residents' Handbooks archived at EK Central Library.
39 EKDC, Annual Reports 1954, 1955.
40 Smith, *East Kilbride*, 60.
41 EKDC, Annual Report 1956; EKDC minutes, 31 December 1955 [copy at EK Central Library].
42 EKDC, Annual Report 1956 (para 17).
43 Ibid.
44 EKDC, Annual Report 1967.
45 EKDC, Annual Report 1968.
46 Smith, *East Kilbride*, 131.
47 Ibid.
48 Ibid.
49 EKDC, Annual Reports 1954, 1961.
50 EKDC, Annual Report 1957.
51 Close et al., *Lanarkshire and Renfrewshire*, 297.
52 'Fort Apache', *Scottish Daily Express*, 14 April 1965.
53 Ibid.
54 Smith, *East Kilbride*, 37–45.
55 Ibid., 39.
56 EKDC, Annual Report 1962.
57 EKDC, Annual Report 1969.
58 EKDC, Annual Report 1964; 'Development Plan for St Leonards', *East Kilbride News*, 24 February 1967.
59 EKDC, Annual Report 1965.
60 'Cheers – on the 15th floor', *East Kilbride News*, 15 July 1966.
61 EKDC, Annual Report 1957.
62 Smith, *East Kilbride*, 45–8.
63 'East Kilbride Plan Extension', *Herald*, 18 August 1966.
64 NRS, SEP15/733, 'Redeployment of Glasgow Population', 27 November 1970.
65 EKDC, Annual Report 1973; Close et al., *Lanarkshire and Renfrewshire*, 291.

66 See e.g. EKDC Minutes, 8 September 1964 [copy at EK Central Library].
67 EKDC minutes, 23 February 1962.
68 EKDC, Annual Report 1957; EKDC minutes, 26 July 1958.
69 EKDC minutes, 20 September 1966.
70 Alistair Kefford, 'Housing the Citizen-Consumer in Post-War Britain: The Parker Morris Report, Affluence and the Even Briefer Life of Social Democracy', *Twentieth Century British History* 29, no. 2 (2018): 225–58.
71 EKDC, Annual Report 1985.
72 EKDC, Annual Report 1988.
73 EKDC, Annual Report 1985.
74 Miles Glendinning and Diane Watters, *Home Builders: Mactaggart and Mickel and the Scottish Housebuilding Industry* (Edinburgh: RCAHMS, 2015), 177.
75 EKDC, Annual Report 1996.
76 'First of the New Towns', *Evening Dispatch*, 25 October 1946.
77 *Hamilton Advertiser*, 16 November 1946.
78 Darling and Fair, 'The Core, part 1'.
79 EKDC, Annual Report 1951; Louise Campbell, Miles Glendinning and Jane Thomas, *Basil Spence: Buildings and Projects* (Edinburgh: RCAHMS, 2007), 305.
80 EKDC, Annual Report 1955.
81 EKDC, Annual Reports 1957, 1960.
82 *Glasgow Evening Times*, 30 April 1964.
83 EKDC, Annual Report 1964.
84 Ibid.
85 Ibid.
86 EKDC, Annual Report 1965, 1973.
87 EKDC, Annual Report 1980.
88 EKDC, Annual Report 1981.
89 *East Kilbride News*, 20 March 1981.
90 EKDC, Annual Reports 1981, 1983.
91 EKDC, Annual Report 1991.
92 *East Kilbride News*, 3 April 1964; *Scottish Grocer and Provision Trader*, 3 July 1965; *Scottish Licensed Trade News*, 28 April 1967; *National Guardian*, 16 September 1967.
93 EKDC minutes, 27 July 1962.
94 'East Kilbride's Civic Centre', *Scotsman*, 11 July 1968.
95 NRS, SEP15/193/59, memo by JJ Farrell, 10 April 1963.
96 'East Kilbride Amenities', *Scotsman*, 11 May 1955; see also SEP15/264, 'Community and Recreational facilities in New Towns' – 16 September 1959.
97 *National Guardian*, 30 June 1951.
98 NRS, SEP15/264, 'Notes of Meeting held on December 4th' [1959]; SEP15/193/46B – written question from Patrick Maitland in Commons, 1 December 1958.
99 'They Want More Fun and Games in East Kilbride', *Glasgow Evening Citizen*, 6 November 1959.

100 'Official Opening of the Dollan Baths', 27 May 1968. Copy at East Kilbride Central Library.
101 NRS, SEP15/264, 'Youth Problems in East Kilbride'.
102 NRS, ED27/515, 'Draft Brief to Architect'.
103 'East Kilbride', *NTR*.
104 Ibid.
105 Ibid.
106 Ibid.
107 Ibid.; 'Motorola to Set Up New Plant in Scotland', *Financial Times*, 18 April 1969.
108 'Tax Headquarters for E. Kilbride', *Herald*, 27 July 1963; 'More office work for Scotland', *Herald*, 31 August 1963.
109 SLA, EK9/7, 'East Kilbride Goes to Town'; 'Corporation Can Start Building', *East Kilbride News*, 13 April 1978.
110 EKDC, Annual Report 1982.
111 Smith, *East Kilbride*, 49.
112 SLA, EK 9/22, 'East Kilbride: Open for Business'.
113 'Projecting New Town', *Herald*, 5 March 1969; 'Whistlestop Tour of America for Mr Young', *East Kilbride News*, 14 August 1970.
114 EKDC, Annual Report 1984.
115 *East Kilbride News*, 1 September 1983.
116 *East Kilbride News*, 17 October 1987; SLA, EK9/7/8, 'Peel Park Campus'.
117 Brian Edwards, 'Building Study', *Architects' Journal* 201, no. 7 (27 April 1995): 34–5.
118 EKDC, Annual Report 1990.
119 'East Kilbride', *NTR*.
120 EKDC, Annual Report 1969.
121 EKDC, 1988 Development Plan review.
122 Matt Macdonald, *East Kilbride History and Guide* [1963], n.p.

2

Glenrothes

Glenrothes was designated in 1948, a year after East Kilbride. Perhaps even more than East Kilbride, its origins and history embody particularly clearly the idea that the new towns might serve as vehicles for – and representations of – the modernization of Scotland. Glenrothes was conceived in ambitious terms as a centre for the expansion of the coal mining industry in Fife, a move which was intended to take up the slack created as the older Lanarkshire coalfield was wound down. Mining itself was given a new image: the new colliery buildings, overseen by architect Egon Riss, contrasted in their monumental concrete modernism with the more ad hoc quality of older mining infrastructure (Figure 2.1).[1] Meanwhile the new town, located within a rural setting, promised a new urbanity and a sense of experiment, architectural and social, that is sometimes overlooked. As we shall see, the notion that the Welfare State might be an enabler of opportunity was implied from early in the new town's history, and some of the planners' ideas looked ahead to themes which would become commonplace in the 1960s. Yet this experimental approach had its limits. John Gifford, writing in the late 1980s, thought Glenrothes 'undistinguished'.[2] Similarly, at the opening of a 1970 exhibition, it was suggested:

> The criticism has sometimes been made that Glenrothes is not 'advanced' in the sense that Cumbernauld is supposed to be 'advanced'. Our reply to this is that our philosophy over all the years that we have been building the town has been quite simply that it will be a prosperous place that people will like to live in. […] however clever the planning may be, it is the quality of life lived by the residents that makes the town.[3]

Such a perspective chimes with the kind of pragmatic, positive 'mainstream modernism' which we have already encountered in East Kilbride.

It was not only in its conception that Glenrothes tells the story of a 'modern Scotland'. Industrial change – a hallmark of Scotland's post-1945 experience – came suddenly and dramatically to the town. During the 1960s and 1970s, Glenrothes experienced a dramatic shift from 'heavy' industry (i.e. mining, albeit 'modern' mining) to electronics and computers. The development of Rothes Colliery progressed slowly, prompting proposals to scrap the new town early in the 1950s; indeed, building operations were suspended in the middle of the decade.[4] The hiatus was temporary, but, amid technical difficulties, the colliery closed in 1962. Subsequently, a new focus on accommodating Glasgow overspill was accompanied by a revised masterplan, presented at the

FIGURE 2.1 Rothes Colliery (© RIBA Collections).

time as almost the 're-starting' of the new town, with new assumptions about planning, traffic and housing. Glenrothes, boosted by a vibrant publicity campaign, became known during the 1980s as part of Scotland's 'Silicon Glen'. Here, then, is a clear example of the flexibility of the 'new town idea', as is explored in the following discussion, which considers the evolving masterplan as well as the town's housing and central areas, and its public architecture.

Initial visions, c. 1948–60

Glenrothes was, like East Kilbride, the product of the post-war emphasis on planning – regional planning in particular. In May 1946, the Secretary of State, Joseph Westwood, identified Fife as a potential location for new towns, primarily to serve the coal industry though with an eye on industrial diversification.[5] Two locations – Lochgelly-Cowdenbeath and Leslie-Markinch – were considered; the latter became Glenrothes.[6] These proposals were formalized in Frank Mears's 1948 *Regional Survey and Plan for Central and South-East Scotland*, the 'east of Scotland' counterpart to the Clyde Valley Regional Plan, which was discussed in Chapter 1 and the Introduction.[7] Covering the Borders, the Lothians and Fife, Mears proposed that the Fife region be developed with urban 'constellations' combining existing and new settlements, a significant idea which though clearly indebted to Ebenezer Howard's vision of a network of linked new towns nonetheless echoed avant-garde interwar proposals for polycentric linear cities; it also anticipated the multi-centre new towns proposed in the late 1960s in Scotland and England (discussed in Chapter 5 of this book). The Leslie-Markinch area was of particular interest to the newly formed National Coal Board (NCB), which had in mind the creation of a 'megapit' employing around 4300 miners.[8] Arthur Woodburn, Westwood's successor as Secretary of State, argued in 1948 that there was to be 'almost another industrial revolution' which would shift coal production from the west to the east of Scotland.[9] The aim was a new town population of 30,000, with a balance between mining jobs and other forms of employment.[10]

As was also the case in East Kilbride, the new town's location was much debated.[11] Vocal objections came from the National Farmers Union and the local paper mills, and involved concerns about the loss of productive farmland and disruption to the supply of water.[12] Markinch was proposed as an alternative core for the new town, paralleling the way in which East Kilbride was to grow from a single village, but here it was decided that an existing town would impose too many limitations on development.[13] Glenrothes would sit between the towns of Markinch, Leslie, Kinglassie and Coaltown, abutting but not including these existing settlements.[14] As in East Kilbride, key personnel came from existing local government and new town networks.[15] The first chief architect was E.A. Ferriby, previously architect to the Northern Ireland Housing Trust, but he soon departed for Bracknell Development Corporation and was replaced by Peter Tinto.[16] Tinto had previous experience working for local authorities, including as a senior architect for Glasgow Corporation Housing Department from 1922 to 1945, and then at Paisley Corporation.[17]

The Department of Health for Scotland (DHS) took a close interest in the early plans for the town, preparing an initial masterplan as it had done for East Kilbride (Figure 2.2).[18] This move was unsurprising, given the Scottish Office's wish, discussed in the previous chapter and the Introduction, to encourage improved standards of planning and design along with social reform. In 1948, Arthur Woodburn spoke of how he 'hoped the raising of the standards of life generally in

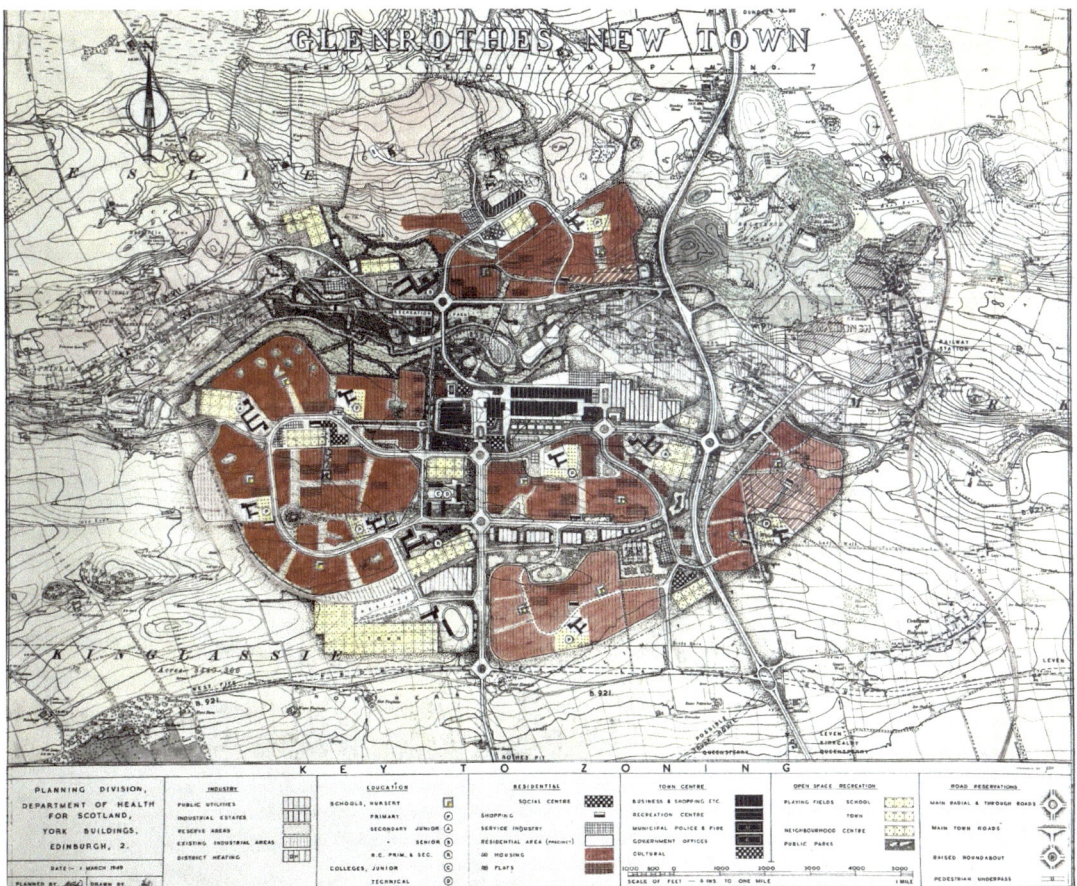

FIGURE 2.2 Initial Glenrothes masterplan, by the staff of the Department of Health for Scotland, 1948 (© Fife Cultural Trust, courtesy of Fife Council).

the new town of Glenrothes would be a beacon to which other towns in the future would look for light and guidance in their work'.[19] Seven iterations of the master plan were developed.[20] The DHS planners' report on their proposals invoked familiar critiques of 1930s estates in calling for variety of housing type and design: 'such a scheme would greatly assist architects to avoid the large scale design generalizations which are characteristic of extensive inter-war projects.'[21] There was also a quiet radicalism in the planners' focus on individual opportunity. The town would, they said, offer 'maximum freedom of choice to [the] individual' through their lifetime.[22] Although the proposals reflected what was emerging as planning orthodoxy in their neighbourhood-based layout – with three neighbourhood units, each broken down into smaller precincts that were based on a primary school – the planners also used the small size of the projected town to advance a critique of the neighbourhood idea:

> In Glenrothes, where the town centre is easily reached from all parts of the town, it is considered that the emphasis will be thrown on the centre as the common social nucleus of the whole population. While social centres have been zoned in the main residential areas, large parts of these areas are more conveniently served by the town centre, and at the same time a shopping survey now nearing completion indicates that it is unlikely that 'neighbourhood' shopping centres can be supported.[23]

In saying this, the planners articulated the kind of thinking which would become prominent ten years later in the plans for Cumbernauld, where the town centre was very much intended as a single focus for the whole new town.

The in-house Glenrothes Development Corporation (GDC) planners produced their own Outline Plan in 1951 (Figure 2.3).[24] It was closely based on the DHS scheme, much more so than the equivalent proposals for East Kilbride. There were to be three neighbourhoods, each sub-divided into precincts of approximately 3765 people (in 1200 homes), with a primary school and a small shopping area. Two-storey houses, not flats, were to dominate – a move that, in the context of rural Fife and its tradition of cottage living, was in type, if not in style, less obviously a break from precedent than East Kilbride's construction of houses as an alternative to Glaswegian tenement flats. Nonetheless three- and four-storey flats and maisonettes would also be introduced, intended primarily for single people and families without children; in some cases, seven or eight storeys were adopted. The aim was to increase densities in some precincts, especially near the town centre, for practical reasons as well as the 'improvement of the architectural effect', a goal framed in terms of contrast with earlier practice in that the result would be 'a genuine urban character rather than that of the large housing estate so characteristic of inter-war development'.[25] There would by implication also be greater social mix than those estates. Dense 'urban' areas would contrast with expansive areas of green space, including tree shelter belts intended to add variation in height to housing areas, as well as playing fields and public parks. John Coghill, deputy chief architect and planning officer from 1953 to 1977, later argued that greenery added value to the town. He claimed that rather than being inspired by the Garden City Movement, the Corporation hoped to emulate the greenery of St. Louis, USA, as discussed in a 1954 *Illustrated London News* article.[26] The development corporation also mapped out two industrial areas at the Queensway and Viewfield, each within walking distance of the housing areas. The plan suggested that there was 'no reason why the industrial buildings should not constitute a positive architectural advantage',

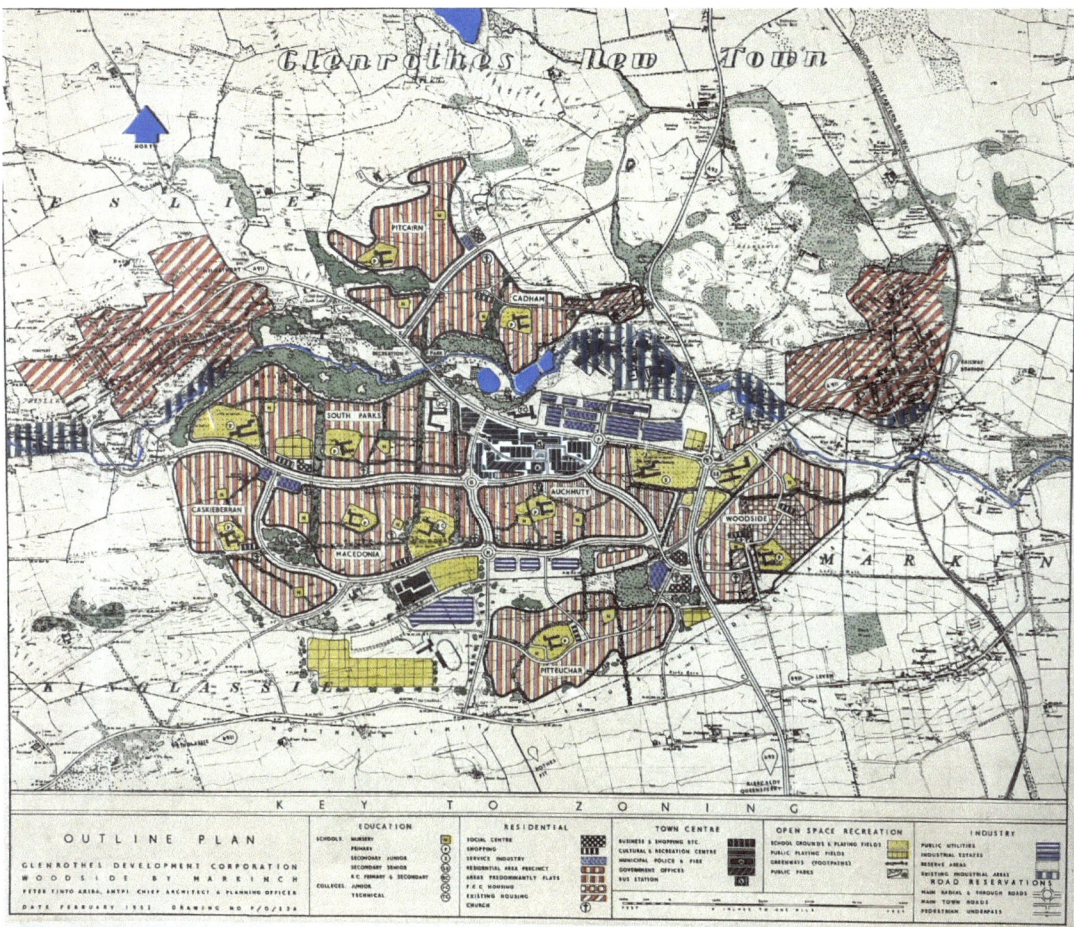

FIGURE 2.3 1951 Glenrothes masterplan, produced by the Development Corporation (© Fife Cultural Trust, courtesy of Fife Council).

yet also suggested the use of planting belts to shield the view of factories from the roads.[27] Great effort was also made to describe the concept for the town centre, which was to adopt a 'unified design'.[28] It was expected to cater for the people of Glenrothes and surrounding areas, and therefore was to contain a mixture of shops, offices, governmental departments, cultural buildings and flats.

New visions: The 1960s

Whereas East Kilbride enjoyed a flying start with the arrival of Rolls Royce and the government's engineering laboratory, progress was slower in Glenrothes. To some extent, slow progress was expected, because the new Rothes Colliery would only be built up gradually. Essentially, the National Coal Board outlined how many miners were needed each year during the build-up; this in turn dictated the town's initial rate of growth, including the number and location of new houses and the provision of amenities.[29] In the meantime, few other employers showed an interest in the town, especially because the kinds of financial incentives available elsewhere were not on offer.[30] There were shortages of labour in Fife, but Glenrothes was conceived as a self-sufficient new town, not as a dormitory for other parts of the region. The media – and residents – began to debate whether the town was a 'flop'.[31] As early as 1951, the incoming Conservative government considered whether Glenrothes should be made the responsibility of the county council, which would have meant it losing its 'new town' status.[32]

Rothes Colliery was not the breakthrough that might have been hoped. Despite claims that the pit boasted reserves that would last 100 years, the mine quickly faced complications.[33] Problems related to geology and water ingress hampered production and eventually led to complete closure in 1962. Though keen to stay in Glenrothes, many miners were forced to find work elsewhere. There was further consideration of abandoning the new town, and in 1967 GDC's General Manager R.S. Doyle explained that the project had faced the risk of a premature end.[34] However, the purpose, size and plan of the new town were rethought – something which, perhaps counter-intuitively, involved an increase in 1963 in the population target from 32,000 to 55,000, as well as a new focus on Glasgow overspill, and an eventual target of 70,000. In the light of the new emphasis on the new towns as industrial growth points, Doyle believed that 'no industry of any size would consign its future to a town of 32,000'.[35]

Whereas East Kilbride's growth had prompted incremental additions to the masterplan, in Glenrothes, a more fundamental revision was undertaken, described as 'a new town [...] on top of a new town'.[36] For architect Merlyn Williams, the task of imposing a 'phase II transportation and land use pattern' on a 'phase I concept new town' was harder than urban renewal.[37] In 1966, William Gillespie and Associates were appointed as landscape consultants.[38] That same year, a Transportation Plan and new interim plan were published,[39] with the revised masterplan following four years later.[40] The new plan not only provided for the extra housing and employment now projected but also imposed a new road layout. A revised hierarchy of roads was proposed: a box of fast freeways, a supplementary grid of highways, then spineways leading to serviceways and finally to house groups (dubbed 'clusters') on culs-de-sac. Although infused with fashionable jargon and reflecting the growth of car ownership as well as new planning theories, these labels in fact described a system not far removed from the precinctal arrangement of the 1951 plan, though the local shopping areas were now understood to have wider catchments than hitherto and greater use of Radburn layouts was projected.[41] The increased population targets – to be achieved with the existing Designated Area – implied higher densities, an approach which would also promote a renewed emphasis on 'urbanity'. The new approach can best be seen in Glenrothes' 'Western Neighbourhood'. While this area was originally broken into three precincts in 1952, each containing their own shops (South Parks, Macedonia and Caskieberran), the planners now fitted five (with the addition of Tanshall and Rimbleton) which all shared the central Glenwood Shopping Centre. This was a relatively unusual approach, but was also used in Harlow new town.[42] Methods changed again in the 1970s. While in previous approaches primary schools stood as the defining factor of each precinct, now 'dwelling clusters' stood within 'containment areas'. In this iteration, each dwelling cluster did not necessarily hold enough people to warrant a primary school and thus multiple clusters shared a school.[43]

It was not only the plan which was revised but also the purpose of the town. The 'new' Glenrothes would become a centre for electronics manufacture – something which had begun even before the closure of the pit, with the arrival of Beckman Instruments in 1958 and Hughes Microelectronics in 1960.[44] Boasting a clean atmosphere and a plentiful supply of advance factories and vacant sites, Glenrothes came during the 1960s and 1970s to form a key part of the Scottish 'Silicon Glen',[45] with prominent companies such as Burroughs Machines Ltd, Brand Rex, General Instruments and Apricot Computers.[46] By 1965 one industry was settling in Glenrothes each month, and by 1966 large companies such as Elliott Automation and Associated Electrical Industries had arrived. While employment in the town stood at just 940 jobs in 1962 when Rothes Colliery closed, this number had risen to 7,442 by 1973.[47] By 1974 electrical engineering made up 24.73 per cent of the town's employment, with paper printing and publishing the second largest sector at 12.98 per cent.[48] There was a weighting towards education and retraining in electronics within the town's key educational institutions.[49] While occupied floor space in 1962 was 260,000 square feet, by 1966 this had reached 1,000,000 square feet.[50] Used for the first time in Britain in Glenrothes, the 'Tilt Up' system for rapidly constructing factory buildings was adopted by GDC.[51] Concrete was cast in situ, then lifted into place using cranes.

GDC, like its contemporary in East Kilbride, actively marketed the town from the 1960s onwards As explained by Pocock in 1970, 'in an age when strictly non-economic factors are recognised as having a part to play in deciding among alternative locations, the efforts of the new town have even included a publication to show that the climate of Fife was in several respects equal to that of South-east England'.[52] Tactics included a series of state visits by foreign leaders, advertisements in magazines and newspapers as far afield as China, marketing films in multiple languages, and television adverts both at home and abroad.[53] Despite these attempts, the story of Glenrothes was not solely one of success. The economic slowdown of the late 1960s and early 1970s took its toll. Most significantly, the Burroughs Machines factory proved to not be as successful as first anticipated, and by 1974 was employing just 430 of the expected 1000 people. Whitehall government officials were so concerned about unemployment-related social unrest in the town that special incentives primarily used to attract new industry to Glasgow were extended to Glenrothes.[54] There were also concerns about the new town's isolated location, with Fife surrounded on three sides by water. Even after the Forth Road Bridge opened in 1964, road connections remained poor, and the town lacked its own railway station. Aiming to minimize the impact of this and to attract foreign industrialists, an airfield was opened in 1964; Glenrothes was the first new town in Britain to build one.[55] The airfield brought the town to within half an hour of Scotland's main international airports. According to Beckman Industries executives, this airfield gave a 'psychological advantage in showing those who might be thinking of coming here, the progressive attitude of Glenrothes'.[56]

Housing

Glenrothes' housing attracted little comment from John Gifford in the *Buildings of Scotland*, while David Cowling summed it up in similar terms to East Kilbride: 'it shared […] the knack of doing the normal very well.'[57] But while it is Glenrothes' public buildings – especially its churches – which have attracted previous historians' attention, the town's housing is also worth close examination. It is true that, in many ways, the story of housing design in Glenrothes is familiar. It echoes East Kilbride and the English 'Mark 1' new towns, with an initial emphasis on terraced three-bedroom houses giving way during the 1960s to greater typological variety, more overtly modernist designs with monopitch and flat roofs, and more complex layouts (Figure 2.4). As in East Kilbride, one might understand this story not only as one of 'reforming' the Scottish dwelling – the concern of the Scottish Office, made particularly clear in the Westwood Report – but also as its Anglicization, as English models (of, for example, terraced housing) were imported. The visual impact of housing was also stressed in ways that echo wider, Britain-wide interest in 'Townscape' planning theories, that is, the urbanization of the English Picturesque. This broad characterization, however, ignores the particularities of the Glenrothes experience, as well as the diversity of the results. On the one hand, the development corporation certainly took a pragmatic approach, with architect John Coghill remembering that 'our original idea was to make Glenrothes a homely place that people would want to live in rather than a town which would be distinguished by its modernity, and I think that was the right decision'.[58] However, their approach, especially in the 1960s, at times tended towards a radicalism of the sort more usually associated with Cumbernauld. At the same time, wider debates about density and urbanity were given a particular local flavour. John Coghill spoke of the initial aim for Glenrothes to be 'like little seaside villages', presumably of the kind found on the Fife coast.[59]

The earliest housing was provided by Fife County Council, which had already been planning development in the area, and comprised semi-detached cottages with steep roofs, dormer windows and formal gardens.[60] The corporation took over with Woodside 2 in 1952; this area was the first to be developed, along with Auchmuty.[61] Typologically, early development corporation housing was not unlike that provided by the council, with similar steep roofs and dormers, and small paned steel windows, plus coloured roughcast used as a 'Scottish gesture'.[62] There was nonetheless greater emphasis on variety in both plan (with some wide-fronted designs, whose layout reflected the recommendations of the Westwood Report, plus pend houses), form (projecting windows) and materials (facing brick, tile hanging, timber weather-boarding – all perhaps 'English' materials).[63] As the 1950s progressed, there was increased use of terraced layouts, perhaps reflecting the preference of the Westwood Report for this arrangement as a contrast with inter-war cottage layouts. Three-storey flats were added to add further diversity, both visual (in the spirit of contemporary 'Townscape') and potentially also social (Figure 2.5). In this latter respect, a small amount of housing for the elderly was provided in small numbers at 'Coronation Cottages'.

FIGURE 2.4 Mixed development in Glenrothes, with bungalows for older residents alongside houses (Collection of Miles Glendinning).

FIGURE 2.5 Saltire Award-winning housing at Woodside (© Fife Council).

By the early 1960s, private-sector builders were constructing small numbers of houses for sale, and plots for one-off designs were also available. However, the development corporation remained the major provider of new housing, and, though some properties were purchased by tenants, it had a substantial management role. Its approach nonetheless evolved. For example, the layout of the popular South Parks and Rimbleton precincts reflected increasing levels of car ownership, with lock-up garages and winding roads intended to slow down traffic; some higher-rental properties had with their own garages.[64] Provision for cars was accompanied by greater emphasis on the pedestrian experience, with a segregated pedestrian network and, in time, the growing use of Radburn layouts, not least in the Macedonia and Tanshall precincts (1964–7), where fronts of homes faced central pedestrian walkways and green spaces; parking was to the rear.[65] Visually, the housing in these areas took various forms. Rimbleton designs were simple in form but diverse in texture and colour, with some featuring timber and painted infill panels for added variety. South Parks 4 was intended as a high-amenity area with correspondingly increased rents. It featured extensive use of brick screen walls as well as tile-hanging (perhaps showing the influence of the work in East Anglia of the architects David Tayler and Herbert Green, or Eric Lyons' Span estates around London). Variety was not inevitable, however. Macedonia's terraces were more uniform, with roughcast, simple timber windows and flat roofs giving a somewhat box-like form.[66] Similar designs were used in Tanshall, though pitched roofs were reintroduced (Figure 2.6). On several sites, industrialized building systems were tried, including, in South Rimbleton, the Hall Kincorth system of concrete cross wall construction with concrete panel and timber infill, and the Hawthorn Leslie system, using a steel frame with asbestos panels and flat-roofed timber porches. The Jespersen concrete-panel system, used in Livingston's mid-1960s developments, was also implemented in Glenrothes, especially for flatted developments. From 1966 to 1969, nine Jespersen five-storey 'walk-up' maisonette blocks were constructed in Caskieberran and Rimbleton.[67] This period also saw the construction of the town's only high-rise block, a 1967 Wimpey designed tower named Raeburn Heights, in South Parks.[68]

During the 1960s, increased emphasis was placed on landscaping. In Caskieberran (1966–9), the same basic house types were used as in Tanshall, but were now gathered around landscaped courts with increased variety of finishes. Lest it be thought that the trend was one of ever-increasing design complexity, Newcastle neighbourhood saw the same types reworked in visually simplified forms. However, the idea of a 'total housing environment' reached its apex in the Pitteuchar neighbourhood (1970–7) where the housing, though constrained by the limits of the new 'indicative cost system', was arranged around a dense, decidedly 'urban' layout akin to

FIGURE 2.6 Aerial view of Tanshall (© Crown Copyright: HES).

the compact planning then being used in Cumbernauld (Figure 2.7).[69] Houses were varied in roof form, with wall finishes and colour introduced in various ways including different roughcasts and paintwork. Increasing demand saw some housing built by private contractors. Planting was used for effect: the architects later recalled that the formal 'rose bed' approach of early schemes had now been decidedly jettisoned in favour of a more 'natural' approach.[70]

There were repeated attempts by planners to increase the proportion of flats. In order to house the 55,000 people envisaged to form the town's eventual population, in 1970 it was proposed that the northern areas of the town be developed with clusters of ten-storey point blocks surrounded by low slab blocks stepping up the steep slopes, while the southern precincts would adopt high-rise blocks set within parkland.[71] As populations never reached the estimated numbers and mine workings in the area continued to present difficulties, this vison never reached fruition, though increased numbers of flats were nonetheless constructed.[72]

Tighter cost limits affected developments during the 1970s, forcing a simpler aesthetic in Stenton and Cadham (1977–82) as well as economies such as the omission of car ports, but there was still scope for creative design. Cadham saw mono-pitched rows of housing clinging in an echelon pattern to steep hillsides with lush planting and, in David Cowling's words, 'some of the finest pedestrian ways in any of the Scottish new towns, rich in drama and foliage, light and shade'.[73] Layouts were adjusted to take advantage of the often hilly topography, with one type featuring first-floor living rooms from which open views could be obtained. It had been decided that pale roughcast would be jarring against the backdrop of the hillside, so muted tones were adopted.[74] Painted smooth bands – a vernacular Fife detail – were introduced around windows, invoking the kind of 'vernacular modern' style which was also seen in Cumbernauld and especially Irvine. Experiments were made with road layouts in order to reduce traffic speed and provide parking without compromising on the sense of urbanity felt to result from tightly arranged layouts.[75] These experiments culminated in the 'pedestrian/car paths' of Collydean (1977–82), where routes around

FIGURE 2.7 Architects' impression of proposed Pitteuchar housing, *c.* 1970 (© Fife Cultural Trust, courtesy of Fife Council).

the houses were essentially wide footpaths shared by cars and pedestrians – a form of layout derived from Dutch practice which was also used in Irvine as a critique of segregated Radburn planning.[76] Innovations were made in terms of process. In Pitcoudie at the end of the 1970s, for example, a method of sequencing was adopted in which each trade would visit the site only once, with claimed savings in time.[77]

There was optimism at the end of the 1970s that the new layouts evolved in Collydean would be developed further in Balfarg (1982–8), but the moratorium on the construction of public-sector general needs housing which was in place for much of the 1980s saw the development corporation's role reduced. In 1982, 515 Corporation houses were built, but the number fell thereafter and none were completed in 1985 or 1988; there were just eight completions in 1986 and the numbers were below 100 in 1987, 1989 and 1990.[78] In parallel, more than 4000 homes were bought by their tenants.[79] In total, 12,622 homes of various shape and size were built by GDC up to 1994.[80] Together, they demonstrate the creativity of the public sector in this period, and the ability of its designers to respond to the particularities of the site as well as changing needs.

A particularly distinctive feature of the residential areas was the provision of art. Glenrothes was the first of the Scottish new towns to appoint a 'town artist', in 1968.[81] David Harding was given the broad remit of 'adding individuals' experience to the town'.[82] Followed by Stan Bonnar and Malcolm Robertson, the artists transformed Glenrothes' public spaces, especially in and

FIGURE 2.8 Public art in Glenrothes: hippos by Stan Bonnar (© The Scotsman Publications Ltd.).

around housing areas, with marching hippos, toadstools, murals, crocodiles, henges and giant lilies (Figure 2.8).[83] Many of the sculptures and murals became local meeting points, especially for children. By 1991 over 100 sites across Glenrothes featured artwork.[84]

Public architecture

Despite the DHS's initial reluctance to encourage local centres, GDC's approach accorded with 'Mark 1' practice in providing neighbourhood shopping areas. That at Woodside (1951–5) is a particularly clear example of the idea, frequently expressed in wartime planning reports, that these centres should bring together commercial and community uses (Figure 2.9). Rows of shops define two sides of a pedestrianized square, with shops above; a community hall forms the third side of the square. This layout was described by Anthony Wheeler, GDC senior architect, as 'a little village hall grouping round a square'.[85] His turn of phrase evoked the kind of imagery which frequently suffused discussions of planning in the 1940s and 1950s, in which villages and small burghs were held up as exemplar forms for their supposedly strong sense of community and socially mixed basis – all qualities which were, it was suggested, lacking in inter-war suburbs. In this respect, Woodside, like The Murray in East Kilbride, reflected the drive to offer a new model of Scottish urban development and to stimulate a supposedly 'improved' approach. However, rising levels of car ownership meant that, while later neighbourhoods also gained centres, the significance of these places was gradually reduced.

Wheeler also provided initial plans for the town centre, proposing a location north of the Auchmuty neighbourhood.[86] In many ways, his proposal was an expanded version of the Woodside neighbourhood centre, with two pedestrian squares and a mixture of uses (Figure 2.10). Commercial imperatives would be tempered by civic, religious and cultural buildings. At its core

FIGURE 2.9 Woodside neighbourhood centre (© Crown Copyright: HES).

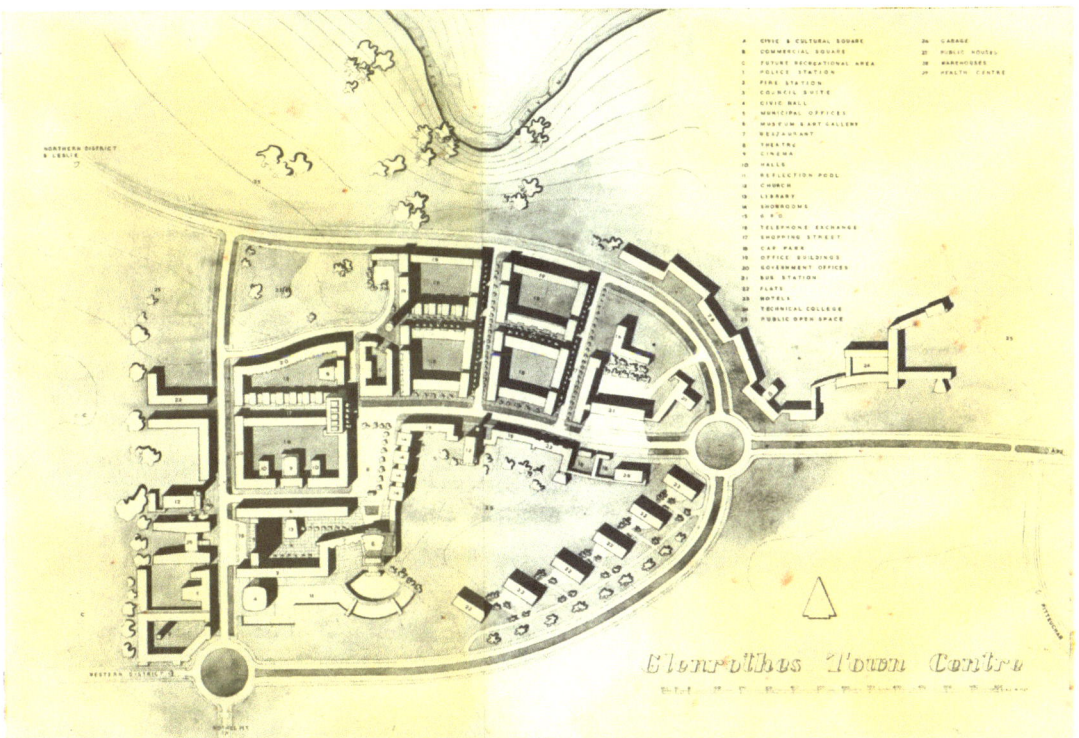

FIGURE 2.10 Plan of proposed Glenrothes town centre by Anthony Wheeler (© Crown Copyright: HES).

FIGURE 2.11 Perspective drawing by Anthony Wheeler showing his vision for Glenrothes town centre, 1950 (© Crown Copyright: HES).

would be a civic and cultural square housing the town's municipal offices, library, museum, theatre and restaurant. Wheeler's approach coupled elements of formal Beaux-Arts planning – akin to the initial plans for East Kilbride – with a more informal, cheerful aesthetic derived from Scandinavia (with wavy rooflines anticipating the style of the Festival of Britain); monumental buildings were located at axial points (Figure 2.11 and also Figure 0.6). These buildings included a cantilevered library, to the north of the civic square, and a curved theatre. Their prominence reflected the value ascribed at this time to these sorts of buildings in wider debates about community, citizenship and leisure, as well as the emergence of the civic theatre as a new type of building after the Second World War.[87] As realized, however, commercial uses came to dominate. First, the slow growth of the town meant that the first central shops to be built were temporary.[88] The first permanent phase was completed only in 1964, a pace of development which was slow within new town terms, and was the first of four phases to be constructed across a thirty-year period.[89] This incremental approach was described by Gifford as 'LEGO architecture' with 'a new piece added almost every birthday'.[90] The first phase contained Lyon Square, a semi-open air space. Also included was Albany Gate, with its clock tower, reminiscent of southern English new towns (Figure 2.12).[91] After a 'study mission' across Britain and Scandinavia in 1971,[92] by 1976 the second phase

FIGURE 2.12 Glenrothes town centre and clock (© Fife Council. John Porteous, Edinburgh).

had been completed, adding eighty-five shops. At its opening it was the largest heated indoor shopping centre in Scotland.[93] Further phases followed in 1982 and 1993, the latter consisting of twenty-two shops and the Rothes Halls, a multipurpose complex including a large 500-seat hall.[94] Housing theatre shows, concerts, exhibitions and conferences, the Rothes Halls finally provided the town with facilities dreamt up in the 1950 plan for the town.[95] A number of office buildings were constructed, including in 1979–80 a headquarters building for the newly constituted Fife Regional Council (designed in-house by GDC's architects with elevations of precast concrete).

Critical reception was mixed. The initial phase, for example, was characterized by the architectural press as displaying a 'strong sense of isolation', being set back from busy roads by large carparks on all sides with much of the building's exterior consisting of loading bays[96] Internally, while the shopping centre was seen as a 'skilful and well thought out design', there was criticism of the glazed roof, with one article questioning whether its addition had been a 'sudden and arbitrary decision'.[97] Yet while such negative views suggest that the ambition that the new towns be exemplars of design quality was less than evident, where the town centre was concerned such a conclusion surely misses the point. Although initial hopes of civic and cultural excellence may have foundered, Glenrothes centre, like East Kilbride before it, reflects a search for new types of urban space. As a modern centre, it demonstrates a pioneering, if nonetheless quietly pragmatic, approach by the development corporation, one attuned, perhaps, to commercial realities and consumer expectations, rather than avant-garde experiment. As a centre with a wide catchment, it also reflected the original idea that Glenrothes could become part of a wider 'constellation' of Fife communities.

The provision of leisure facilities also evolved. During the early years of the town, community provision was sparse, with most halls, libraries and health centres not arriving until the completion of the neighbourhood centres. In 1966, it was reported that increasing pressures were being placed on the then existing community facilities in the town.[98] Reasons were cited including increased car ownership, more leisure time, changing patterns of recreation and growing levels of affluence.[99] Provision increased from the mid-1960s; the 1970s and early 1980s was a key period in the construction of community and leisure infrastructure. As with shopping, a three-tier hierarchy divided facilities into those affecting the entire town, broader neighbourhoods and finally individual precincts.[100] By 1967 a policy for the construction of a small meeting room in each precinct was underway, with such spaces under construction in Rimbleton and Macedonia.[101] Elsewhere, community facilities were often shoehorned into existing buildings or those primarily intended for other uses. In Newcastle, a community wing was added to the primary school, while in Stenton an old farm steading was converted into a community space.[102] Most substantial of all, however, was the Lomond Centre in Woodside of 1975–6, designed by Fife County Council's architects. It provided a multi-use community space, within a spreading, low-rise polygonal building whose geometric forms recalled recent theatres in such places as Sheffield. By 1995 there were twenty-eight community meeting places, youth clubs and halls across the town.[103] Community sports facilities were also provided, with athletics facilities, sports pavilions, tennis and squash courts, a swimming pool, ice rink and dry ski-slope being built.[104] The majority were contained within the Fife Institute of Physical and Recreational Education, opened in 1970, and were intended to cater for both Glenrothes and the broader Fife region (Figure 2.13).[105] They were complemented by commercial leisure facilities, the provision of which was increasingly attractive to operators as the population increased.

Within the housing areas, the principal public buildings comprised schools, designed principally by the local authority, and churches. Some of the latter are among the key works of post-war Scottish architecture. St Paul's, Glenrothes (1957) – the town's only Roman Catholic church – marked a decisive turning point in the work of the architects Gillespie Kidd and Coia (GKC), breaking

FIGURE 2.13 Fife Institute of Physical and Recreational Education (JR James Archive/Flickr. CC BY-NC 2.0 DEED).

FIGURE 2.14 St Columba's Church (© Courtesy of HES (Wheeler and Sproson Collection)).

with the abstracted historicism of their earlier designs for a simple modernist aesthetic inspired by Scandinavian practice. A largely low-slung collection of buildings, compact in plan, it suggests a particular modesty in tune with the landscape, with, internally, light, texture and movement being carefully handled.[106] Similarly modest (built for just £37,000), Wheeler and Sproson's St Columba's (1961) was for the Church of Scotland, with a centralized plan that was both novel in its contrast with many other churches but which also harked back to pre-Reformation precedents (Figure 2.14).[107] Wheeler subsequently reflected on the novelty of the design, which included a large mural by Alberto Morrocco, seeing it as more innovative than its GKC near-contemporary.[108] It was, he said, 'the key church among the ones I designed', its well-detailed vault and tower being particular points of pride. Wheeler suggested that its modernity embodied the entire idea of the new town as an 'experiment' as well as being critical to the formation of a new, progressive community. 'You needed the right kind of minister', he recalled. 'It had to be modern, because, in a new town, the whole spirit of the place was to make it attractive to new generations.'[109]

Conclusion

The story of Glenrothes is one of the messy reality of new town construction. Whereas East Kilbride enjoyed a stellar start and grew incrementally, Glenrothes teetered on the brink of cancellation more than once, and the planning and economic assumptions which had underpinned its conception were revisited. Many of GDC's loftiest ambitions were never achieved, and in 1995 over 31 per cent of the town's land remained undeveloped.[110] One 1966 critic dismissed the town's apparently ad hoc approach to planning, which, 'in the sense of an understanding of the need for a disciplined town structure', it was suggested had become an afterthought.[111] Yet Glenrothes came into its own by the 1970s, finally able to supply the jobs, housing, shopping and community facilities its pioneers had dreamt of at designation. Its architecture reflects the same 'mainstream modernism' we encountered in East Kilbride, pragmatic but also concerned with setting an example for others to follow. This is especially true of the housing, which deserves greater attention than it has hitherto received. The town centre may lack the considered approach of Wheeler's early designs, but grew by the 1990s to be a successful regional centre.

Glenrothes, even in its revised form, was neighbourhood-based. But within just a few years of designation, the idea of a neighbourhood-oriented town was being increasingly challenged by factors including the rise of car ownership as well as planners' growing interest in compact urban forms. Cumbernauld, begun in 1955, would adopt a somewhat different approach, though one which in some ways developed DHS's initial thinking for Glenrothes as a town focused on a single centre.

Notes

1 Miles Glendinning, *Rebuilding Scotland: The Post-War Vision* (East Linton: Tuckwell, 1997), 18–20; Gary A. Boyd, *Architecture and the Face of Coal: Mining and Modern Britain* (London: Lund Humphries, 2023), 263–8.
2 John Gifford, *Fife* (New Haven and London: Yale University Press, 1988), 231.
3 Fife Archives [FA], GDC/11/198/3/4, 'Master Plan Exhibition – Opening Remarks', 1970.
4 'Scottish Notes: Glenrothes Standstill', *Official Architecture and Planning* 19, no. 3 (March 1956): 146.
5 J.B. Cullingworth, *Environmental Planning Volume III: New Towns Policy* (London: HMSO, 1979), 33, 38–40.
6 Ibid., 57 and 86–7.
7 Frank Mears, *Regional Plan for Central and S.E. Scotland* (Edinburgh: Central and SE Scotland Planning Advisory Committee, 1948).
8 David Cowling, *An Essay for Today: The Scottish New Towns 1947 to 1997* (Edinburgh: Rutland Press, 1997), 29.
9 '15 Years to Build Glenrothes: Mr Woodburn Meets New Corporation Balanced Community', *Scotsman*, 6 November 1948.
10 Cullingworth, *New Towns*, 61.
11 Alistair J.D. Wood, *40 Years New Glenrothes* (Glenrothes: Wood, 1989), 12.
12 'Glenrothes', *New Towns Record* (Planning Exchange CD-ROM set, 1996) [*NTR*].
13 Wood, *40 Years*, 11.
14 F.R. Stevenson, 'Planning and Development in Scotland', *Town Planning Review* 26, no. 1 (April 1955): 5–18 (p. 10).
15 'Glenrothes: Mr Woodburn Appoints Corporation Eight Members', *Scotsman*, 27 October 1948.
16 'From AN ARCHITECT'S Commonplace Book', *Architects' Journal* 109, no. 2828 (21 April 1949): 355.
17 'Glenrothes: Appointment of new Chief Architect', *Architects' Journal* 111, no. 2884 (18 May 1950): 600.
18 FA, GDC/17/69/15/1, 'Corporation told to pack up'.
19 '15 Years to Build Glenrothes', 6 November 1948.
20 FA, GDC/198/3/19/445, 'DHS Outline Plan 7'.
21 Ibid.
22 Ibid.
23 Ibid.

24 FA, GDC/11/198/5/2, 'Outline Plan, 1952'.
25 Ibid., 9–10.
26 'Glenrothes', *NTR*; Arthur Bryant, 'Our Note Book', *Illustrated London News*, August 1954, 316.
27 FA, GDC/11/198/5/2, 'Outline Plan, 3'.
28 Ibid., 2–3.
29 Wood, *40 Years*, 39.
30 Ibid., 39–41.
31 Ibid., 41–2.
32 Ibid., 43.
33 '"Tombstones" of Rothes Mark Double Death: Job-For-Life and Home Lost', *Guardian*, 12 July 1962.
34 'Diversity in Glenrothes', *Financial Times*, 28 February 1967.
35 Ibid.
36 FA, GDC/17/69/15/1, 'A New Town Created on Top of a New Town'.
37 FA, GDC/11/198/2/4, 'Interim Planning Proposals, 1966'.
38 Gillespie also worked in Cumbernauld: see Chapter 3.
39 FA, GDC/10/126/1/4/282, 'Transportation Plan'.
40 FA, GDC/185/1/3/385, 'Glenrothes Master Plan, 1970'.
41 Anthony Goss, 'Neighbourhood Units in British New Towns', *Town Planning Review* 32, no. 1 (April 1961): 66–82 (p. 70).
42 Mark Llewellyn, 'Producing and Experiencing Harlow: Neighbourhood Units and Narratives of New Town Life 1947–53', *Planning Perspectives* 19, no. 2 (2004): 155–74.
43 FA, GDC/185/1/3/385, 'Glenrothes master plan, 1970', 37.
44 'The Day When a "New Town" Loses Its Tag: Growing Pains of a Scottish Community', *Guardian*, 10 September 1958.
45 'Growth and Environment', *Financial Times*, 28 February 1967.
46 FA, GDC/11/17/1/58, 'Statistical Data 1974'.
47 Ibid.
48 Ibid.
49 D.C.D. Pocock, 'Economic Renewal: The Example of Fife', *Scottish Geographical Magazine* 86, no. 2 (September 1970): 123–33.
50 'Diversity in Glenrothes', 28 February 1967.
51 FA, GDC/13/159/48/2-4, 'Southfield 10, Tilt Up No 1 Advance Factories, Architects' Drawings'.
52 Pocock, 'Economic Renewal'.
53 E.g. FA, GDC/16/131/2/14-18, GDC/16/104/2/4-6, 'GDC Promotional Material'.
54 Jim Phillips, 'Deindustrialization and the Moral Economy of the Scottish Coalfields, 1947 to 1991', *International Labor and Working Class History* 84 (2013): 99–115.
55 'Airfield Puts Scots New Town Ahead', *South China Morning Post*, 31 August 1964.
56 Ibid.
57 Cowling, *Essay for Today*, 46.
58 'Architect Who Helped to Make Glenrothes "A Homely Place"', *Glenrothes Gazette*, 2 July 1998.
59 'Glenrothes', *NTR*.

60 'Impressive Progress at Miners' New Town', *Guardian*, 13 December 1954.
61 Wood, *40 Years*, 29.
62 FA, GDC/11/17/5/9, 'Thirty Years of Housing in Glenrothes 1950–1980', March 1987, 1.
63 Ibid., 2.
64 Ibid., 3.
65 Ibid.
66 Ibid., 9–11.
67 Cowling, *Essay for Today*, 46.
68 'Glenrothes', *NTR*.
69 FA, GDC/11/17/5/9, 'Thirty Years of Housing', 12–13.
70 Ibid., 15.
71 FA, GDC/185/1/3/385, 'Glenrothes Master Plan, 1970', 63.
72 'Glenrothes', *NTR*.
73 Cowling, *Essay for Today*, 46.
74 FA, GDC/11/17/5/9, 'Thirty Years of Housing', 8.
75 Ibid., 15, 18.
76 Ibid.
77 Ibid., 17.
78 FA, GDC/11/17/5/10, 'Glenrothes Housing Trends and Issues', 1990.
79 Ibid.
80 FA, GDC/11/17/7/4, 'Factfile 1995'; 8.
81 'Glenrothes', *NTR*.
82 Ibid.
83 Cowling, *Essay for Today*, 45.
84 'Glenrothes', *NTR*.
85 Anthony Wheeler, interviewed by Miles Glendinning, May 1995.
86 Historic Environment Scotland Archives, DP 418744, 'Glenrothes Town Centre'. Drawing, signed on Mount 'HA Wheeler', 1950.
87 Elizabeth Darling and Alistair Fair, '"The Core": The Centre as a Concept in Twentieth-Century British Planning and Architecture. Part One: The Emergence of the Idea', *Planning Perspectives* 38, no. 1 (2022): 69–98; Alistair Fair, *Modern Playhouses: An Architectural History of Britain's New Theatres, 1945–1985* (Oxford: Oxford University Press, 2018), 9–26.
88 'Glenrothes', *NTR*.
89 Ibid.
90 Gifford, *Fife*, 232.
91 Cowling, *Essay for Today*, 38.
92 GDC, Annual Report 1971, 101.
93 'Glenrothes', *NTR*.
94 FA, GDC/15/78/1/1, 'Glenrothes Kingdom Centre – Phase Four Extension'.
95 'Glenrothes', *NTR*.
96 'News: Glenrothes – Town Centre', *Architects' Journal* 143, no. 17 (27 April 1966): 1054–5.

97   Ibid.
98   'Glenrothes', *NTR*.
99   Ibid.
100 Ibid.
101 GDC Annual Report 1967.
102 'Glenrothes', *NTR*.
103 FA, GDC/11/17/7/4, 'Factfile 1995', 21.
104 Ibid.
105 'Glenrothes', *NTR*.
106 Johnny Rodger, 'Towards the MacMillan and Metzstein Years', in *Gillespie, Kidd & Coia: Architecture 1956–1987*, ed. Johnny Rodger (Glasgow: Lighthouse, 2007), 11–20.
107 Diane Watters, 'St Columba's, Glenrothes: A Post-War Design Laboratory for Reformed Worship', *Architectural Heritage* 12 (2001): 66–87.
108 Anthony Wheeler, interviewed by Miles Glendinning, May 1995.
109 Ibid.
110 FA, GDC/11/17/7/4, 'Factfile 1995', 22.
111 'News: Glenrothes – Town Centre', 1054.

3

Cumbernauld

Cumbernauld is set apart from Scotland's other new towns by the fact that, in addition to the Scottish-specific political and cultural values that structured its development, it was a highly prominent participant within a global intellectual discourse of modernist architectural and planning innovation.[1] Internationally, it was the very first large-scale realization of an urban planning theory which prized density and intensity, conceived in the 1950s under the slogan of 'urbanity' and today sometimes bracketed under the misleading heading of 'Brutalism'. This innovation meant that, within Britain, Cumbernauld was the pioneer 'Mark 2' new town. It offered perhaps the most compelling image yet of the 'modern Scotland' being created by the new towns, reiterating once more the drive to offer an exemplar of careful planning and design (Figure 3.1). In 1967, with around 10,000 official overseas visitors being received annually, Cumbernauld won the prestigious American Institute of Architects RS Reynolds Award for Community Architecture, in competition with the Swedish satellite town of Vällingby, and Tapiola in Finland. The award jury proclaimed that

> the town centre and the roadway system, the heart and circulation system of Cumbernauld, bring together the urban environment and the automobile into a powerful resolution. The residential areas of Cumbernauld may remind one of a medieval hill town or even a nineteenth century mill town but not the centre. It is designed for the millennium and the dreams of the 1920s and 30s are being built on a hill near Glasgow.[2]

Reflecting this fame, the development corporation in 1963–4 commissioned a book documenting the town's conception and design. Ultimately never completed, its intended title, *The Building of a New Town*, reads as a confident, even competitive, response to the London County Council's 1961 book *The Planning of a New Town*, which records the unbuilt project for a Cumbernauld-esque new town at Hook, Hampshire.[3] Hook was planned; Cumbernauld was actually realized.

The initial rationale for a new town at Cumbernauld echoed that for East Kilbride, stemming from the proposal in Patrick Abercrombie and Robert Matthew's 1946 Clyde Valley Regional Plan, that a proportion of Glasgow's population and industry should be moved away from the city. Having been identified as a potential new town location by Abercrombie and Matthew's team, Cumbernauld was eventually designated in 1955, after earlier conflict between Glasgow Corporation and the Scottish Office relating to the desirability of so-called 'overspill' had abated; the *Preliminary Planning Proposals* were issued in April 1958.[4] The designated area took in 4150

FIGURE 3.1 Towers and terraces: the high-density urbanity of a 'Mark 2' new town (© RIBA Collections).

acres and an existing population of 3,000, largely concentrated in two villages, Cumbernauld and Condorrat; the aim was a self-contained town of 50,000 people. The site was not only restricted in size but also set on a hill, between 260 and 480 feet above sea level. This exposed setting would impact on layout plans for housing areas, for example in the ubiquitous use of bridged pends and underpasses to maximize shelter (Figure 3.2). In the early 1960s, in response to the general refocusing of the Scottish new towns programme towards economic modernization, the target population was raised to 70,000. By 1967, over 5600 houses had been completed and 6100 jobs had been provided, and in 1973 the designated area was doubled in size by a 3,638-acre addition to the north-west. However, it was only in 1989 that the initial population target of 50,000 was achieved.

By the 1990s, in striking contrast to its initial architectural acclaim, and amid wider public denigration of modern architecture and planning, Cumbernauld had acquired a distinctly negative popular reputation within Scotland, and was for a time largely forgotten within international architectural discourse. At a local level, the roots of the stigmatization of Cumbernauld began with the functional problems of the futuristic concrete Town Centre, but maintenance and management problems affecting system-built housing also fuelled the negativity, as did the institutional neglect that followed the winding up in 1996 of the paternalistic Cumbernauld Development Corporation

FIGURE 3.2 Pedestrian path and bridged housing at Seafar (© Architectural Press Archive/RIBA Collections).

(CDC) and the transfer of its assets to an unsympathetic successor, North Lanarkshire Council. Renewed academic and heritage interest in post-war architecture during the 1990s could not stop the part-demolition of the Town Centre megastructure after 1999.[5] In 2003, Cumbernauld's international profile began to re-emerge. With no significant targeted preservation protection, it was placed in the 'top twenty' of endangered twentieth-century modern heritage by international conservation body ICOMOS. But Cumbernauld Town Centre was twice rejected for heritage 'listing' by Historic Scotland, in 1992 and 2023, as was a 1996 request to the local authority by the international heritage watchdog DOCOMOMO to designate local Conservation Areas in the Kildrum and Seafar residential districts. In the quarter-century since then, demolitions have continued, including all the multi-storey towers that gave the town its landscape profile, and soon, perhaps, the rest of the original Town Centre.

Reflecting the avant-garde architecture-planning status of Cumbernauld, this chapter does not set out to describe its entire built environment. It excludes from detailed consideration traditional monumental public buildings such as churches or community complexes such as schools, which were of little importance within the overall concept (although these, perversely, are now the structures picked out for heritage protection).[6] The chapter is concerned above all with planning and architectural innovation, and so focuses on the most innovative aspects of the project: its overall urban plan and concept; its boldly conceived Town Centre; and its equally innovative housing designs, which provided the world's first large-scale realization of the 'low rise high density' patterns that would eventually sweep away the old modernist ideal of the isolated tower block in open space.

Planning and urban landscape

Cumbernauld was the only new town to be designated in 1950s Britain. Compared with the earlier new towns, such as East Kilbride and Glenrothes, or those around London, it adopted a radically new planning approach, and for this reason it quickly became known as a 'Mark 2' new town. Overall, although the town was to be much lower in density than overcrowded Glasgow, it reacted against the spaced-out neighbourhood units of the 'Mark 1' towns, with their low-density housing and industry. Cumbernauld would instead be planned at higher densities, and the Town Centre would be a single focus for the whole new town. In this departure the planners were encouraged by the Scottish Office, which, as we saw in the previous chapter, had toyed with the idea in some of their initial plans for Glenrothes. Although urban density and concentration were increasingly advocated at this time by avant-garde planners and architects (not least in the writings of the international Team 10 group), there were also practical considerations, as Scottish Office planner Robert Grieve recalled:

> We were forced by a growing agricultural lobby not to build on the best land, and because of mineral substance between Cumbernauld and Glasgow, and the fact that it was surrounded by coal strips, only a very small area was really available to build on. Other considerations included the fact that we were very heavily pressured by environmentalists, including the development corporation's architect, to build an 'urbane' development. So the new town was designated and the team was set up. The Architect and Planning Officer, Hugh Wilson, came from Canterbury. He took that job because we said to the corporation that it would have to be built at densities greater than Garden City levels. That's why – because he was very keen on urbanity. I'd meet up with Wilson's architectural staff in a pub in Cumbernauld village, and we would drink a pint or two of beer. We would debate what urbanity was.[7]

Such planning innovation was made possible by the distinctive organizational structure that resulted from new town designation, here as elsewhere. The use of an administrator-led development corporation offered a degree of insulation from the sort of local political pressures which applied outwith the new towns and which could have generated high-output, low-rent mass housing solutions. Instead, Cumbernauld, like the earlier new towns, prioritized the high-quality, coordinated design of both buildings and landscapes under the aegis of Hugh Wilson, who was appointed in 1956. Almost all housing developments were designed by CDC's own housing architects, initially (from 1957) in a single large group led by Roy Hunter, who had come to Cumbernauld from Stevenage new town, and then in several groups of more variegated character. Hunter led the Northside group, and a separate Southside group was formed by Derek (W.D.C.) Lyddon, another designer who made a career in the new towns programme by subsequently moving to Skelmersdale and then to the Scottish Office (Figure 3.3). Bridges and other road engineering works were designed with great consistency under CDC's Chief Engineer Alex Scott. An initial landscape plan was prepared in 1957 by consultant Peter Youngman; William Gillespie was eventually appointed as staff landscape architect. All the elements were tied together not only by Gillespie's pervasive landscaping schemes but also by the design work of 'Town Artist' Brian Miller, including mural paintings and bespoke utility objects such as special colour-coded street signs.

FIGURE 3.3 Derek Lyddon in conversation with a colleague in Cumbernauld (Miles Glendinning).

Following a brief discussion with Hunter and Lyddon, who argued for a location in the valley just south-east of the ridge, Wilson decreed that the central area was to be on the very crown of the hill.[8] It was designed under the architect Geoffrey Copcutt as a single, multi-level, multi-purpose building complex, exemplifying the ideal of the 'megastructure'. This term emerged in the 1960s, not least with reference to Cumbernauld, meaning a multi-functional and potentially extendable structural framework, filled with more ephemeral units. Around the Town Centre, the seven residential areas formed an elongated doughnut-shape (Figure 3.4). These areas featured a continuous 'carpet' or 'mesh' of buildings, low in overall height but, as already noted, deliberately more dense (or 'urban'/'urbane') than the Garden City or inter-war international modern patterns. Their governing concept was that of enclosed space in the Camillo Sitte tradition, rather than open or flowing space. The housing nonetheless kept a foot in the older 1940s/1950s pattern of mixed development and picturesque 'Townscape' planning by using tower blocks as important vertical accents.

Writing in 1964 for an architectural audience, Wilson summed up the overall concept and the typically modernist design organization that enabled its realization:

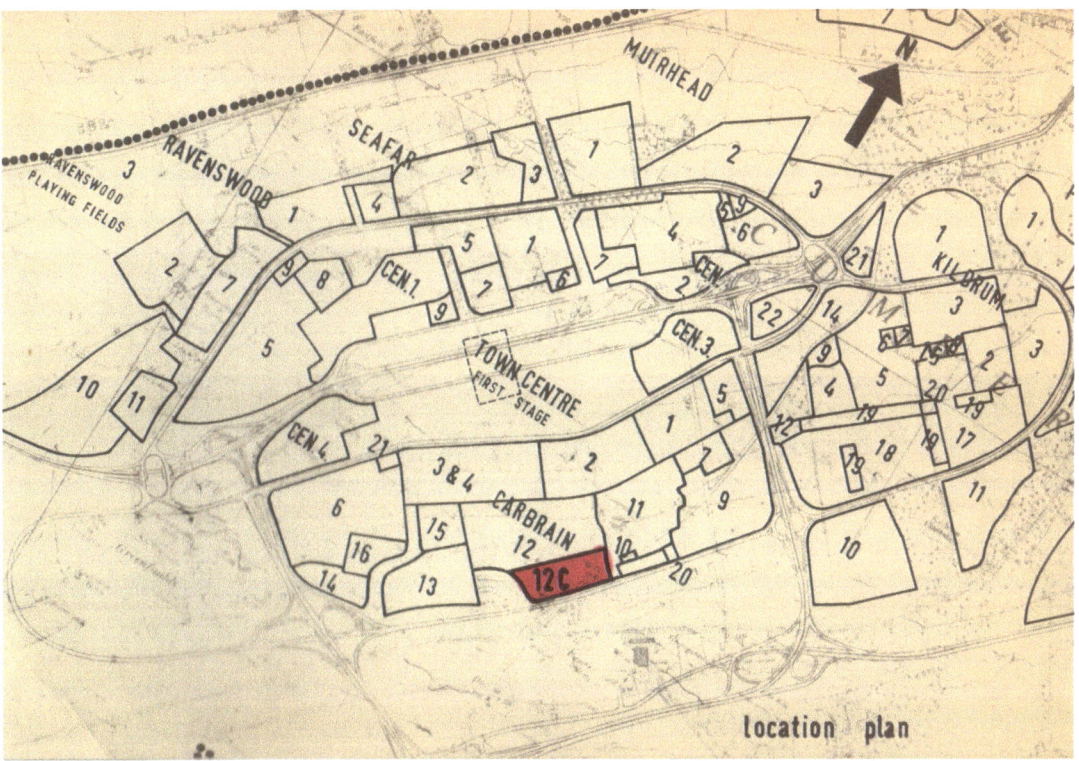

FIGURE 3.4 Layout plan of Cumbernauld showing housing area names and development numbers (Collection of Miles Glendinning).

> I want to see a compact urban area [...] the neighbourhood unit is not an essential element of good town design [...] too rigid use zoning can produce a negative approach to planning problems [...] Vehicles and pedestrians should be separated [...] the car parking problems of central areas call for fresh study [...] We have the opportunity to design a cellular town, the houses within walking distance of the centre, with planting used as an integral part of the development and with levels that can be exploited to provide interest in the grouping of buildings. My office will be organised on a group basis with planners, architects, landscape architects and engineers working side by side.[9]

The initial realization seemed to live up to these hopes. The following year, Richard Crossman (then the Minister for Housing and Local Government in Westminster) toured Cumbernauld with Hugh Wilson and Dame Evelyn Sharp, the powerful civil servant who oversaw new towns practice in England. Crossman enthused that

> Cumbernauld is built on the top of a long, high, bleak ridge. It's a very grey Scottish town, which has settled into the ridge with an enormous lot of roads and a fascinating variety of modern houses. Up-and-down houses, vertical houses, horizontal houses, and everything, including the churches, fitting into the style, everything done in a tremendously austere, exhilarating, uncomfortable style.[10]

This, he noted, was 'the kind of thing which Dame Evelyn and I are excited about, in contrast to the cosy, garden-suburb atmosphere of Stevenage or Harlow or Basildon' – about which 'the Dame, of course, was contemptuous. She loves Cumbernauld'.

The original seven residential areas were clustered into two zones: the north-west side of the ridge (Northside) looking towards the Campsie Fells, where the Muirhead, Seafar and Ravenswood areas were built; and the flatter south-east side (Southside) sloping away from the Town Centre, which comprised Carbrain, Kildrum, Park and Greenfaulds. Uneasily reflecting the difficulty of extending this highly integrated concept to accommodate increases in population targets, several later satellite areas were added: the expansion of Cumbernauld Village; Abronhill to the north-east (from 1964); and in the late 1960s, to the south-west, Condorrat, which integrated a pre-existing village. A new extension zone to the north-west, separated from the existing town by what was then the A80 road, was designated in 1973 and developed in the 1980s and 1990s with the Balloch, Wardpark North, Castlecary, Westfield and Blackwood areas, setting a new trend for private-led housing development, planned conventionally, which continues today (Figure 3.5).

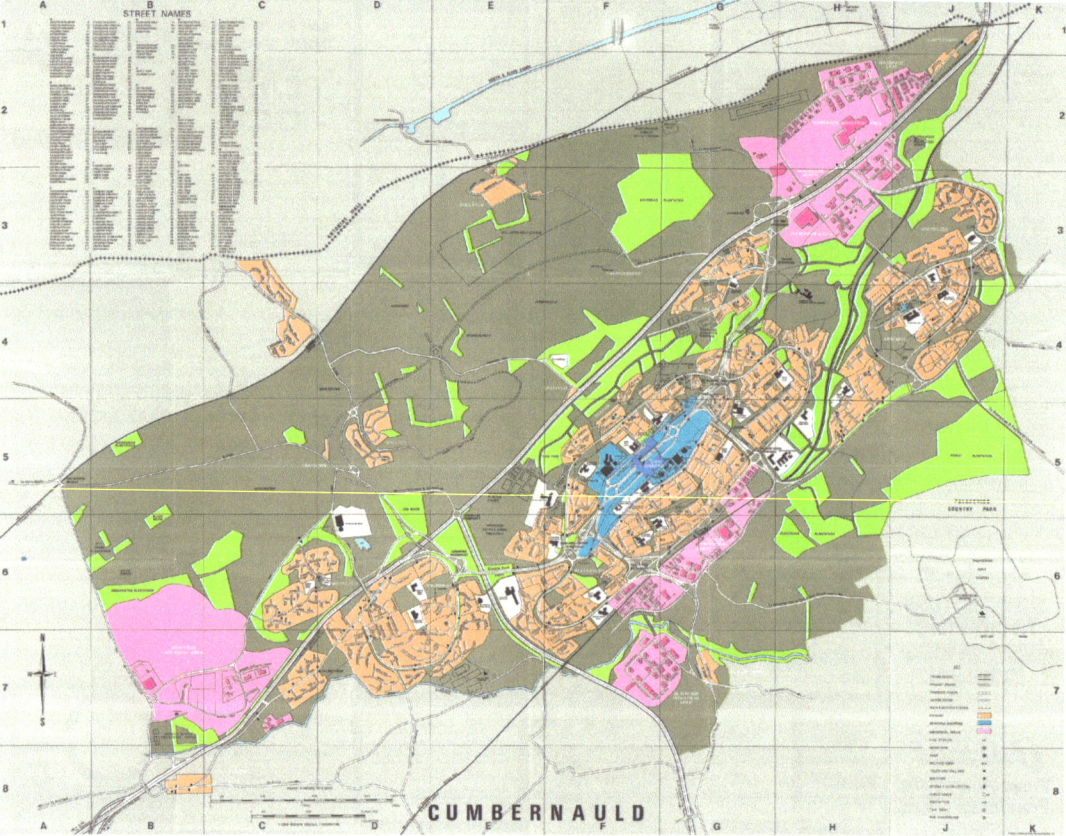

FIGURE 3.5 Early 1980s plan of Cumbernauld, showing the majority of the housing areas (orange) clustered around the town centre (blue) with industrial areas on the perimeter (pink). Subsequent development has taken in the area towards the top of the plan (Collection of Miles Glendinning).

The original town development zone was organized around a hierarchical road network, laid out from 1958 to 1959, which segregated foot and vehicular traffic and systematized cross-town movement in a manner which anticipated the influential Buchanan report (*Traffic in Towns*) of 1963. Priority was given to pedestrians, with pathways allowing the most direct point-to-point routes. In landscape terms, there was a stark contrast between the two planned ways of moving through the town: the small-scale, often tree-lined internal footpath network, and the bold, somewhat monumental incisions of the traffic system, whose main feature was an expressway 'A' road running from north-east to south-west, right through the Town Centre megastructure. The rest of the original 1958 network comprised an oval distributor loop 'B' road surrounding the whole town, augmented by an additional loop road to the south-west, and with two transverse 'B' routes: Jane's Brae, between Carbrain and Greenfaulds, and the B8045, which connected the town to the Abronhill satellite area. The focal points of this motor-age vehicular network were two massive 1960s grade-separated interchanges at either end of the two-centre zone, the first built being Muirhead-Braehead to the north-east, originally planned as an inverted-trumpet grade-separated interchange.

In each housing area, smaller-scale ring roads gave local access to housing, schools and sometimes industrial areas, with the immediate access to housing groups typically being on foot in an example of Radburn-style planning (Figure 3.6). Key to the layout was a dense layering of culs-de-sac, bridges and underpasses, belts of contoured grass and preserved or newly planted trees designed by Gillespie's staff. Clusters of circular 'bubble' garages were built throughout the town; the first and best examples survive at Kildrum, Park and Abronhill. In each residential

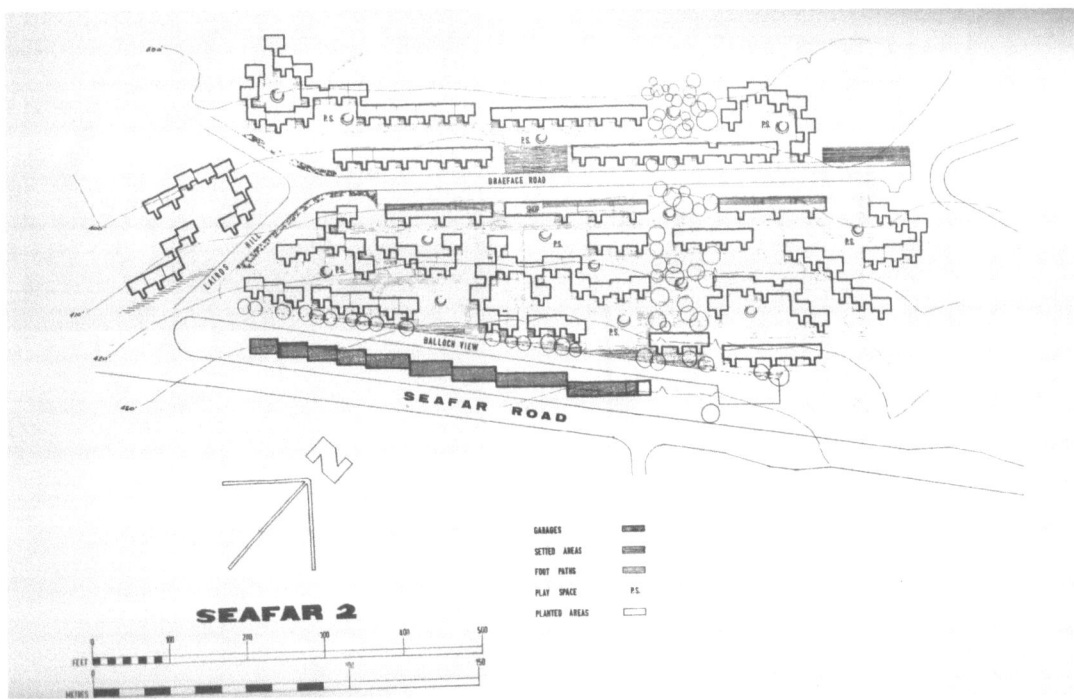

FIGURE 3.6 Plan of Seafar 2, showing the 'carpet' of housing (Miles Glendinning).

area, a local shop was built for every 300 houses, usually comprising single-storey roughcast structures with deep black fascias, large pyramidal roofs and timber lining internally. A sense of local continuity was conveyed by naming the areas after the farms that had previously occupied the compulsorily purchased sites, some of whose steading buildings were re-used for community functions. Granite setts sourced from Glasgow Corporation's contemporary slum-clearance areas were re-purposed as landscaping elements, for example as cladding for embankments or as pathway edges. Recycled boulders uncovered in site-formation work were dispersed in the landscape in an evocation of 1940s–50s Scandinavian urban design, becoming highly valued by the townsfolk as meeting points (e.g. Figure 3.3)

Town Centre

Cumbernauld's Town Centre was built as a single, multi-level, multi-purpose megastructural complex at the summit of the designated area (Figure 3.7). It was initially constructed in two phases, the first being officially opened in 1967. However, the first models and sketches were published in 1962–4, accompanied by the breathless language of technological enthusiasm, especially in Geoffrey Copcutt's own piece in the May 1963 issue of *Architectural Design*.[11] By 1966, similarly boosterish rhetoric informed Cumbernauld's corporate promotion efforts, with CDC reports excitedly recording that 'air hostesses admired the model of Cumbernauld Town Centre when on display at the West London Air Terminal', while a 1970 brochure noted that the completed Phase 1 included 'the largest supermarket in Scotland' and boasted that 'there is nothing like [the Centre] in Britain, or, for that matter, in the world'.[12]

The town-centre zone formed an elongated rectangle aligned north-east to south-west. The original planning concept called for a staged, linear-style development, starting in the middle and extending at either end. Phase One (1963–7) comprised two principal elements. The larger was the main commercial, administrative and (originally) housing block located to the south-east of the dual carriageway and formed of a gigantic, squat, tiered structure that originally stepped up from south to north. Its lower south section contained two-storey covered parking, with,

FIGURE 3.7 Cumbernauld Town Centre (© Architectural Press Archive/RIBA Collections).

above, a supermarket and civic podium, and offices. Its higher north section is crowned by a semi-freestanding horizontal range of porthole-windowed units (originally penthouse flats, empty as of 2024). An elaborate network of ramps knitted together the various levels. The second element of Phase One was a spur to the north, which directly continued the main shopping concourse for a short distance across the dual carriageway.

The main element of Phase One consists of a massive reinforced concrete skeleton, built in ruggedly shuttered form, containing a labyrinthine and typically megastructural diversity of infill structures: shops, library, civic offices (Figure 3.8). In Copcutt's words, this was 'a central infrastructure of highways and walkways, layers and ledges promising shelter, warmth and family freedom'.[13] The linear 'penthouse' block which crowns the whole structure is supported by a separate line of six slab columns, punching their way up through the rest, and proudly exposed at either end in hammer-head cross-section form, with grey concrete protuberances.

North of the expressway is Phase Two (1968–72), a three-storey block with horizontally banded windows. Attached to its south-west side was the Golden Eagle Hotel, with a glazed wall directly overlooking the expressway. Designed by Sam Bunton and built in 1966–7, it was demolished as early as 1982. The interior of Phases One and Two originally featured exposed concrete walls and waffle-slab ceilings, subsequently mostly filled in. The modest Central Library on the uppermost level is a rare survivor; the adjacent spacious deep-plan Town Hall was closed in the 1990s.

FIGURE 3.8 Cumbernauld Town Centre, interior as it appeared in the 1970s (Miles Glendinning).

By the late 1960s, the same architectural fashion-led press that had enthusiastically welcomed Copcutt's Town Centre was already turning against it: 'the least appealing features of urban life are faithfully reproduced [...], a misplaced attempt to combine widely different movement systems', reported *Architectural Design* in 1968.[14] An 1976–7 RIBA-funded study, *Cumbernauld Revisited*, was authored by two architects, Jim and Krystyna Johnson, who had lived and worked in Cumbernauld from 1961. It argued that 'the brilliance of the design blinded people to certain practical weaknesses'.[15] The Centre was 'more attractive on paper than it would to a harassed mum pushing her pram up those exposed ramps on a typically wet and windy Cumbernauld day'.[16] Similarly in 1981, Lionel Esher concluded that 'only a state monopoly would have dared assault a female clientele with so much raw concrete'.[17] Yet the megastructure also had significant social advantages. The concrete terraced structure on the south-east side, stepping down towards North Carbrain, provided townsfolk with an impressive open-air 'civic podium', where almost all interested children in Cumbernauld in the 1970s and 1980s passed their cycling proficiency test.

Phases One and Two became increasingly dilapidated from the late 1980s onwards, and significant alteration and piecemeal demolition began. The linear 'extensibility' of the megastructure was abandoned, and new, utilitarian box-like shopping structures were built randomly around it. In a protracted scheme of 1995–2005, the lower levels of the original terraced megastructure, sloping down south-eastwards to North Carbrain, were removed to allow construction of a new, flat-roofed mall of utilitarian character, the 'Antonine Centre'. As of 2024, this new mall is itself now not only plagued by water leaks but is also commercially insolvent. Behind it, the surviving monumental fragments of the old megastructure still cling to life amid the chaotic banality of the new, market-led Town Centre 'vision'.

The original housing zone: Southside

The architectural fireworks of the Town Centre contrasted sharply with the surrounding belt of housing, which was treated as a restrained yet highly variegated backdrop. The 1958 preliminary masterplan envisaged an unprecedentedly high (for the new towns) average housing density of eighty-one persons per acre, which required the CDC architects to develop a substantially new design approach. The Northside and Southside housing zones were designed in contrasting ways. The Southside's layout was deliberately compact and urban, with a homogeneous and overtly modern treatment including flat-roofed housing dominating areas like Carbrain, while Kildrum has 'vernacular'-inspired terraces arranged in rows with outshots. By contrast, the natural landscape was far more prominent in the steeper Northside (Muirhead, Seafar and Ravenswood), which had a more abrupt and even picturesque layout. The satellite area of Abronhill, to the east of Kildrum (from 1964), shared some aspects of both zones. The planners aimed to provide choices: in size and type of house, as well as quality.[18]

Within the Southside, the development that became known as Park was the first area to be developed from 1957–60, being located on the north-east shoulder of the hill, on a flat and open site. In parallel, the southern section of Kildrum and Carbrain was designed and built from 1958 onwards. The architectural design and layout of the early developments, built before the full road network, was highly varied. Early on, private architectural practices were involved while Wilson built up his staff. In 1956, Kildrum 1, the first housing project commissioned by CDC, was awarded to Gillespie Kidd & Coia, with ninety-eight terraced houses (completed 1958) and four- and five-storey balcony access slab blocks (1959–61), all laid out in square courtyard layouts. The first CDC-designed Radburn-planned development, Park 1, designed in 1957–9 and built by Weir Housing as a higher rental managers' development on the edge of the Town Park, presented a strong contrast to this, with its mixture of single-storey timber-clad houses, staircase-access maisonettes and miniature point blocks; timber-cladding was also used for a group of adjacent private housing (Figure 3.9). Subsequently, terraces came to dominate, in what we might consider a 'modern vernacular' style. As many of the CDC designers were English, the use of dense rows set along lanes reads like a hybrid of nineteenth-century English industrial terraces and traditional Scottish village housing, both very different from the long-established Scottish urban tradition of tenemental housing. The use of roughcast in various shades of grey concealed the use underneath of cheap industrial bricks, of the kind common in nineteenth-century miners' rows, and accentuated the 'traditional Scottish'/vernacular image.

The Kildrum area pioneered Cumbernauld's idiosyncratic street numbering and naming system, which significantly accentuated these areas' sense of complexity (Figure 3.10). Each development at construction stage was simply known by area and section number – for example, Kildrum 1, or Kildrum 5 – but post-completion the densely packed rows were identified within a hierarchy of street names, street numbers and number suffixes. In Kildrum 17/18, for example, Clouden Road was not only the name of the main access road but was also attached to two-storey rows of housing on its south side, each row comprising around half a dozen houses. Rows each had their own 'number', and each house within the row a letter-suffix: for example, 34a-34g Clouden Road. Variations of topography dictated a flexible approach to the Radburn system. Owing to the sloping character of southern Kildrum, each Radburn access path there was bounded by the retaining wall of the next row, whereas in other areas, such as southern Carbrain, some housing had pathways at the front and at the back, accessed through a garden gate. In all cases, however, the primary concern of the planners and architects was to avoid 'front and back' facades along traditional 'streets', and to provide privacy.[19]

The 'Town Park' – also locally known as 'Cumbernauld Field' – originated as the landscaped policies of Cumbernauld House, designed by William Adam in 1731, and taken over by CDC as

FIGURE 3.9 Timber-clad housing, Park 1 (© Architectural Press Archive/RIBA Collections).

FIGURE 3.10 Plan of Kildrum 17, showing Clouden Road housing (Collection of Miles Glendinning).

its headquarters in the manner typical of new town development corporations. In the late 1950s, however, these policies, whose Picturesque contoured layout had replaced the formal vistas and avenues of the Adam era, were opened to the public.[20] Extended from 1958 with low-rise office annexes built using the timber gridded Vic Hallam 'Derwent' system (originally developed for school construction), Cumbernauld House served as CDC's headquarters until the 1996 wind-up, conveniently and cleverly located near the owner-occupied housing areas where the CDC design professionals and civil servants lived (locally identified as 'the bought houses'); the historic house was converted to private flats in the early 2010s.

As in the other new towns, most of the original housing stock built by CDC was for rent. And it was within this rental stock, accordingly, that the most celebrated, award-winning set-pieces of housing design are to be found, mostly by CDC architects and featuring accentuated contrasts between the work of different 'groups', in keeping with the tradition established by Robert Matthew in the London County Council Architect's Department after 1950. (A few developments continued to be designed by outside agencies, such as Park 3 by Matthew's Edinburgh University Housing Research Unit (1963–70), which consisted of a complex gridded network of low-rise flats plus rows of terraced houses monumentally linked by long pends (Figure 3.11).[21]) The first housing area in north Kildrum to be designed in-house was Kildrum 3, Afton Road, designed in 1957–8 and built in 1958–9 by the Scottish Special Housing Association (here acting simply as contractors) using their trademark no-fines concrete system. This extensive area of over twenty rows introduced many of the recognized standard features of CDC housing layouts. It adjoined the Kildrum ring road and had Radburn-style pedestrian-vehicle segregation, with an internal footpath network and a variety of built forms including two-storey 'vernacular' terraces. Those at the west end of the site feature shallow swept-down roofs, with sunny-side private gardens allowed by the shallow slope (1:12). To their east were miniature point blocks with split monopitch roofs, and two-storey terraces with distinctly 'Stevenage' style detailing, including white bargeboards. Immediately adjacent to the west, the 278-unit Kildrum 5 (Mossgiel/Ellisland/Kyle Roads) was designed by leading CDC architect Ron Simpson in 1957–8 and built in 1959–61. It took a different approach (Figure 3.12), with two-storey terrace houses on zig-zag layouts and medium-rise flats

FIGURE 3.11 Park housing by Edinburgh University's Housing Research Unit (Photo: Alistair Fair, 2022).

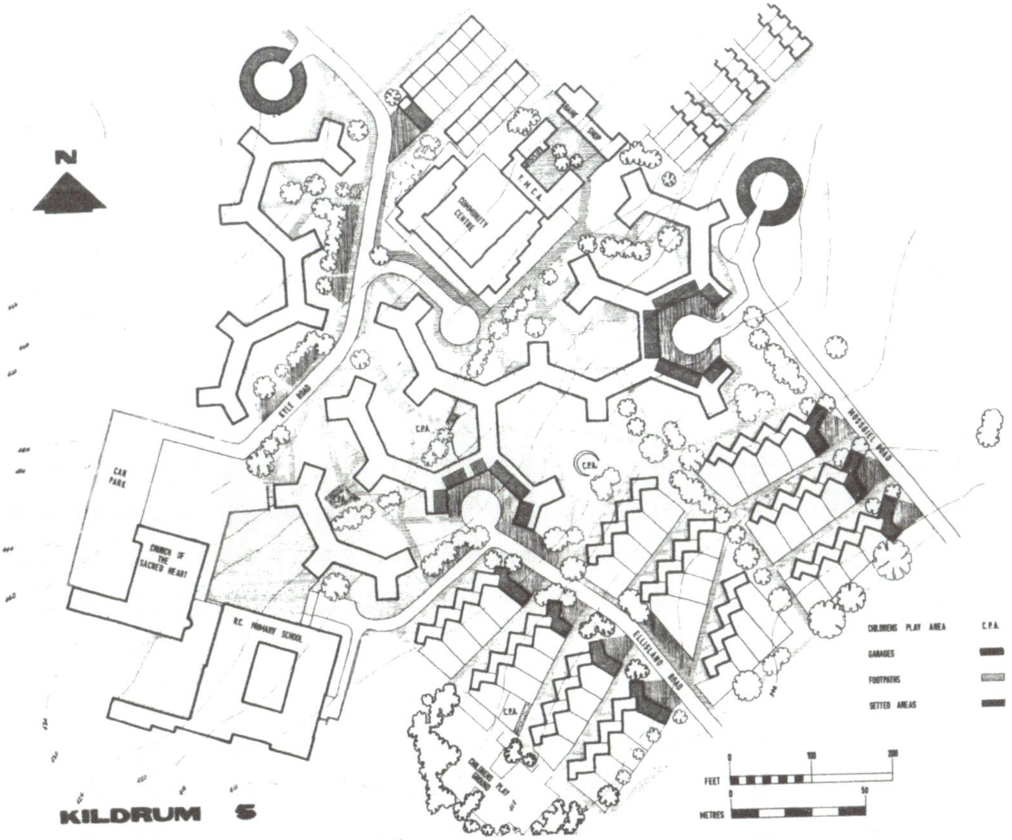

FIGURE 3.12 Kildrum 5 (Collection of Miles Glendinning).

in a continuous honeycomb pattern around courtyards. This pattern was inspired by Backström & Reinius's 1947–8 'star' project at Gröndal near Stockholm, but here the blocks were arranged in a more irregular and picturesque way. In contrast to the strongly coloured Swedish originals, they were more subtly coloured in grey roughcast, with pastel-coloured gable ends and open ground-floor drying areas. Simpson's special circular 'bubble' concept for grouped lock-up garages was first trialled here.

All those areas, however conceptually varied, were low-rise in profile. However, a further, more striking contrast was provided by Kildrum 22, the tallest of the clusters of tower blocks designed by CDC and built using prefabricated Bison construction from the mid-1960s for high-rental 'executive' occupiers. Clustered around the Muirhead-Braehead interchange, three slender point blocks, two of twelve storeys and one of twenty storeys, were grouped around a three-level concrete multi-storey car park. Explicitly intended by Lyddon, Hunter and Wilson to provide a San Gimignano-like visual marker, all the towers were successively demolished from the late 2010s by Sanctuary Housing Association, for reasons that seem to have been motivated by aesthetic prejudice as much as practical management factors.[22]

In the southern sector of Kildrum, Lyddon's team had their first opportunity to design a large area on the low-rise high-density 'vernacular' lines that would ultimately predominate in the town. The most important section was the 525-dwelling Kildrum 17/18 development of 1960–5 (Clouden/Kenmore Roads, Moss Knowe, Doon Side). Set in dense rows along internal paths with steep, swept-down roofs over repetitive outshots, and with unwindowed gable ends, the houses were suggestive in a general way of 'terrace house vernacular'. Houses had a galley-kitchen with a north-facing window at the 'front', reputedly designed to enable mothers to 'keep an eye on the weans' (i.e. children). A belt of single-storey patio houses (courtyard-plan terraces) on Clouden Road to the east of Kildrum 17/18, and also replicated at the western end of Kildrum, was initially popular with 'arty types' in the 1970s.[23]

The largest single element of the pioneering Southside zone, if not of the whole original town, was the Carbrain housing area, immediately to the south-west of Kildrum. Its development process was divided into north and south sectors – a division not generally recognized by residents – and the area was bounded by the North Carbrain and South Carbrain local ring road. The southern sector of Carbrain was, essentially, a straightforward development of Kildrum South on the same lines, by the same CDC architectural group.

Variations in topography, however, dictated significant design differences, in line with Wilson and Gillespie's strong emphasis on landscape *genius loci*. The northern part of Carbrain, designed and built from 1960 and directly abutting the Town Centre, was a far flatter site. Thus, by contrast with Kildrum, the design approach of Lyddon's architects here was more overtly modernist, with long, flat-roofed terraces a little reminiscent of Oud's 1930s Kiefhoek housing in Rotterdam, laid out on grids. To maximize privacy, the houses were single-aspect, with windows on the wide-frontage windows, as at Seafar, Northside (below). In Carbrain 1, 2, 3 and 4 (1960–8), the grid created a network of miniature public squares, and rows of setted parking spaces, in addition to the houses' individual gardens. As a contrast, and to maintain densities, in Carbrain 5 (1964–5) the CDC architects inserted a more picturesque grouping of four medium-rise blocks with horizontal glazing, surrounded by extensive landscaping and trees.

South Carbrain was a far more steeply graded site, and here multi-level or split-level housing types influenced by slightly earlier Northside developments (see below) were built from 1963 to 1972. Owing to the site constraints, gardens tended to be small, despite the homes often accommodating larger families: the terraced rows were clustered together. The first phase was the 525-unit Carbrain 9 (Millcroft and Greenrigg Roads), designed in 1963 by Lyddon's team and built in 1964–7 by Holland Hannen & Cubitts. It comprised a mixture of innovative, higher-density house-types, including narrow-frontage, three-storey flat-roofed terraces stepping down the slope with pend access to the terraces below, some with integrated garages: the houses had timber fronts with a lighter roughcast than in Kildrum.

At the southernmost perimeter of Carbrain South, the area was given a more monumental face by a south-facing array of five six-storey barrier blocks, linked by a rear elevated walkway (to Millcroft Road) at first-floor level. Unlike most of Cumbernauld's higher flats, this development has (as of 2024) so far stubbornly escaped refurbishment and demolition. In the early decades, the only recognizable social division between housing areas was that between the very few 'bought houses' of the professional classes and the overwhelmingly predominant CDC rented stock, and thus no area was stigmatized. But the introduction of medium-rise slab blocks, some system-built, in Kildrum and Carbrain, was bound up with a subtle decline in the social status of those areas from the late 1970s, an issue that grew in prominence following 'Right to Buy' in the 1980s.

The original housing zone: Northside

The Northside housing zone, whose design was led by Roy Hunter, included the Muirhead, Seafar and Ravenswood areas. Reflecting its far steeper topography, facing directly across to the Kilsyth Hills, it was given a more abrupt and even picturesque layout, influenced very strongly by Gillespie's input and by the modernist ideal of 'Scandinavian forest landscaping'. In 1995, Gillespie recalled the genesis of the resulting concept:

> On the Northside, as we were building on a hilltop, we could bring in the distant scenery as an integral part of the local landscape. That affected everything we did, as it comprises a constant backdrop. The Northside is developed on steep slopes, so there are two sides to all the developments, a road side and a footpath side. On one early occasion, around 1958, Bill Thomson, the planner, and Roy Hunter, the architect, and myself (who were doing the Northside) were walking across the Northside before any houses existed there! We were wandering along, wondering, 'What are we going to do here?' And Bill said, 'Wouldn't it be wonderful if it was like Norway and Finland and we had a big forest we could build into it?' We all agreed, and decided there and then, 'Let's build a forest on the Northside!' So the 'forest', we designed and planted. Then at Seafar, we integrated existing trees with buildings, to create flowing spaces in a very natural setting, including boulders and other features. The background of the hills is ever-present – we drew it in. And the tower blocks formed part of the formula – they were built as much as sculpture as anything else![24]

Hunter's Northside designs evoked the architectural past in a 'romantic', almost organically evolved way, in contrast to the relative order of the Southside (Figure 3.13).[25] The Northside

FIGURE 3.13 Housing at Seafar 2 (© Architectural Press Archive/RIBA Collections).

housing (designed from 1958) was divided topographically: the southern part, next to the Town Centre, was gently sloping (1:10 to 1:15), while the northern outer slopes were steeper (1:7 average). The subsoil conditions allowed only specific house-types, either low-rise houses or slender tower blocks on deep piles, and a belt of impressive multi-storey point blocks was built amid the trees and rocks. The outer, northernmost belt of the landscape was divided by small valleys and tree belts which were retained and became a 'play forest' with recreation and play spaces.

The early and gently sloping area of Muirhead 4 (Grieve/Mitchell/Mitchison Roads, designed from 1959 and built in 1961–5) comprised larger single-aspect terraces, similar to Kildrum. Complementing the taller group at Kildrum 22, the outcrops of twelve-storey 'Bison' prefabricated blocks at Muirhead 6 and Seafar 3 (1964–7), comprised two- and four-person 'executive flats' – all within easy walking distance of the Town Centre, like everywhere else in the original housing zone. Strongly contrasting with these, in scale at least, were the award-winning Seafar housing projects. The Northside housing designed by Hunter's CDC architects pioneered several of the standard house patterns for the town – although, regardless, its original flatted slab block (Fleming Road, Seafar 1) was demolished alongside those elsewhere in the town in 1999.

Seafar 1 (Lennox/Seafar/Fleming/Fergusson Roads, 1960–3) established the town's standard pattern of single-aspect houses with gardens on sloping sites. The houses themselves were laid out in rows aligned according to sunlight requirements, with monopitch roofs. Seafar 2 (Lairds Hill/Balloch View/Braeface Road, designed 1959–60, built 1961–3) was a 147-house project on the steeper northern edge of the Northside. Built at quite a high density of eighty-five persons per acre, it comprised a different pattern of 'terrace' house, with split-level sections and featuring no gardens, and set in long rows running parallel to the contours on the lower slopes, linked by pends. The irregular groups, with their entrance porches, light-harled walls and irregularly disposed wooden windows, were set in an intensely integrated landscaping scheme, embracing rocks, shrubs and heather turfing, and strongly ramped and contoured. Both Seafar 1 and 2 won Saltire Society Housing Design Awards on completion (Figure 3.14).

FIGURE 3.14 Housing at Seafar (© Crown Copyright: HES).

Abutting the Southside zone, to the north-east of Kildrum and Park, was the first major extension to the original housing area, Abronhill, which was developed from 1965 onwards. Located overlooking over a natural gorge, on a 170-acre site, it was built as a miniature version of the main town, planned in a self-contained way to avoid compromising the integrity of the original housing belt. It included its own mini-town centre, local ring roads and low, but dense clusters of housing set around a belt. Today the built fabric of Abronhill is, on the whole, in better condition than that of the original sectors of the town.

Cumbernauld as urban vision: Early reception

In the early and euphoric international evaluations of Cumbernauld as a whole, the housing zone was assumed to be an integral and successful part of the avant-garde vision. The AIA jury in 1967 argued:

> [T]he architects have evolved a 'Cumbernauld idiom' in keeping with Scottish tradition and in harmony with the site [...] the town, though only partly complete, has already a real sense of community and place, endearing it to both residents and visitors. The architects have achieved townscape on a shoestring since the entire budget has been extremely limited. The most effective urban design has been gained at moderate cost with a limited palette.[26]

Equally, the housing was not a key issue for the mainstream architectural press in Britain, in sharp contrast with the polemical architectural early attacks from 1968 against the Town Centre. For example, in 1966, the London-based design journalist and author Mary Gilliatt wrote a personal evaluation of the town in *Country Life*. It followed her fourth visit, and by that time, she noted, 20,000 people had been accommodated in 4,000 new dwellings. She posed pragmatic questions about the success of the town as an updated 'blueprint' for urban planning in the 1960s. 'Is the town standing up firmly to the acid test of daily living?' she asked. She confidently reported on the 'good mixed population' – mostly young people in their thirties who were 'hand-picked' for levels of cleanliness! Perhaps reflecting the long-established English preference for brightly coloured brick finishes and busy Picturesque detail, Gilliatt suggested that there was overall 'still too much monotony, too much grey everywhere, too little change in the light and shade'.[27]

Sociological investigations, too, seemed to suggest a general positivity towards the town and towards their new homes. In 1967, CDC commissioned a household attitude survey from the University of Strathclyde's Sociology Department, which reported that Cumbernauld was 'a friendly town in which most of the people are mostly satisfied [...] and three-quarters of its residents considered that they had bettered themselves by moving to the town'.[28] Journalist Alistair Borthwick reported that in the late 1960s, 'the children I saw (they went about in shoals) were having a whale of a time with never a car to bother them'.[29] And the 1970 promotional film *Cumbernauld: Town for Tomorrow*, commissioned by CDC and directed by Robin Crichton with a commentary by Magnus Magnusson, talked of 'small sturdy cottages set to the wind' and hailed its 'engineering for pedestrians' and segregation of footpaths and roads as 'brilliantly legible'.[30]

However, the first critiques were visible by then, at first in the far distance. In 1969, the journalist John Sinclair of the *Scots Magazine* cautioned that 'first impressions of Cumbernauld can be a bit daunting. The mass of regimented concrete leaves the individual feeling he is pretty small beer'.[31] And in the 1977 *Revisited* study (detailed above), the resident architects reflected on the town's 'dour and undemonstrative appearance to visitors [...] disliked by many Scots and by most English visitors when they first see its grey, unrevealing form on their hilltop'.[32] In that same year, Ferdynand Zweig, sociologist and free-market economist, authored *The Cumbernauld Study*.[33] He claimed that planners had made it difficult for people to drive to the centre and regretted the absence of 'street life' in the footpath system. Hugh Wilson vigorously contested these criticisms of the 'imagined ills of Cumbernauld', arguing that 'people can and do meet on the footpaths, that have schools, corner shops, halls, churches and playgrounds sited along them, but you can certainly not meet in a motor car' and concluding that Zweig's views 'could do harm to the cause of creating a decent setting for life in the motor age'.[34]

The strong disparity of scale between pedestrian and motor traffic infrastructure increasingly seemed excessive. The 1977 *Revisited* study claimed that the large road system in some areas effectively cut the town into neighbourhoods. The four-lane expressways were a 'scar in what was intended to be a unified urban fabric', but within each area, 'there is no doubt people appreciate the separate footpath system, especially for the safety it gives children'; in this respect, it concluded that Cumbernauld 'has to be explored on foot to be understood' and 'once in and among the houses, people can be won over'.[35] Housing was on occasion now highlighted for criticism. The 1977 study noted criticisms of the 'tightly packed housing, like miners' rows'. But elsewhere, the media and townsfolk were still mainly positive. Gilliatt praised the 'astonishing variety in house types and shapes, with thoughtful gradations of roofs so that everyone gets a fair share of sunlight and a view down the hill to the woods'.[36] This positive phase of media and popular reception of the Cumbernauld environment culminated triumphantly in Bill Forsyth's 1980 romantic comedy, *Gregory's Girl*, set incidentally in Abronhill rather than the original housing zone. Here the complexity of the housing layouts and the footpath network, and the mature landscaping, in combination, provide an immaculate, almost paradise-like setting for the comedic coming-of-age adventures of the young cast. Even although the town's physical reality since then has slid into decay and 'old age', the urban setting of Cumbernauld celebrated in the film will remain for posterity as a perfect and unsullied vision of the town's modern innocence.

Conclusion

In architectural and planning terms, Cumbernauld enjoyed an international status far higher than the other Scottish new towns. Within Britain, its only conceivable rival in this respect was the later Milton Keynes. But whereas Milton Keynes was in some ways bound up with a retreat from concentrated urbanity, instead reflecting new ideas of flexibility and mobility through a low-density gridded layout of sometimes postmodern housing, Cumbernauld was the product of 1960s late modernism, and demonstrated an approach of unqualified daring and risk-taking. As the AIA jury argued in 1967, it was unashamedly 'designed for the millennium'.[37] Its architectural-planning concept and its realization represented in many ways a huge gamble, and this chapter has set out to highlight its key elements: the plan, infrastructure, housing design and landscaping.

As late as 1980, it seemed that the vision of the CDC's planners, architects and landscape architects had triumphantly paid off, but after the abolition of the development corporation in 1996, Cumbernauld fell victim to an insidious process of dilapidation, redevelopment and demolition, including most recently the excision of all its tower blocks and, in the process, its shrivelling to invisibility in distant views. Narratives of failure, stigmatization and self-hate gathered pace after 2000, with media-generated anti-awards, such as the 'Crap Towns' competition of 2003. The infamous 'Plook on a Plinth' 'award' of 2001 compared Cumbernauld to Kabul, and, uniquely, it was singled out a second time in 2005. Yet at the same time, its international architectural reputation, especially that of the Town Centre, began to subtly revive as part of the 'Brutalist heritage' movement. The 2020s seem likely to witness an unexpected 'race' between, on the one hand, the continuing physical degradation of the town, including the likely demolition of the remaining part of the megastructural Town Centre, and on the other hand, the increasingly detached revival of its international architectural reputation. Which of the two will 'win' is, as of 2024, highly unclear!

Notes

1 This chapter draws on the Cumbernauld entry (written by Diane Watters and Miles Glendinning) in Rob Close, John Gifford and Frank A. Walker, *Lanarkshire and Renfrewshire* (New Haven and London: Yale University Press, 2016), 232–62. See also Miles Glendinning, 'Cluster Homes: Planning and Housing in Cumbernauld New Town', *Twentieth Century Architecture* 9: *Housing the Twentieth Century Nation* (2008): 132–46; Miles Glendinning and Diane Watters, 'Cumbernauld New Town: Reception and Heritage Legacy', *Architektura & Urbanizmus, Journal of Architecture and Town Planning Theory* 46 (2012): 271–87; Jessica Taylor, 'Cumbernauld: the Conception, Development and Realisation of a Post-War British New Town', PhD dissertation, University of Edinburgh, 2010.

2   'Report of the Jury for the 1967 R S Reynolds Memorial Award for Community Architecture Awarded to Cumbernauld', *American Institute of Architects Journal,* July 1967, 36–58.
3   Though unpublished, partial drafts survive in manuscript form.
4   Cumbernauld Development Corporation, *Cumbernauld New Town, Preliminary Planning Proposals*, 1958 and *Cumbernauld New Town, Planning Proposals, First Revision* [1959].
5   E.g. Miles Glendinning and Diane Watters, 'Cumbernauld and Kilsyth: Tour by the Architectural Heritage Society of Scotland, 25 June 1994' [authors' collection].
6   For more about those buildings, see Close et al., *Lanarkshire and Renfrewshire*, 232–62.
7   Robert Grieve, interviewed by Miles Glendinning, 1987.
8   William (Bill) Gillespie, lecture at Royal Fine Art Commission for Scotland, 17 August 1995 [authors' notes].
9   'Wilson on Cumbernauld', *Architects' Journal* 139, no. 2 (8 January 1964): 65–6.
10 Richard Crossman, *The Diaries of a Cabinet Minister*, vol. 1 (London: Book Club Associates, 1975), 158–9.
11 Geoffrey Copcutt, 'Cumbernauld: New Town Central Area', *Architectural Design* 33, no. 5 (May 1963): 210–25.
12 Cumbernauld Development Corporation, *Welcome to Cumbernauld*, brochure, 1970. Its front cover photograph shows CDC architect Krystyna Johnson and other mothers dragging the 'weans' up the pathway beside Maclehose playpark in Kildrum.
13 Copcutt, 'Central Area'.
14 Stephen Mullin, 'Day Tripper', *Architectural Design* 38, no. 9 (September 1968): 408–11.
15 Jim and Krystyna Johnson, 'Cumbernauld Revisited', *Architects' Journal* 166, no. 40 (5 October 1977): 637–49 (p. 644).
16 Ibid.
17 Lionel Esher, *A Broken Wave: The Rebuilding of England* (Harmondsworth: Penguin, 1981), 249–50.
18 'Housing', chapter in the unpublished Cumbernauld Development Corporation book, 'Building a New Town', 1964 [copy in the possession of Miles Glendinning].
19 Ibid., 4–5.
20 Close et al., *Lanarkshire and Renfrewshire,* 244–5 [entry on Cumbernauld House, by Aonghus Mackechnie].
21 For a detailed discussion of Park 3: Alistair Fair, 'Privacy, the Housing Research Unit at the University of Edinburgh and the Courtyard House, 1959–70', *Architectural History* 65 (2022): 327–58.
22 'Way's Paved for Flats Demolition', *Cumbernauld News*, 23 January 2012.
23 'Arty types': Diane Watters' recollections of local terminology from childhood, 1970s.
24 William (Bill) Gillespie, lecture at Royal Fine Art Commission for Scotland, 17 August 1995 [authors' notes].
25 Roy Hunter, interviewed by Jessica Taylor, 20 November 2007; Close et al., *Lanarkshire and Renfrewshire*, 248.
26 'Report of the Jury', 36–58.
27 Mary Gilliatt, 'Anatomy of a New Town', *Country Life* 140, no. 3631 (October 1966): 830–2.
28 Ibid.
29 A. Borthwick, undated newspaper cutting, Edinburgh College of Art Cumbernauld Archive.
30 Scottish Moving Image Archive, 2227, *Cumbernauld: Town for Tomorrow* (1970), dir. Robin Crichton.

31 John Sinclair, 'Exciting Days at the Cottage', *Scots Magazine*, January 1969, 31.
32 Johnson and Johnson, 'Cumbernauld Revisited', 644.
33 Ferdynand Zweig, *The Cumbernauld Study* (London: Urban Research Bureau, 1970), 5.
34 Ibid.
35 Johnson and Johnson, 'Cumbernauld Revisited', 644.
36 Gilliatt, 'Anatomy'.
37 'Report of the Jury', 36–58.

4

Livingston

Livingston, with a population in 2023 of nearly 60,000, is the second largest settlement in the Lothian region after Edinburgh. Designated in April 1962, the new town was planned by an in-house team, initially under Chief Architect and Planning Officer (CAPO) Peter Daniel, the former deputy architect of Peterlee New Town in England.[1] It took in a landscape shaped by coal and shale mining as well as farming; at the core of the designated area was what the development corporation's housing manager in 1977 described as 'a small village still draped in the dustsheet of the 19th century'.[2] Livingston's master plan – the work of Livingston Development Corporation (LDC) – was shaped by ideas of mobility (especially the use of the private car), flexibility and the relationships between the new town and its wider region.[3] In this respect it offered an early exploration of themes which became significant in 1960s new town planning across Scotland and internationally. The integration of the existing landscape was an essential and original feature of the plan; Daniel's greatest reputed success at Livingston was in diverting the proposed line of the new M8 motorway away from the Almond Valley.

Peter Daniel's tenure was short, as he was dismissed in August 1964.[4] However, his bold, innovative vision set the course for his successors, and even in 1965 a newspaper report hailed Livingston as 'Daniel's Dream Town'.[5] His 1963 'Interim Report on the Preparation of the Master Plan' proposed that Livingston would 'break away from the established form of new town concept which still persists in its attempt to relate the artificially created new town to conventional town form'; it would offer 'a planned environment which vigorously employs modern techniques of building to create different ways of living set in a balanced environment of humanism […] new architecture and in the spirit of our age'.[6] For Daniel, writing in 1964, Livingston represented a new phase in the new towns programme: 'the building of Livingston would have less to do with the traditional techniques of the old, 1948 new towns than with evolving techniques of town design and production, and I was determined that this new town should look to the future.'[7] An open-ended grid plan, set out in a loosely framed set of proposals rather than a detailed blueprint, anticipated the slightly later plan for Milton Keynes in England (Figure 4.1). Yet at the same time, the 'districts' set within Livingston's grid squares in some ways revisited the 'Mark 1' idea of a town divided into smaller units, albeit now described using an American term. And although Livingston rejected the concentration of Cumbernauld's plan, in other ways it looked to its immediate Scottish predecessor.[8] The design of the housing areas, in particular, echoed Cumbernauld in such matters as density and traffic planning, though the pioneering if problematic

FIGURE 4.1 'Welcome to Livingston': drivers orientate themselves within the grid plan (© West Lothian Archives and Records Centre).

use of prefabricated, standardized construction systems in some of Livingston's early estates gave them a distinctive visual character.

Livingston was to be a centre for new employment and economic growth, the place where, as Daniel put it, 'the industrial society of Scotland in the 1960s has its birth'.[9] It was an early embodiment of the 'growth point' ideas set out in the 1961 Toothill report on the Scottish economy (discussed in the Introduction to this book), and it formed part of a broader regional strategy concerned with the economic and infrastructural modernization of central Scotland.[10] It was noticeably successful, resulting in high-status industrial and commercial zones whose design, by the 1980s, was decidedly postmodern and, particularly at the pioneering Kirkton Campus, reflected the high-quality, technology-focused 'business park' model seen also in East Kilbride. Deliberate 'Americanisms' fuelled the impressive and aggressive promotional campaigns by LDC to attract business and industry in the 1970s and 1980s – most notably 'Make it in Livingston'.

In plan, Livingston remains divided into two parts: south and north of the Almondvale district, where the town centre is located. This chapter will first examine the genesis of the overall plan and its early development, and will then move on to focus on the central area before turning, more briefly, to housing design and density. The chapter is rooted in field survey. It also draws on the uncatalogued archive of Peter Daniel, deposited at the University of Edinburgh.[11] The chapter examines the town as designed, built and lived in – a slightly different emphasis from the picture presented in LDC's powerful and clever promotional campaigns. That detailed story has already been expertly covered by previous historians, in particular the works of Elspeth Wills, Emma Peattie and William Hendrie.[12] Indeed, Livingston is rare amongst Scotland's new towns in that it already has four histories devoted to it. The first was published as early as 1977 by LDC's Leslie Higgs, whose role as Housing and Social Relations Officer – a first for Scotland – allowed him to produce a vivid 'on the ground' account.[13]

Livingston has, with a few exceptions, been overlooked by architectural historians in favour of the avant-garde late-modernist set pieces of Cumbernauld and Irvine. David Cowling's 1997 survey remains the best architectural account to date.[14] Not all histories have been so balanced, however. In 1994, for instance, architectural critic Charles McKean dismissed Livingston's 'desultory housing'.[15] And by contrast with Colin McWilliam's enlightened praise of the town in 1977, the revised *Buildings of Scotland* volume of 2024 concludes of Livingston that 'overall there is little spectacular architecture'.[16] This, however, was precisely the point. Livingston restated the

FIGURE 4.2 'A new urban landscape': Livingston's plan was shaped by ideas of mobility and flexibility, with separation of traffic and pedestrians (© West Lothian Archives and Records Centre).

goal of modest excellence which had been the key in East Kilbride (as discussed in Chapter 1). One 1964 report concluded that the 'standards to be achieved, techniques used [...] should be more advanced in a rapidly expanding town with its eye on the 21st century than the established ways of semi-rural area'.[17] It laid down themes which would be at the core of 1960s planning in Scotland and beyond. In its well-balanced architecture, road infrastructure, landscaping and built legacy, Livingston was arguably a *model* 'Mark 3' new town, 'a new urban landscape of exceptional quality' (Figure 4.2).[18]

Designation

The designation of a small new town in the East Calder/Midcalder area of West Lothian had first been proposed in 1948 in the Mears plan for east-central Scotland.[19] Mears anticipated the enlargement of these two villages to a total of 7,000 people, with new employment to balance the declining mining industry. This approach paralleled the 'small new town' formula which Mears also proposed for Fife (and which had led to the designation, albeit on more expansive lines, of Glenrothes). It was not until April 1962, however, that Livingston was designated. The immediate motivation was the continuing need for Glasgow overspill, with some 80 per cent of a planned incoming population of 70,000 people being intended to come from the city.[20] An initial source of employment existed in the form of the British Motor Corporation's factory at nearby Bathgate, which was expanding.[21] But designation also had other, more novel goals. It would serve as a means to transform the landscape, scarred as it was by mining.[22] The designation order suggested that the rundown appearance of the designated area served to 'deter industrial growth' while also being unattractive to potential residents.[23] The Secretary of State for Scotland anticipated that the Livingston project might bring land back into productive economic use, or at least improve its appearance, leading the *Architects' Journal* to conclude that Livingston 'could be an important exercise in the intelligent control of the environment'.[24] The use of new towns provisions to effect urban and rural landscape improvements would subsequently be developed elsewhere, especially in the English new town of Dawley (later renamed and expanded as Telford), which the *Architects' Journal* suggested would have much to learn from Livingston.[25]

Although Livingston was deemed to be far enough away from both Edinburgh and Glasgow to develop its own identity,[26] the earlier new town ideal of closely defined self-containment was to some extent abandoned in favour of a broader approach which conceived Livingston, physically and economically, at the centre of a large urban region of some eighty square miles. This region would act as a single interconnected market for goods and services, linked by railway lines and especially by the new M8 motorway (which would run between Edinburgh and Glasgow, passing to the north of the designated area); a further motorway or expressway would run south of the town, upgrading the A71 road. The Geddesian idea of regional contexts and connections had been at the core not only of the Mears plan but also the Clyde Valley Regional Plan, and had underpinned the designation of East Kilbride, Glenrothes and Cumbernauld. However, regional considerations would now take on a new significance in the new towns planning process. In this respect, the draft designation order for Livingston recommended the preparation of a scheme of development for the wider West Lothian area, so that questions of industrial growth, the development of agriculture and transport, and social facilities might be considered in a co-ordinated way.[27] Similarly, the advertisement for the town's chief architect and planning officer in 1963 described Livingston as 'a bridge between Scotland's two great industrial centres […] an economic link between Edinburgh and Glasgow'.[28]

Livingston's regional contexts were elaborated in the newly established Scottish Development Department's 1963 report *Central Scotland: a Programme for Development and Growth*.[29] The report, which looked across the central belt from Glasgow to Edinburgh, noted the growing contribution to the economy of modern light industry (especially electronics) and the service sector, and noted the potential of the central Scotland region to accommodate this sort of growth. It reprised the idea of 'growth points' set out by the 1961 Toothill report on the Scottish economy, calling for a concerted 'modernisation exercise' based on 'major focal points […] growth areas', which included all of the new towns designated to date plus Irvine (suggested as a potential further new town); the performance of the new towns was described as 'outstanding'.[30] This change would be supported by broader infrastructural improvements, co-ordinated planning and financial inducements: investment in public services and facilities was essential for an 'up-to-date industrial economy' to develop.[31] Subsequently, Livingston was identified as a key strategic sub-regional centre – the first time a new town had been understood in this way – in the *Lothians Regional Survey and Plan* of 1966, prepared by the architect-planners Robert Matthew and Percy Johnson-Marshall, and the economist Donald Robertson.[32] Looking beyond the designated area, they projected an eventual regional population of some 180,000, a figure far higher than the earlier new towns which echoed similarly expansive thinking in England (where it was the consequence, in part, of evidence that the population was growing more rapidly than had been previously expected).[33] Livingston itself was also to be bigger than its predecessors. The 1962 designation order adopted growth plan estimates for the 'greater' population of 70,000, rising to 100,000 in 1990. Percy Johnson-Marshall retrospectively acclaimed Livingston's sub-regional and growth-area concept as 'a stroke of imagination unusual in a Government Department […] a proposal for a new kind of plan undertaken in a new kind of way', which reflected a 'new idea of a new town within a new growth area or region'.[34] It was hoped that the model could be applied across Scotland with further economic benefits,[35] and indeed Johnson-Marshall was subsequently involved in preparing a regional plan for the Borders which reconceived the area as a 'regional community' offering the amenities of a city dispersed across a sequence of connected settlements.[36]

The master plan

On the whole, collaborative group design typified public-architectural practice here, as in other new towns. The chief exception is Peter Daniel's own personal grid-plan concept, his unrealized early plans for the town's central area and his 're-creation' of Livingston's landscape. Many new town architects saw themselves as a cut above other post-war public designers, and Daniel maintained that his main challenge was 'to protect my staff from negative interference' from the development corporation's powerful administrators, above all the first General Manager, Brigadier Arthur Purches (1962–71 – ex-Glenrothes), with whom Daniel had a difficult relationship.[37] Daniel's eventual sacking in August 1964 followed an escalating personality clash with Purches, who increasingly lost patience with what he saw as Daniel's unworldly approach and with the costs implicit in his team's plans; from Daniel's point of view, the 'bombastic' Purches 'couldn't resist meddling and interfering' in professional matters.[38]

Daniel's appointment in summer 1962 had followed a lengthy search. An initial round of interviews included such candidates as the Scottish Special Housing Association's Harold Buteux and Cumbernauld Town Centre designer Geoffrey Copcutt.[39] The post was in fact offered to Jack Whittle, then working at the London County Council, but he surprised the panel (which offered him the job on the day of the interview) by suggesting that he wanted to consult his wife before making a decision.[40] Whittle decided not to proceed, and so further interviews were held in the autumn, with a new shortlist that included, alongside Peter Daniel, the London architect Edward Hollamby (who withdrew, to become borough architect at Lambeth) and Derek Lyddon (who had worked at Cumbernauld and subsequently would move to Skelmersdale).[41] The emphasis on landscape no doubt partly explains the choice of Peter Daniel. He had particular expertise in this field, and in 1962 chaired a ground-breaking conference on landscape policy in Scotland.[42] For Daniel, the landscape aspect of the masterplan was key. The designated area was, he said in *c.* 1963, 'picked over, discarded, surrounded by heaps of man's rubbish; I seek the recreation of this landscape'.[43]

Daniel's LDC team, as established during 1963, had a strong interdisciplinary structure – at least at the top. High-level roles combined planning and architecture, and illustrated the pan-British make-up of new town design teams, which were often dominated by mobile and transient designers from London or southern England – as in the case of Daniel's early design workforce. Staff lists from 1964 set out a hierarchy below Daniel headed by two principal architects of planning and design (P. Clapham, and Denis Martin Browne, an architect and town planner, who returned to London in the 1970s).[44] A senior planner post was soon afterwards filled, in 1964, by Dr Peter McGovern, who had worked on the 1961 Belfast Regional Plan with Robert Matthew and Percy Johnson-Marshall, and remained in post at LDC until 1967. Below them, four 'Group Architects' were listed in 1963 including D. Ashdown, a Liverpool-trained planner-architect; Jim Latimer, Belfast-born, who had worked for RMJM; and J.R.B. Palmer. Below that tier was a senior architect post and thirteen assistant architects; there was a female landscape architect, Miss M.S. Paynter, who was soon joined by two assistants, and seventeen forestry staff.[45] After Daniel's departure, the interdisciplinary focus was diluted and a clearer division between planning and architecture was established, although the same commitment to landscape continued. Daniel's successor was W. Newman Brown (1966–82), followed by Gordon I. Davies (1982–96). Prior to 1982, Davies had worked on two other new towns: Skelmersdale (early 1960s) and East Kilbride (mid-1970s), in the latter case with responsibilities including some of the abortive planning of

Stonehouse new town.[46] Livingston's first chief engineer was D.D. Paterson (1963–69), followed by J. Munro (1969–84) and N.C. Bowman (1984–8).

The designated area of 6692 acres was double the original size of Livingston's predecessor Cumbernauld, and accommodated around 2000 people at designation. An initial plan of 1963 and a revised master plan of 1966 differed little in concept, both envisaging a loose, flexible grid, although the later plan extended further south to reduce planned residential densities to forty-six persons per acre (Figure 4.3). Unlike East Kilbride and Glenrothes, where the DHS had prepared an initial plan, in Livingston the proposals were those of the development corporation (and Daniel's team) from the outset. The grid was overlaid onto the splendid natural site topography of the Almond valley, which runs east to west through the southern range of the town. Daniel emphasized that, unlike Cumbernauld, Livingston was to be a valley town, not a hilltop town.[47] Livingston's main north-south dual carriageway (Livingston Road, A899) vaults high above the river on the concrete Almond Valley Bridge, designed by the LDC in 1972 but indicated in Daniel's early sketches in recognition of its visual as well as practical significance. The view to the south, across the Lothian plain to the distant Pentland Hills, was identified from the outset as one of the town's best attributes,[48] and remains impressive. In 1979, indeed, LDC named its first six-storey office block 'Pentland House'.

Physically, Livingston's plan was based on the principles of hierarchy and interdependence: first between adjacent housing and industrial districts (the latter predominantly located on the outskirts), then within the town as a whole and finally between the sub-regional roads which served the sub-region, and linked it to the national road network. Mobility was a spur to planning innovation, going 'beyond a concentration of radial roads on a central point'; 'with increasing personal and commercial mobility it is all the more necessary to evolve a different form and all the more feasible to do so'.[49] In this respect, the idea that traffic demanded a new approach to planning, involving extensive segregation between pedestrians and vehicles, echoed Cumbernauld, but the planners also had in mind the unbuilt Hook new town plus Colin Buchanan's influential 1963 report, *Traffic in Towns*.[50] The resulting arrangement of Livingston's main routes in grid form reflected the rectilinear property boundaries and bands of woodland found in the northern part of the designated area, especially around Dechmont and Livingston Station village (some of which survive in the built-up town). It also evoked the work of the Greek planner Constantinos Doxiadis in the 1950s and 1960s, for example at the Pakistani capital, Islamabad. Furthermore, the grid responded to a desire for 'flexibility in execution and expansion',[51] an aim of many designers at this time,[52] in that it provided a basic but adaptable framework for development, formed but not too prescriptive.

Livingston stands as a pioneering attempt to develop an urban form which would offer maximum flexibility of design at each stage of development. As initially proposed by Daniel in a March 1963 concept drawing dreamt up as a '"small glass of whisky job" in the small hours of the morning' at his historic home, Borthwick Castle, the plan took its cue from the planned motorways to north and south (Figures 4.4 and 4.5). These were to be joined by a transverse link road, onto which a succession of 'cross-sectional slices' of urban development would be bolted, one after another, each including a portion of the central area and linear park. Daniel summarized this concept of an 'expanding linear town', focusing on 'this sort of great spine which would link the two motorways, while the valley would flow through the middle as a sort of green open space'.[53] The first to be started was the eastern strip, with the Knightsridge, Ladywell, Howden and Murieston districts following at the end of the decade. Second, the grid's flexibility enabled the town, or any part

FIGURE 4.3 Livingston, initial master plan (© West Lothian Archives and Records Centre).

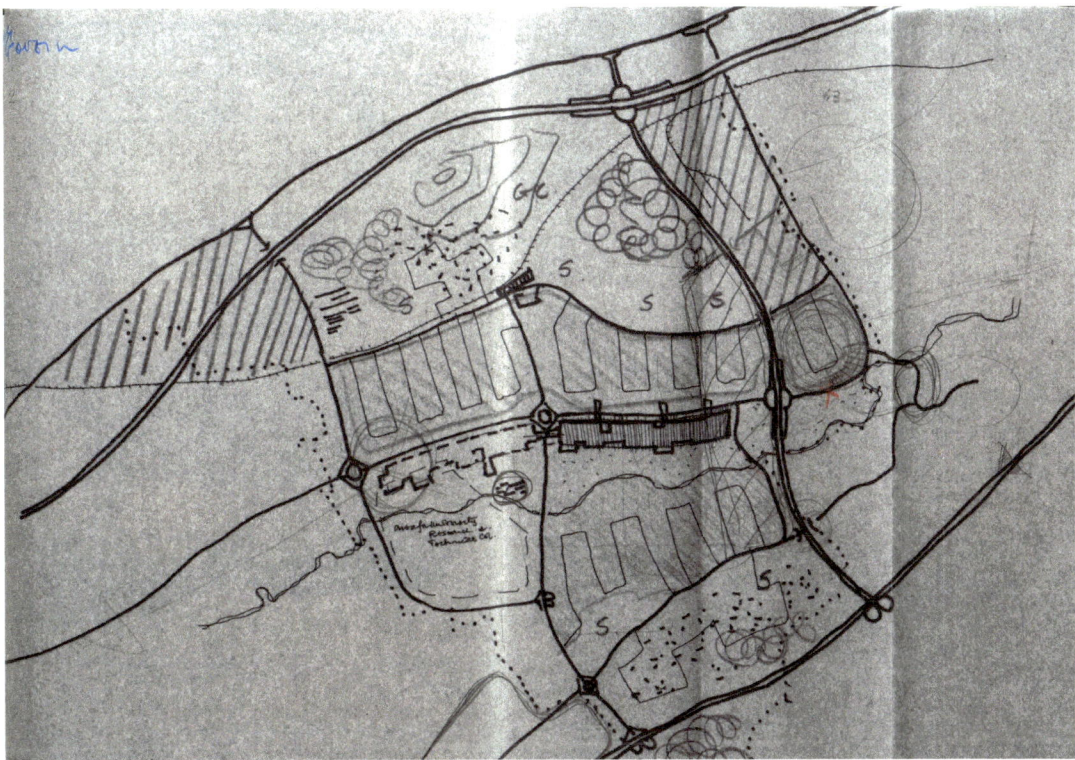

FIGURE 4.4 Early masterplan sketch by Peter Daniel (University of Edinburgh Heritage Collections, with the additional permission of West Lothian Council).

of it, to grow more (or less) than intended – or in unexpected ways – within the basic layout. LDC's planners were aware of the work on flexible planning by Richard Llewelyn-Davies and John Weeks, who discussed this subject with reference to hospital design on several occasions after 1960.[54] As in Weeks' Northwick Park hospital (1963–72), the aim at Livingston was that 'a strong communication pattern' would be the basis of planning, 'an open ended plan which is capable of incorporating unforeseeable growth and change of varying scales and intentions while still maintaining a complete form'.[55] The plan for Livingston in fact pre-dates the application of this idea at an urban scale by Llewelyn-Davies and Weeks themselves in their master plans for Washington new town (1965–6) and Milton Keynes (1967–70).[56]

As built, the town deviated little from the final plan. The road pattern gave access to central urban functions both for townsfolk and for visitors (via the A899 Livingston Road north-south spine road), while at the same time connecting regional roads direct to industrial areas. Twelve housing districts (some with adjacent small business centres) and four large industrial districts were distributed within the traffic grid. This grid was hierarchical in character and structured by the grade-separated (elevated and ground level) north-south Livingston Road and three parallel sub-routes. Crossing those are several east-west sub-routes – the main one being the dualled Cousland Road (A715) which connects with Livingston Road at the Cousland Interchange. Livingston Road features a further three interchanges. Numerous roundabouts are sited at the remaining intersections of the

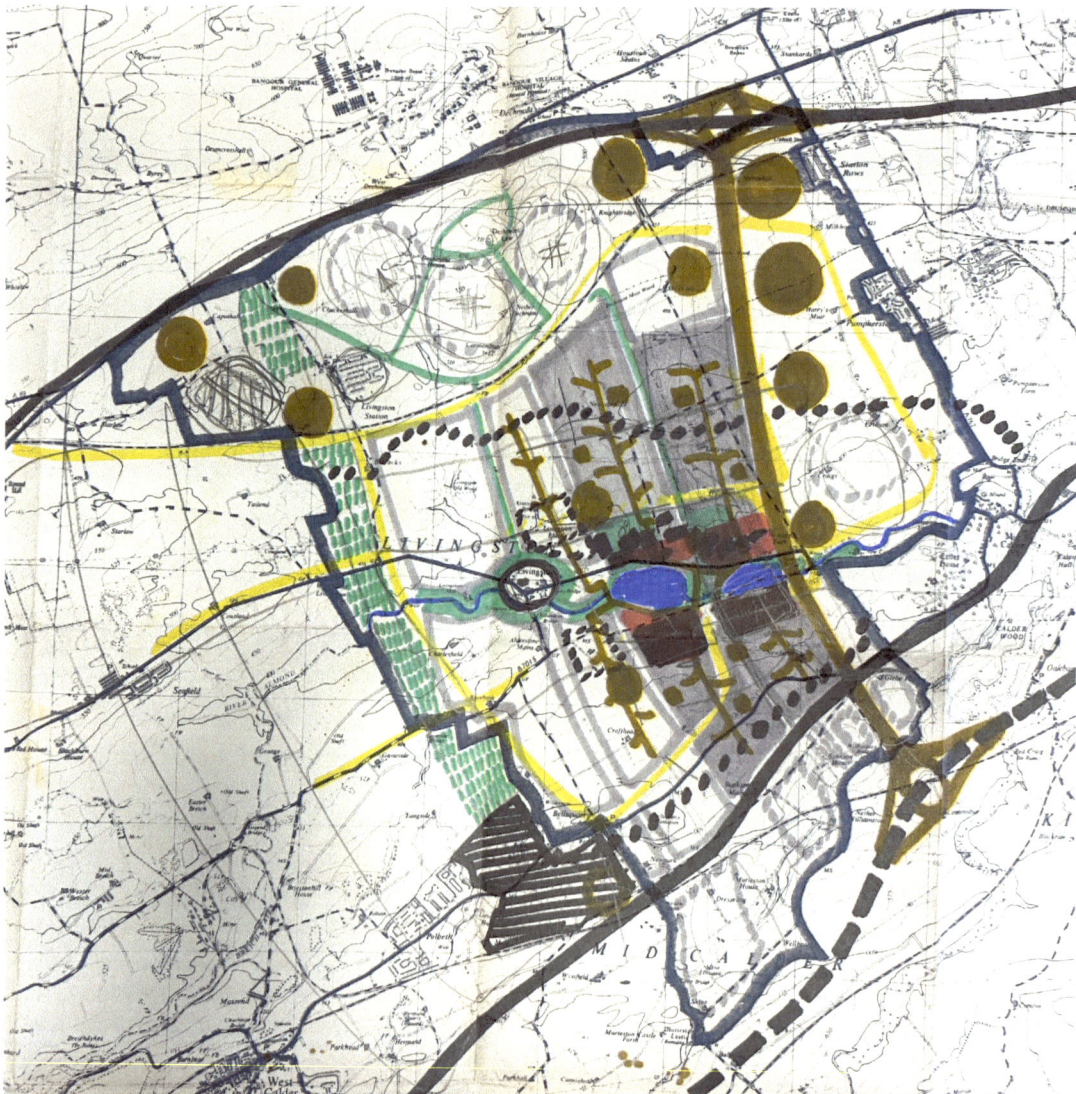

FIGURE 4.5 Masterplan sketch as of May 1963 (University of Edinburgh Heritage Collections, with the additional permission of West Lothian Council).

main road grid. The grid defines the extent of each residential/industrial district, and its elements are known as 'Town Roads'. *Within* each residential district, there is a single peripheral road – essentially a district ring road – which serves the houses and most of the public buildings. These were designated 'District Roads',[57] and their road-signs are colour-coded. Finally, cul-de-sac roads spur inwards from the District Roads and lead to car parking and garages, and, of course, access paths to the houses.

The brilliant clarity of this road-grid concept, Colin McWilliam argued in 1977, made Livingston 'one of the easier new towns to find your way about in'.[58] That clarity is now somewhat obscured, owing to the mature belts of trees which shelter the housing districts; only the roofs are now glimpsed from the main roads. Livingston was designed for the car, and one parking place was allocated to each house. While the grid accorded primacy to the car at a macro level, it equally enabled the maximum segregation of vehicles and pedestrians within the residential districts, as a result of which Livingston stands as an unmatched exemplar of Radburn planning in modern Scotland. Linear pedestrian walkways within each district link to other districts, and ultimately to the Centre (as in Cumbernauld). In addition, there is a town-wide system of 'natural' pathways ('Greenways'), some built on raised embankments and sheltered by trees, linking the town to the countryside beyond. The Almond valley was to be a linear green 'lung' running through the heart of the town.[59] Both pathways and open-space parkland were major aspects of Daniel's plan. In 1974, car ownership was at 60 per cent, but public transport was problematic up to the late 1980s, and there was a twenty-year wait for a rail service.[60]

The Centre

Livingston's thriving commercial, civic and recreational centre now forms a wedge-shaped district, named Almondvale. The site, chosen by Daniel, is located in the south of the town and dominates the southern slope of the valley. The Centre comprises two main elements: a long southern rectangular strip housing a privately run shopping mall, and new retail and business parks to its west. In the late 1970s, initial buildings to house civic functions were built on its north and south periphery. To the north lies the picturesque Almondvale Park. During the late 1980s, the park's role as a setting for leisure activities was joined by a new remit as Livingston's main civic and educational zone, including the Almondvale Stadium (1994–6) as well as the rebuilt headquarters of West Lothian Council (2009).

The design of the Centre was complex and multi-phased, embodying in microcosm the interest in flexibility which shaped the town plan as a whole. An early proposal was produced by Daniel in 1963, but like a 1966 design (in which Daniel's influence was also clear) it remained on paper.[61] These early schemes were ambitious in character (Figures 4.6 and 4.7). They were clearly inspired in their linear planning and complex multi-level arrangement by the contemporaneous Cumbernauld Town Centre designs – not surprisingly, owing to the prominence of the latter in

FIGURE 4.6 Town centre model, mid-1960s (University of Edinburgh Heritage Collections, with the additional permission of West Lothian Council).

international discourse.⁶² Daniel's first concept sited the Centre on both sides of the River Almond, linked by bridges:

> in the central valley is the focus of the town [...]. Buildings are linked as in a chain along the valley's length, shelter traps what northern sun there is for the town's benefit. Here winds the Almond River, cleaned of man's pollution. And from the entrance gateway, see how the town must be moulded to the land.⁶³

Crucially, the sloping site identified by Daniel proved functionally 'ingenious' and could accommodate services, roads and multi-storey parking below the main pedestrian level, taking advantage of the slope of the valley sides – as in the earlier proposals for the unbuilt Hook new town, where, in contrast to Cumbernauld's hill-top town centre, the central area was to straddle a valley.⁶⁴ The plans for Livingston show four free-standing but closely linked trapezoidal blocks, irregularly placed, each spanning the river from east to west. The scheme, which linked northwards to Howden and south to Dedridge, and also to the proposed District Hospital, incorporated riverside squares and shops, and high-rise flats.

However, both the 1963 and 1966 schemes posed engineering and economic challenges. In 1971, the Scottish Office instructed that the new Centre should be built and managed privately, adopting the approach seen in East Kilbride and which would also be followed in Irvine. Protracted design negotiations ended in 1972 when private architects Hay, Steel, MacFarlane & Partners of Kilmarnock were contracted by Ravenseft Properties. A grand bird's-eye view sketch design from the north-east, dating from *c.* 1972, was most probably by these newly appointed private architects. This extensive scheme showed two large slab blocks and two tower blocks surrounding the low-lying shopping accommodation. Classically inspired in its general layout, it featured long rows of poplar trees lining the regular pathways to east and west. It copied Daniel's plans for the northern town park and created a new 'lake' with an array of public buildings running down from Almondvale Boulevard. A concept drawing illustrates the impressive curved South Road bending into Howden and the new Howden Bridge crossing the Almond below.⁶⁵

By contrast with the ambitious unbuilt schemes, the 1972 scheme has a simple rectangular linear block.⁶⁶ Its low-lying slabs remained the main element carried forward. The Centre was planned to be built in three phases. The first phase was on the eastern-most part of the rectangular grid (now forming the centre section), and the original main entrance to the Centre was through

FIGURE 4.7 Detail of town centre model, mid-1960s, showing multi-level, multi-functional planning on the lines of Cumbernauld (© West Lothian Archives and Records Centre).

an underpass from the south (Dedridge), and via ramps and bridges to the north. Work eventually began on site formation in 1973, and the first phase of the new Livingston Regional Centre (as it was initially known) was opened in 1976. Echoing the way that the earlier new towns had included new types of urban space, it was anchored by a large Woolco superstore, an early example of a 'one stop' shop.[67] As first built, the Centre comprised 220,000 square feet – reportedly, it is the largest enclosed shopping centre in Scotland. Claims of the 'biggest' and 'best' were common in post-war new town narratives; we have noted similar claims in Glenrothes and East Kilbride.

Architecturally, Phase 1 was sleek in profile, straightforward in plan and clad in red brick: 'built well of mulberry coloured brick', reported McWilliam in 1977.[68] It was flat-roofed, and the dark brick cladding and oversized white projecting signage had a site-sensitive late-modernist aesthetic. Inside, it had two linked glass and steel topped-lit internal squares with planting and informal, fashionable furniture (Figures 4.8 and 4.9). On the whole, Phase I was built as planned. The perceived 'safety' of the developer-led model adopted by LDC from the early 1970s most probably ensured the Centre's commercial success. By 1978, LDC sought expansion (two years prior to a nationwide economic recession), but Ravenseft delayed the first interior refurbishment of Phase 1 until 1989–90. The private developer model frustrated the LDC architects, but the corporation welcomed the completion of a new roundabout in February 1990 that would link the M8 motorway to the Spine Road, enabling quicker access to the Centre.

The expanded Centre initially adopted what were thought to be 'Americanisms' for street and roundabout names, notably 'Boulevard' and 'Avenue'. As it expanded and became multi-functional, practical names were introduced to aid out of town visitors navigate: for example, 'Multiplex Roundabout' or 'Retail Park Roundabout'. There was even a 'Bubbles Roundabout' at the eastern edge of Almondvale Boulevard, originally named to refer to the swimming pool built by the local authority in 1992–4.

The design and construction of Phase II (west of Phase I) spanned 1989–96. This large extension more than doubled the Centre's footprint; it was also brick-clad and included the re-cladding of sections of Phase I, to unify the Centre externally. It provided a new major superstore (a neo-vernacular Safeway opened in July 1996 by Robin Cook MP), forty-three shops and nine kiosks. In terms of design, it completely abandoned the low-key aesthetic of Phase I, its gaily ornamental post-modern frontages featuring 'Mockintosh' (i.e. Charles Rennie Mackintosh-esque) and neo-Art Deco design collages. Diverse and eclectic detailing included: black ironwork; green, white and

FIGURE 4.8 Town centre, internal square (© West Lothian Archives and Records Centre).

FIGURE 4.9 Town centre mall (© West Lothian Archives and Records Centre).

black facings; and long neo-Gothic dormer windows. Massive brick and glazed entrances at the south and north sprouted tall, pagoda-like pavilion towers. The mall was top-lit by a ridge of glazing with white fenestration, and the westernmost part had a massive glazed clock tower high above. Street furniture, mostly now removed, comprised tall bright-red lamp posts topped with clusters of red semicircle lamps, and red bollards. A year after its opening, Cowling acclaimed the 'turreted affair [...] with a magnificent town clock',[69] and argued that the re-styled Centre could become a 'strikingly attractive destination' for the region, and even for Edinburgh. On completion in August 1996, it was renamed the Almondvale Centre, and when completed was 550,000 square feet in area (including phase I).[70]

Extensive further structures were added after 1997, included Phase III (west of Phase II, but aligned east-west), whose overall configuration featured an irregular enclosed crooked 'street' (Almondvale Avenue), built in red brick and topped with a silver curved roof. Westwards, a free-standing extension, the rather humdrum Almondvale Retail Park of 1996 (adding further 130,000 sq. ft) still adhered to the controlling grid plan. The Livingston Designer Outlet (2000) was even more flamboyant than the post-modern Almondvale Centre, with a shopping galleria and a classically inspired, half-domed multi-storey car-park. By 2012 the Centre (excluding the Designer Outlet) comprised approximately 925,000 square feet. Its economic success was highlighted by its purchase in 2014 by HSBC Investments for £224 million.[71]

Housing

Quality rented housing and new sustainable 'communities' were central aims for post-war new town designers. Reflecting late-modernist ideas of 'urbanity', as were already being explored in Cumbernauld, the housing areas in many of the 1960s new towns, rather than being dominated by open space, were often deliberately compact and urban. In Livingston, the houses were to remain low in overall height, configured in the form of a 'carpet', as at Cumbernauld (Figures 4.2 and 4.10). Initially, Daniel planned densities of up to 200 persons per acre around the Centre, a level similar to Cumbernauld's anticipated highest density, and matching the highest zoned densities in the 1943 County of London Plan.

The 1966 plan proposed 25 per cent flats, but as built LDC provided on average only 10–12 per cent of dwellings in flats and maisonettes of two and three storeys (later extending up as far as

FIGURE 4.10 Housing with footpath access at Pentland Park, by Philip Cocker and Associates (© West Lothian Archives and Records Centre).

five storeys). Livingston was unique among the Scottish new towns in eschewing tower blocks. Terraced houses of two and three storeys with essentially single-aspect plans (for privacy) were the norm, along with two-storey dense culs-de-sac. As built, the average gross residential density was actually only fifty-nine persons per acre. Private housing density was considerably lower still. The designers' holistic approach to townscape is evident in the wayfinding system, with signage integrated into the gable ends of long winding terraces, or on freestanding flat concrete posts. Convention provides for path name and numbers of houses and flats (high to low): for example, 'Lanark Avenue 52-45', sometimes with an arrow pointing to a path, or numbers only in culs-de-sac (as in Deans). Gable ends were also painted with bold contrasting abstract patterns by the town artist, Denis Barnes; a rare survivor is at Nigel Rise 13-10, Dedridge.

LDC planned for an average output of 1000 public rental dwellings annually.[72] The first housing area to be begun, Craigshill, took a distinctive approach, but also ended up being the town's *bête noir* (Figure 4.11). Craigshill I, built from 1964, comprised rectilinear rows of three- and four-storey flats and two-storey houses designed by LDC architects and built by Laing in their Danish-inspired '12M Jespersen' large concrete prefabricated system, supplied from a newly built nearby factory and chosen in preference to 'package-deal' systems from other suppliers including Crudens/ Skarne and Vic Hallam.[73] Daniel evoked a utopian vision of industrial-built futurism, suggesting that

FIGURE 4.11 Craigshill housing, aerial view (© West Lothian Archives and Records Centre).

standardized construction would break with 'the squalid building performance of local builders', as seen in the allegedly poor work of R. Pert & Sons Ltd at the traditionally built Livingston Station housing project in 1963.[74] At the same time, it reflected a strongly practical agenda, namely the need to make rapid progress without overloading conventional local trades; in this respect, industrialization was considered from early on.[75] However, the contract was dogged by materials shortages and the completed houses experienced irremediable damp and condensation problems.[76] Daniel recalled that he 'chose Laings because they were the most respectable firm in Britain and their engineers were Danes, and I thought the Danes were the best engineers in the world. However, even they couldn't get it right'.[77] Known locally as the 'Piano Blocks' on account of their stepped sections (Figure 4.12), Craigshill South was part-demolished and part-refurbished in an exuberant postmodern style in 1987–9; the Corporation's 'Craigshill Initiative' continued into the 1990s (Figure 4.13). Here, as so often elsewhere, the most innovative housing designs and layouts often suffered structurally and socially, and were first to be stigmatized, renovated and/or demolished. Elsewhere in Craigshill, other approaches were adopted, along with conventional construction rather than Jespersen (Figure 4.14). They included: monopitch roofs in the Courts area (by LDC, 1966), white-harled terraces in the Groves (James Parr and Partners, 1966), long terraces with colourfully framed windows (Corston Park, by well-regarded housing specialist Philip Cocker, 1968) and interlinked semi-detached houses (Beauly Drive, by the Scottish Special Housing Association, 1969).[78] Corston Park was one of a few developments in Livingston which won a prestigious Saltire Society design award.

The peak years of housing construction lasted from 1977 to 1981.[79] By this time, LDC had long since returned to traditional building methods, though the principle of low-rise, medium-density housing arranged on culs-de-sac with extensive pedestrian segregation largely remained.[80] Externally, this era of housing designs had links to the developing 'vernacular modernist' movement in Scottish architecture (seen also in Cumbernauld and especially Irvine), with abstracted echoes of single-storey cottage rows.[81] Terraced houses featured quasi-vernacular details, too: contrasting coloured harl and red-brown brick, timber cladding, sloping steep or shallow slate roofs (sometimes red-pantiled), projecting porches and irregular windows with contrasting coloured surrounds. Often accessed by narrow irregular 'paths' on sloping dense sites, with excellent hard landscaping, these residential areas (some impressively intact even today, notably in Ladywell and Dedridge) illustrate the best of Livingston's innovative housing layouts. LDC's architects incorporated these

FIGURE 4.12 Craigshill's 'Piano Blocks' (© West Lothian Archives and Records Centre).

FIGURE 4.13 Before and after: Craigshill as refurbished in the 1990s (© West Lothian Archives and Records Centre).

FIGURE 4.14 Howden East housing, designed by Livingston Development Corporation (JR James Archive/Flickr. CC BY-NC 2.0 DEED).

'old-fashioned' terrace plans and front-facing gardens into more complex 'neighbourhood' housing layouts (as for example at Bloom Court, Livingston Village and Hanover Court, Kirkton). Housing was also designed by the Scottish Special Housing Association (SSHA), notably at Deans Village, for which the Association contracted private architects. Many terraced houses also face large expanses of parkland at Deans, Dedridge and Craigshill. Innovative standardized integral and free-standing garages, and sturdy wooden diagonal-patterned garden fences and gates, also enhance design integrity in these districts; in view of ever-increasing levels of car ownership, LDC allocated one garage per dwelling, and one parking space for every two dwellings.

Consideration was also given to the design of higher-status rented housing for executives which was to be consciously differentiated (and perhaps more conventional) in design terms.[82] In addition, with the owner-occupation target for the Scottish new towns being set at 25 per cent in the mid-1960s,[83] LDC also started to design housing for sale from the early 1970s (at Kirkton, Livingston Village, and in Murieston). By 1978, Livingston boasted 10 per cent owner-occupation. That same year, to serve the same aspirant social group, the Deer Park Golf Course and Club (developed by LDC, 1978, upgraded and extended in 1988 by Muir Group) was opened in Knightsridge North. In the 1980s, private house-building increased, and the 'Right to Buy' legislation resulted in 50 per cent owner-occupation by 1992.[84] The town's most lively red-brick 1980s and 1990s 'high-value' private cul-de-sac housing developments are located off Knightsridge West Road and Golf Course Road, and range from box-standard bungalows to bespoke hacienda-style mansions. The highlight is the massive neo-Baronial six-storey Deer Park Heights flatted complex.

Conclusion

In 1997, a survey by geographers from the University of Strathclyde claimed that Livingston was the 'Second-Best Place to Live in Britain' in a ranking of 189 small cities and towns.[85] It has developed as a commuter town (akin to East Kilbride) and attracts visitors to the Centre and also the subsequent Designer Outlet.[86] Its built heritage value, like that of Scotland's other new towns, remains contested. Livingston boasts surviving modernist public artworks (the best being those by Denis Barnes, from the 1970s),[87] as well as some prominent one-off modernist buildings, such as the swirling concrete forms of St Andrew's Church, by the architects Alison and Hutchison (1969–70) (Figure 4.15).[88] Townsfolk and preservationists now prioritize these 'authored'

FIGURE 4.15 St Andrew's Church (1970) (© West Lothian Archives and Records Centre).

works, as well as the remains of earlier industrial landscapes, above the modernist buildings and infrastructure itself. Such a focus is the opposite of the design hierarchy envisaged by the original designers, though in 2024 the town's early 1980s skatepark was designated as a structure of heritage interest, its cultural influences a symbol of Livingston's connections at that time with North American businesses and their expatriate employees. The mid-1990s decision to protect as historic landscapes surviving shale-bings within sight of Livingston was debated. Described by Daniel, as we have noted, as 'immense heaps of man's rubbish', reassessment was signalled in the 1990 opening of Livingston's Shale Oil Museum (now the Almond Valley Heritage Centre) at a restored 1770s water mill and farm in Kirkton,[89] originally saved by the 1967 Livingston Mill Restoration Group and in use from 1985.[90]

The new towns were central to economic and industrial policy in the second half of the twentieth century in Scotland, and attracting new industries was a priority. How successful was Livingston in turning industrial decline into regional growth? The early to mid-1960s plans were, in retrospect, too ambitious, though there was some notable success. The US-based Cameron Ironworks brought 1200 jobs to the town after 1966, while the arrival of the computer firm NEC at the end of the next decade represented the largest Japanese investment in Britain to date.[91] But neither regional status nor regional growth was really achieved until the new millennium. Livingston's history was ultimately one of steady growth, impacted by recessions, but by the late 1990s, over 40 per cent of all jobs in West Lothian were located there.[92]

Notes

1 'Architect-Planner for Livingston', *Architects' Journal* 136, no. 19 (7 November 1962): 1056.
2 Leslie Higgs, *New Town: Social Involvement in Livingston – An Account of the Formative Years* (Glasgow: Maclellan, 1977), 40.
3 'The Master Plan Examined', *Architects' Journal* 141, no. 15 (14 April 1965): 864–6.
4 'Rumblings at Livingston', *Architects' Journal* 140, no. 21 (18 November 1964): 1158.
5 *Scottish Daily Express*, 9 April 1965, 10–11.
6 University of Edinburgh, Centre for Research Collections [CRC], Peter Daniel uncat. collection [PD] box 46/2, 'Interim Report on the Preparation of the Master Plan for Livingston', 26 June 1963.

7. Ibid.
8. For influence, see e.g.: Thomas Szydlowski, 'Skelmersdale: The Design and Implementation of a British New Town, 1961–1985', MSc dissertation, University College London, 2020, 23.
9. Scottish Moving Image Archive, 6376, *New Town Blues*, dir. John L. Paterson, c. 1963.
10. Scottish Development Department, *The Lothians Regional Survey and Plan*, 2 vols. (Edinburgh: HMSO, 1966).
11. The collection, located in the CRC, is extensive; some eight boxes cover Livingston 1962–4.
12. Elspeth Wills, *Livingston: The Making of a Scottish New Town* (Edinburgh: Rutland Press, 1996); Emma Peattie, *Livingston Lives* (Edinburgh: Luath Press, 2012); William F. Hendrie, *The History of Livingston* (Livingston: Livingston Development Corporation, 1988).
13. Higgs, *New Town*, 51.
14. David Cowling, *An Essay for Today: The Scottish New Towns, 1947 to 1997* (Edinburgh: Rutland Press, 1997), 71–85.
15. Richard Jaques and Charles McKean, *West Lothian: An Illustrated Guide* (Edinburgh: Rutland Press, 1994), 86.
16. Jane Geddes, Ian Gow, Aonghus Mackechnie, Chris Tabraham and Colin Macwilliam, *Lothian* (New Haven and London: Yale University Press, 2024), 560.
17. CRC, PD, box 47/2, 'Responsibility for Developing the New Town', 1964.
18. CRC, PD, box 47/1, Master Plan Review, 1964.
19. Frank Mears, *Regional Plan for Central and S.E. Scotland* (Edinburgh: Central and S.E. Scotland Planning Advisory Committee, 1949), 75.
20. J.B. Cullingworth, *Environmental Planning Volume III: New Towns Policy* (London: HMSO, 1979), 175–8; 'Livingston', *New Towns Record* (Planning Exchange CD-ROM set, 1996) [*NTR*].
21. Cullingworth, *Environmental Planning*, 177.
22. 'Regional Planning and Livingston New Town', *Architects' Journal* 135, no. 21 (23 May 1962): 1112–13.
23. Ibid.
24. Ibid.
25. 'Wanted: New Town and New Country', *Architects' Journal* 135, no. 22 (6 June 1962): 1241; Otto Saumarez Smith, 'Landscapes of Hope and Crisis: Dereliction, Environment, and Leisure in Britain during the Long 1970s', *Journal of British Studies* 62, no. 4 (2023): 988–1010.
26. Cullingworth, *Environmental Planning*, 178.
27. Frederick J. Osborn and Arnold Whittick, *New Towns: Their Origins, Achievements and Progress* (London: Leonard Hill, 1977), 430.
28. Advert: *Architects' Journal* 136, no. 9 (29 August 1962): 85.
29. Scottish Development Department [SDD], *Central Scotland: A Programme for Development and Growth* (Edinburgh: HMSO, 1963).
30. Ibid., 7, 27.
31. Ibid., 15.
32. Osborn and Whittick, *New Towns*, 430.
33. Ministry of Housing and Local Government, *The South East Study* (London: HMSO, 1964), 7–12.
34. Preface to Higgs, *New Town*, 12–13.
35. 'Key Step in Growth of Scotland', *Times*, 18 July 1962, 16.
36. CRC, Percy Johnson-Marshall archive, uncat. folders FR37, FR52, FR76.

37 'Peter Daniel', Dictionary of Scottish Architects, online at www.scottisharchitects.org.uk (accessed on 12 December 2023); see also correspondence regarding criticism of the structure of the architecture and planning teams in CRC, PD box 45/2.
38 'Rumblings at Livingston', 1158; CRC, PD box 48/2, Interview Transcript.
39 CRC, PD box 46/3, Board Minutes 12 July 1962.
40 CRC, PD box 46/3, Board Minutes 24 July 1962.
41 CRC, PD box 46/3, Board Minutes 3 October and 10 October 1962.
42 'Peter Daniel', Dictionary of Scottish Architects.
43 'New Town Blues', dir. Paterson.
44 E.g. CRC, PD box 45/1, 'Staff List February 1964'.
45 Other architects and assistants listed were: B.R. Adams: B. Bagot, D. Bain, T.M. Ball, R.M. Blaikie, E Cameron, N. Collin, J. Dible, J. Dickson, G.R. McSheffrey, D.G. Mason, R.F. Pead, D. Stirling and G. Watts.
46 'Gordon Davies', Dictionary of Scottish Architects, online at www.scottisharchitects.org.uk (accessed on 12 December 2023).
47 Wills, *Livingston*, 31; CRC, PD box 48/3.
48 CRC, PD box 46/2, 'Interim Report'.
49 CRC, PD box 46/1, 'Central Facilities Report', April 1964.
50 Hook influence: CRC, PD box 48/2, Transcript of interview with Peter Daniel, 1996. Buchanan was approached to offer advice on the plan: CRC, PD Box 46/1, Board paper 'The Master Plan for Livingston and Its Relationship to Road Design', March 1964.
51 CRC, PD box 46/1, 'Central Facilities Report, April 1964'.
52 Daniel Abramson, *Obsolescence: An Architectural History* (Chicago: University of Chicago Press, 2016).
53 'The Master Plan Explained', 864; also CRC, PD box 48/3 and 48/5.
54 E.g. 'Planning for Growth and Change', *Architects' Journal* 132, no. 3403 (7 July 1960): 120–2; 'Indeterminate Architecture', *Architects' Journal* 139, no. 22 (27 May 1964): 1183; for LDC awareness, see CRC, PD box 47/2, 'Planning for Growth and Change', 1964.
55 CRC, PD box 47/2, 'Planning for Growth and Change', 1964.
56 Washington Development Corporation, *Washington New Town Master Plan and Report* (Washington: WDC, 1966), 14; Guy Ortolano, *Thatcher's Progress: From Social Democracy to Market Liberalism through an English New Town* (Cambridge: Cambridge University Press, 2018), 93–5.
57 National Library of Scotland, QP4.90.582. *Living in Livingston,* Resident Information Pack.
58 Colin McWilliam, *Lothian* (Harmondsworth: Penguin, 1977), 308.
59 Cowling, *Essay for Today*, 74.
60 Peattie, *Lives*, 239.
61 Wills, *Livingston*, 106–7.
62 E.g. *Architectural Design* 33, no. 5 (May 1963): 206–25 (with Spanish and French synopses).
63 *New Town Blues*, dir. Paterson.
64 Cowling, *Essay for Today*, 77.
65 Peattie, *Lives*, 128.
66 Livingston Development Corporation, *Livingston: The First Ten Years* (Livingston: LDC, 1972).
67 'The Centre', Scottish-Places, https://www.scottish-places.info/features/featurefirst19402.html (accessed on 15 December 2023).

68 McWilliam, *Lothian* [1977], 311.
69 Cowling, *Essay for Today*, 79.
70 Wills, *Livingston*, 111.
71 'HSBC Alternative Investments in £224m Scottish Club Deal', Realassets.ipe.com, https://realassets.ipe.com/hsbc-alternative-investments-in-224m-scottish-club-deal/10005760.article (accessed on 15 December 2023).
72 'Livingston', *NTR*.
73 'New Town Homes Factory Built', *Times*, 24 August 1963; CRC, PD box 45/2, D.M. Browne memo 5 June 1963.
74 CRC, PD box 45/2 and 48/1, Peter Daniel to Peter Dovell, 1 July 1970.
75 LDC, Annual Report 1962–63 [*NTR*].
76 McWilliam, *Lothian* [1977], 309; Wills, *Livingston*, 59–60.
77 CRC, PD box 48/3.
78 McWilliam, *Lothian* [1977], 309.
79 'Livingston', *NTR*.
80 Ibid.
81 Miles Glendinning, Ranald MacInnes and Aonghus MacKechnie, *A History of Scottish Architecture, from the Renaissance to the Present Day* (Edinburgh: Edinburgh University Press, 1996), 480–1.
82 CRC, PD box 48/2, 'House Letting – Segregation'.
83 For more on this: Valerie Wright and Alistair Fair, 'The Opportunity and Desire to Buy: Owner-Occupation in Scotland's New Towns, c. 1950–1980', *Contemporary British History* 38, no. 2 (2024): 219–44.
84 Peattie, *Lives*, 238–9.
85 Cowling, *Essay for Today*, 71.
86 Wills, *Livingston*, 101.
87 Andrew Demetrius, 'A Lesson from the Past: Scotland's New Towns and Their Artists', ArtUK, 2021, https://artuk.org/discover/stories/a-lesson-from-the-past-scotlands-new-towns-and-their-artists (accessed on 15 December 2023).
88 *100 Churches 100 Years*, ed. Susannah Charlton, Elain Harwood and Clare Price (London: Batsford, 2019), 120.
89 Peattie, *Lives*, 244.
90 Wills, *Livingston*, 4.
91 'Livingston', *NTR*.
92 Ibid.

5

Irvine

The designation of Irvine in 1966 reflected a new phase in the Scottish new towns programme. Whereas earlier designations had taken in largely rural sites, here the designated area contained two already substantial towns, Irvine and Kilwinning. The masterplan also demonstrated new ideas. It evolved through a sequence of proposals, produced first by external consultants Hugh Wilson and Lewis Womersley (1965–7) and then revised by an in-house team under chief planner David Gosling (in post 1968–73). The proposals' overall low-density character echoed the 'Mark 1' new towns rather than Cumbernauld's more tightly planned urbanity; the highly dispersed, almost organic layout also contrasted with Livingston's regular grid. Yet at the same time, Irvine's polycentric plan – with a scatter of residential and employment areas separated by landscape belts and main roads – very much reflected contemporary ideas about urban decentralization. The ambition to make a new kind of urban experience culminated in ambitious proposals for a mile-long megastructure connecting the old town centre with the coast, morphing from a shopping centre into a leisure centre as it crossed a river, roads and a railway line before continuing apparently into the sea itself. Irvine, had it been built on these lines, would have made a statement of radical modernity, perhaps even surpassing Cumbernauld as the defining example of late-twentieth-century Scottish urbanism.

Yet much remained unbuilt amid cuts to the new towns programme in the late 1970s and the shift in policymakers' attention towards the regeneration of eastern Glasgow. Large roundabouts await unbuilt flyovers; the first phase of the town centre megastructure crashes into a later superstore before petering out. In this context, the *Irvine New Town Plan*, lavishly published in 1971, is the purest statement of the planners' intentions.[1] Just as 1961's *The Planning of a New Town* records the unbuilt proposals for the development of Hook in Hampshire, the book of the Irvine plan boldly reveals what might have been, its modernity amplified by the use of sans serif typefaces and brightly coloured drawings. Cars are prominent in the imagery, representing the emerging consumer society and the extent to which it increasingly fell within the purview of the 'dynamic social democracy' outlined with reference to this period by Guy Ortolano.[2] However, it would be a mistake to assume that the gap between vision and reality is all there is to say about Irvine. Like Glenrothes, its history demonstrates particularly well the malleability of the new town idea, while the planners' focus on leisure spatialized wider themes in this decade's culture, taking the idea of a 'modern Scotland' in new directions. Irvine's post-1980 development also reveals the vitality of public-sector architecture in a decade more normally associated with diminished public patronage.

Plans

Irvine had become one of Scotland's most significant seaports by the sixteenth century but subsequently lost much of its trade to Glasgow.[3] It was not until the middle of the twentieth century that the area began to regain its economic strength. During the 1950s, Irvine entered a boom period, encouraged by the town's independent and Moderate councillors.[4] International companies such as Skefco, Monsanto and ICI arrived,[5] taking advantage of a location close to Prestwick International Airport.[6] Housing was constructed by the Burgh Council, working with the Scottish Special Housing Association.[7] By 1965, the burgh had increased its population by more than 25 per cent since 1951, while the number employed in the manufacturing industry in the Irvine/Kilwinning area had risen during the previous five years by nearly 30 per cent.[8] These developments contributed to Irvine's selection as a new town.[9] As was also the case with some of the late 1960s generation of English new towns, which similarly involved substantial existing settlements, the established new towns process was in essence adapted to new ends – in this case, to catalyse and organize further growth.[10] But there were three other reasons, too. First, Irvine's designation as a new town would allow closer central oversight of what was done and would mean that development was framed within wider planning and economic contexts. Second, it would also set an example for other local authorities. Given that Irvine's initial postwar development had been independent/Moderate-led, and given that the first proposals for designation date from 1963, when the government was Conservative, perhaps the Scottish Office wanted to make a point to Labour councils. And third, new town status would resolve a particular problem, namely that Irvine Burgh Council lacked full planning powers, but the county authority – which had such powers – was uninterested.[11] Irvine new town would not have a formal 'overspill' agreement with Glasgow, but would contribute to the 'general redistribution of population in central Scotland' as well as its economic modernization.[12]

Although linked with a 1966 White Paper which emphasized the need for Scotland to attract new industries and to create new jobs along with additional and better housing, the designation of Irvine was, as noted above, initially considered during 1963, that is, before the October 1964 election which brought Labour to power.[13] In January 1965, the Secretary of State for Scotland commissioned the consultant firm of Wilson & Womersley to report on the idea and to produce an outline plan.[14] External consultant masterplanners had been involved in the early stages of some of the English and Welsh 'Mark 1' new towns but not any previous designations in Scotland, where outline plans had been overseen either by the DHS (East Kilbride, Glenrothes) or by the development corporation (Cumbernauld, Livingston). Hugh Wilson had formed a planning consultancy in 1962 after his six-year stint at Cumbernauld (discussed in Chapter 3).[15] He was joined in partnership in 1964 by the former Sheffield City Architect Lewis Womersley. In England, they were favoured by Dame Evelyn Sharp, the influential civil servant who oversaw significant parts of the new towns programme there,[16] and between them they secured several English new town masterplans, including Skelmersdale (1962), Redditch (1964) and Northampton (1966).

Wilson and Womersley submitted an 'interim report' at the end of May 1965.[17] By February 1966 the Secretary of State had published the draft designation order, with designation being confirmed in November that year.[18] Six months later, Wilson and Womersley's *Irvine New Town Planning*

Proposals (the 'Wilson Plan') were published.[19] Their plan assumed an increased population of 55,000, but with the capacity for further growth.[20] A desire to be exemplary was clear in their report, echoing the terms in which the earlier new towns had been conceived; it was hoped that the town would be transformative for those who moved there. Wilson and Womersley called for 'a high standard of design [...] the best possible conditions [...]' in order to 'stimulate its citizens and those who visit'.[21] The May 1965 report even suggested that Irvine might be a 'fitting legacy for the 21st century in Scotland'.[22]

While the earlier Scottish new towns focused on a central shopping area (albeit with variations in their adoption of neighbourhood units and radial highways layouts), Wilson proposed a new kind of urban environment, one which was significantly more dispersed than its predecessors. The basic concept was established in the 1965 report and was elaborated in the 1967 proposals (Figures 5.1 and 5.2). The new town would comprise an arc, one mile wide and five miles long,

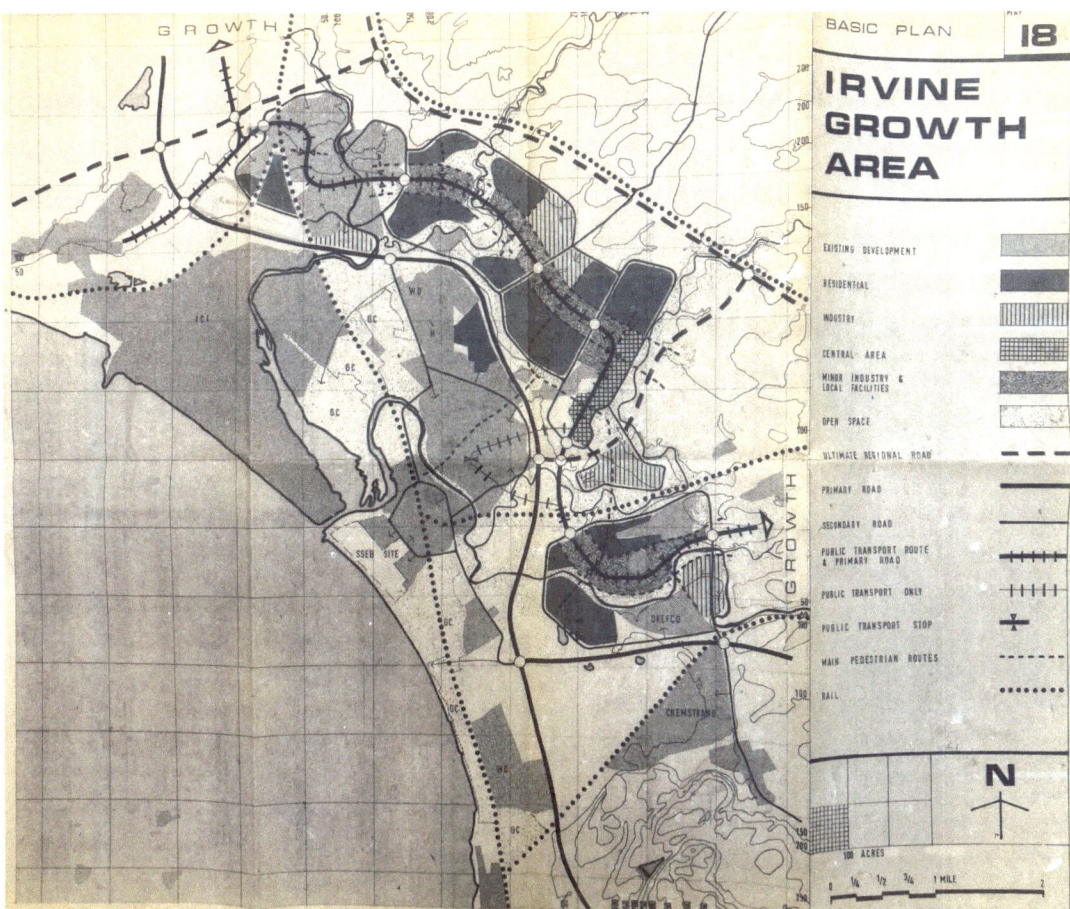

FIGURE 5.1 Wilson and Womersley's initial proposal for Irvine, May 1965, with communities connected by a spine route in a similar manner to their contemporaneous proposals for Redditch (Crown Copyright, The National Archives (T224/1388). Contains public sector information licensed under the Open Government Licence v3.0).

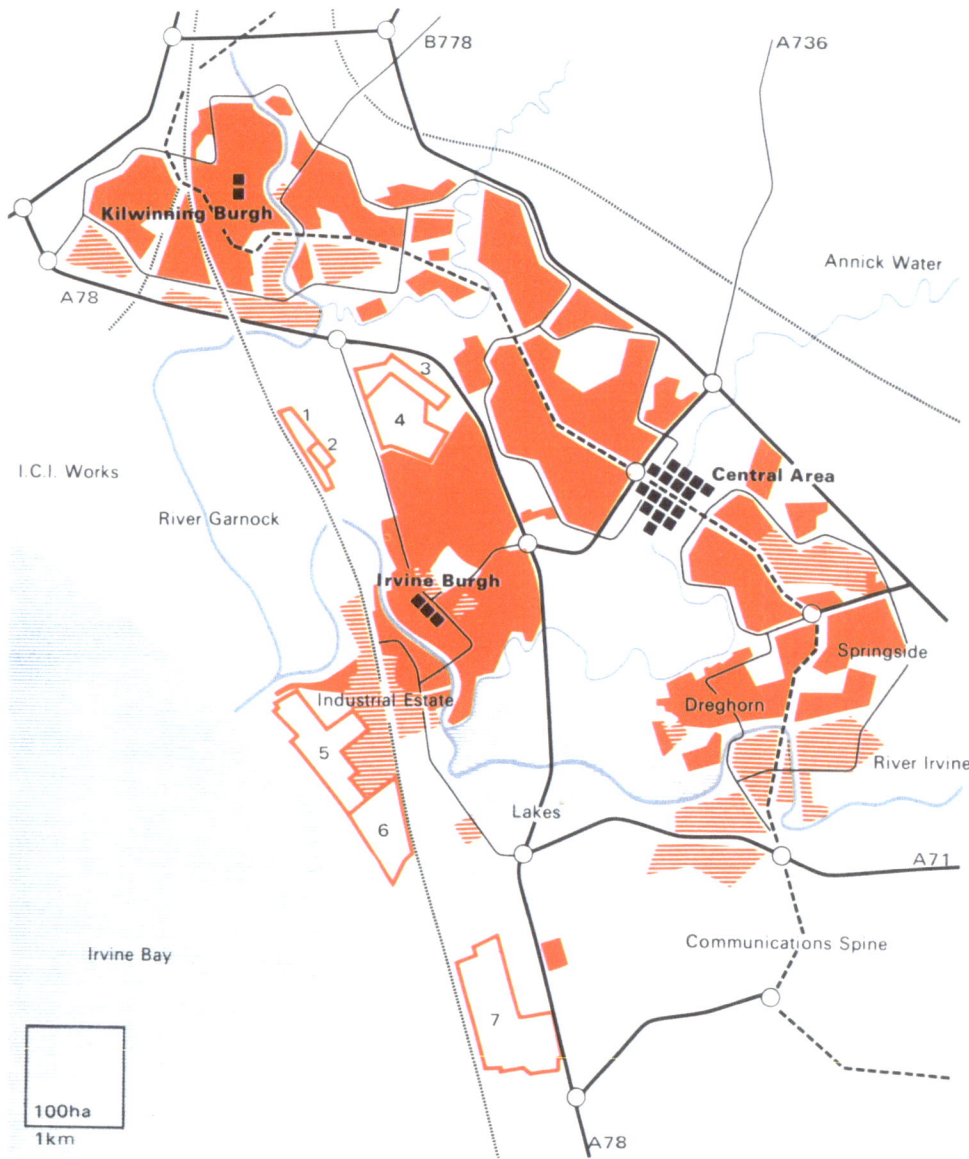

FIG. 1.1 Wilson Plan

1 Bartonholm Tip
2 Ravenspark Hospital
3 Army Vehicle Depot
4 Ayrshire Central Hospital
5 S.S.E.B. Land
6 Rifle Range
7 Dundonald Army Camp

FIGURE 5.2 Wilson and Womersley's developed plan of 1966: the 'Wilson Plan' (© Ayrshire Archives/ North Ayrshire Council).

of discrete units. The new developments would curve around the old town, stretching from Kilwinning in the north to Drybridge in the south.[23] At the core of all this would be a transport route. A major new shopping area would be developed on open land at Girdle Toll, towards the centre of the site.[24] The new town's intended form was influenced by geographical constraints, notably mining subsidence areas. However, this form – which contrasted particularly strongly with Cumbernauld's compact 'urbanity' – also reflected contemporary interest in the impact on urban layout of a high level of mobility, as we have already seen in a different form in Livingston's grid, and also the potential for technology to enable communities to be forged in ways other than simple proximity.[25] Whereas earlier new town planners had emphasized short walking distances, Irvine's residents would be required to travel further, by car or public transport. Wilson and Womersley described their concept as 'beads' of development along the 'necklace' of the transport route.[26] Although anticipating a high level of private car ownership, the planners expected that public transport would become vital as car ownership increasingly generated congestion.[27] This essentially polycentric layout – which was also understood to support flexible growth in that new units could be easily added to either end of the spine – echoed Wilson and Womersley's plans for Redditch (which similarly referred to beads and necklaces) and Northampton, as well as other contemporaneous proposals, including the unbuilt North Buckinghamshire New City (where a monorail was projected),[28] Runcorn (planned by Arthur Ling), Gordon Cullen's circuit-linear 'Alcan' proposals for the Solway Firth and Percy Johnson-Marshall's proposals for the Borders region.[29] Dispersal also informed the plans for Telford, Milton Keynes and Central Lancashire New Town; it was one of the distinctive features of the late 1960s generation of new towns.[30]

Irvine's first chief architect and planner was David Gosling, who began work in November 1967.[31] He had been deputy chief architect and planner at Runcorn from 1965 to 1967, where he took particular responsibility for the central area, 'Shopping City'.[32] During his five years at Irvine, he oversaw two key plans for the town: the 1969 *Interim Revised Outline Plan* and the 1971 *Irvine New Town Plan*.[33] Gosling quickly put together a small team of staff. Irvine Development Corporation (IDC) took up residence in the renovated and extended eighteenth-century Perceton House.[34] From the beginning, it grappled with a complex local government structure, which slowed development. Initially, six local authorities held powers within the designated area, each with its own agenda.[35]

By 1968, it was increasingly clear that the Wilson Plan was, according to Gosling, 'unbuildable'.[36] Surveys revealed that extensive mineworkings and gravel deposits posed a greater risk of subsidence than had been previously supposed.[37] Scottish Office staff despaired, referring subsequently to the 'horrible example' of Irvine.[38] However, studies of the regional economy including the *Oceanspan Report*, the *Metra-Weddle Report* and the Scottish Tourism Board's *Report on Recreation Planning for the Clyde* also suggested the benefits of a new layout, offering a closer relationship with the river.[39] The abandonment of proposals for a power station in the Irvine harbour area also left that site free for recreational development.

Gosling's team produced seven alternative plans, one of which became the 1971 masterplan (Figure 5.3).[40] While the original Wilson Plan had located the central area at Girdle Toll, Gosling resited it within and next to the historic core of the existing town.[41] And, with the power station plans for the harbour area abandoned, Gosling's team now proposed an extensive recreational and

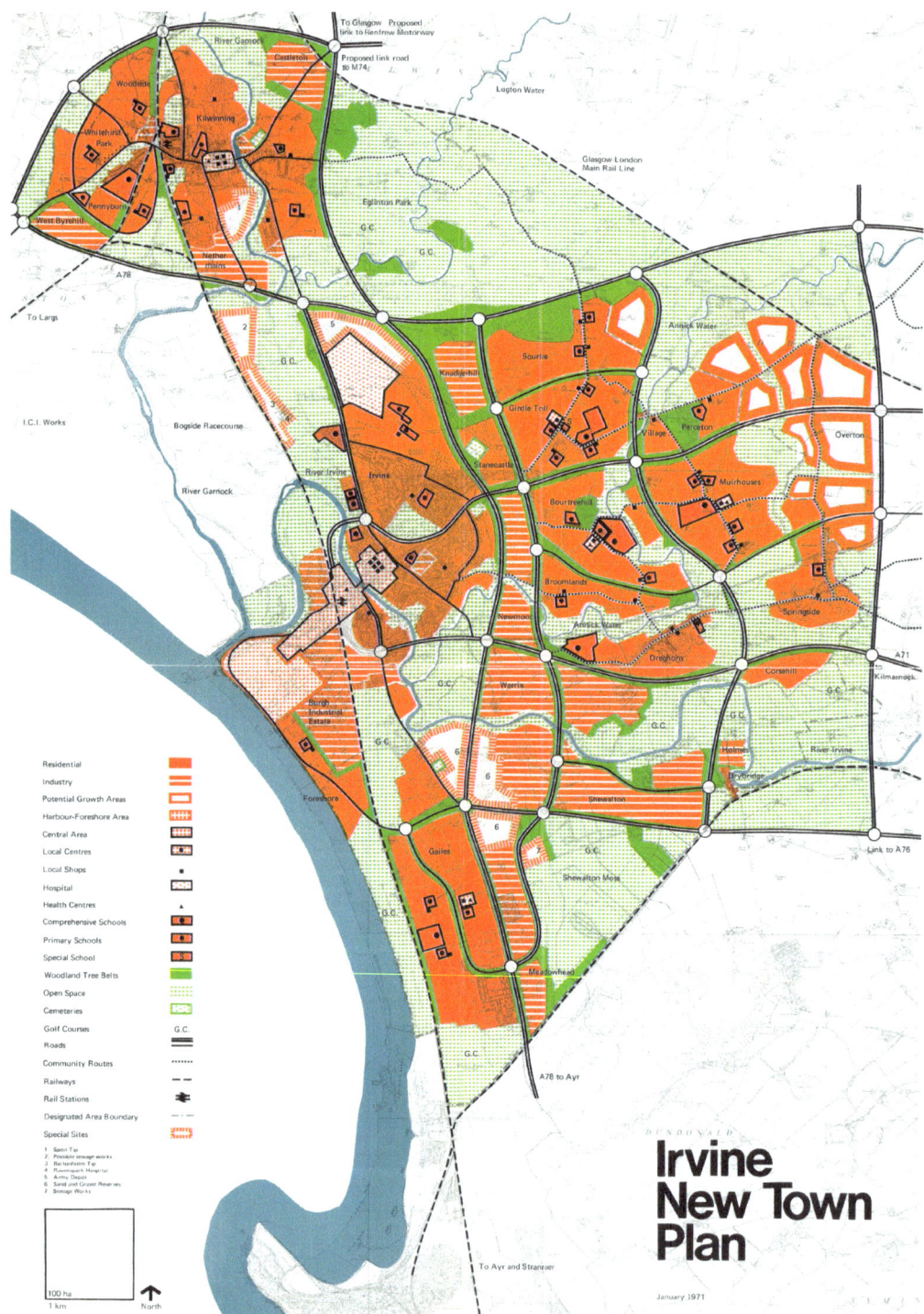

FIGURE 5.3 Irvine New Town Plan, 1971, with the town centre moved to the historic core of the burgh (© Ayrshire Archives / North Ayrshire Council).

entertainment hub on the harbourside, with adjacent 'high amenity housing' in the Gailes area.[42] Ambitiously, but not unreasonably in the light of the early 1960s 'baby boom', the masterplan assumed future populations of 116,000 to 144,000, while a potential city region was projected accommodating upwards of 200,000 people by the end of the century and taking in Kilmarnock, a new port at Hunterston, and the town of Saltcoats.

Ian Downs, IDC's chief architect during 1979–95, later argued that the planners had been 'just super optimistic' in believing that emigration from Scotland would 'go in reverse', leading to unlimited growth.[43] This trend never materialized. Devaluation in 1967–8 dealt a blow to hopes of unfettered expansion, while the Oil Crisis and the economic challenges of the early 1970s compounded the problems. In response, the masterplan was revised in 1983 and again in 1987. These later plans adopted a more cautious approach, with a slower rate of infill development plus a restoration programme to unify and upgrade the town's building stock.[44]

Town centre

Wilson and Womersley's plans of 1965 and 1967 for a shopping centre at Girdle Toll would have involved a substantial development spanning the projected transport spine – the model pioneered by the Swedish satellite town of Vällingby in the 1950s, which was then taken up in differing ways by Cumbernauld and Runcorn and which was also proposed at Hook. However, as noted, in Gosling's 1971 plans the town centre was repositioned, taking a site between the historic Irvine centre and the harbour – a location which related better to the revised overall layout of the new town.[45] It also eased conflict with the existing centres of Kilwinning and Kilmarnock by minimizing the number of large economic centres in the area,[46] and so started to dilute the earlier polycentric ideal. Gosling's deputy, Roger Read, recalled strong support from Irvine traders for the revised proposal, with many trusting they would benefit.[47] Furthermore, the planners believed that the established town centre would provide ready-made character.[48]

The new Irvine town centre was to be dominated by a complex megastructure, a 'comprehensive linear central area',[49] which would ultimately compare in status to the shopping centres in Kilmarnock and Ayr (Figure 5.4).[50] Before designation, the foreshore had been disconnected from the town by the river and a railway line. The new centre would provide a physical connection between the two areas,[51] with a continuous walkway.[52] As planned, new offices and shops in Bridgegate would form the first part of a substantial indoor shopping centre.[53] The centre would then head westwards, replacing the town's historic bridge and including public spaces, a hotel, cinema, restaurants, pubs plus parking spaces for 2400 cars. Leaping over the railway, it would then continue via a transport interchange and harbourside apartments before ending in a sequence of recreational structures strung along the foreshore. With pedestrian circulation on a deck above the traffic and service areas, the megastructural concept was reportedly inspired by similar successful centres such as Yorkdale Plaza in Toronto (also a reference point in East Kilbride, as discussed in Chapter 1) and the Arndale centres in several British towns.[54] Cumbernauld's own recently completed megastructure was no doubt also a key influence – and perhaps a challenge to beat.

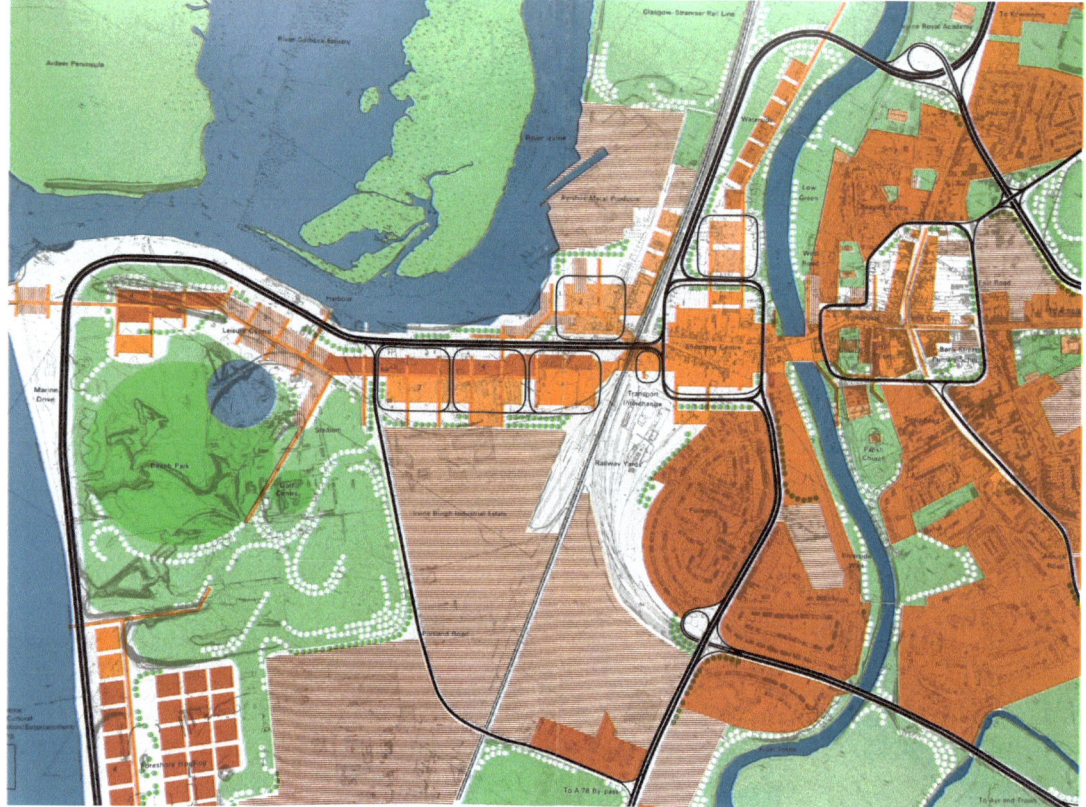

FIGURE 5.4 Irvine's megastructural centre, with shopping to the right and leisure to the left, as imagined by IDC in the early 1970s (© Ayrshire Archives/North Ayrshire Council).

The centre was designed to be built in three phases (1971–4, 1974–7 and 1977–80).[55] The first phase began in 1973 with the construction of Bridgegate House adjacent to Irvine Cross.[56] This mixed office and retail development was intended to accommodate traders displaced by the enabling works for the rest of the shopping centre.[57] Built in materials similar to those of the projected shopping centre, its height was nonetheless kept to that of surrounding buildings to minimize disruption to the skyline while reflective glass was used to minimize its impact (Figure 5.5).[58] While other new towns had primarily converted their historic areas into residential districts, Bridgegate House was praised by Rob Close in his *Ayrshire and Arran* as a bold attempt at 'irrevocably linking the two cultures' of old and new.[59]

The opening of Phase 1 in 1975 received disappointingly little attention, with the *Irvine Times* noting the lack of royal visit: 'No Show as Shopping Bridge Opens'.[60] Subsequently, the planned additional phases of the centre remained unbuilt.[61] In 1983, expansion plans were approved, but IDC officials postponed the project, arguing that expansion should wait until the town reached 70,000 people.[62] Downs explained in a 1995 interview that the decision to terminate the centre with a supermarket was made in the mid-1980s, reflecting a belief within IDC that the full

FIGURE 5.5 The new Bridgegate (photo: Miles Glendinning, c. 1995).

centre would never be realized.[63] In 2019, historian Janina Gosseye noted that the resignation of Gosling in 1973 and the subsequent appointment of John Billingham resulted in a new team left responsible for a plan that was not theirs; over time enthusiasm for the project waned.[64] However, even unfinished, the shopping centre received praise from Opher and Bird in their analysis of British new towns for its connectivity with the historic town centre, becoming a vital element of the town's circulation and avoiding the 'desperate isolation from other activities characteristic of many other new town centres'.[65]

Despite its strongly modern self-presentation and the extent of its demolition work in Irvine's historic centre, the corporation also had a strong interest in conservation. High Street businesses were encouraged to invest in 'facelifting' their properties using a pre-selected range of 'traditional' colours and lettering (Figure 5.6).[66] New buildings were to be built using 'traditional materials and accord sympathetically' with surroundings.[67] Conservation Area surveys were published in 1973 by the architect Henry Roan Rutherford, including plans for Glasgow Vennel, the Seagate, Perceton and Dreghorn.[68] Renovated in 1984, Glasgow Vennel won a coveted Europa Nostra medal for the protection of Europe's cultural heritage.[69] The development corporation was also involved with the restoration of individual buildings. While many of the area's farmhouses were converted into community centres, other key buildings, such as Trinity Church, were restored (Figures 5.7 and 5.8).[70]

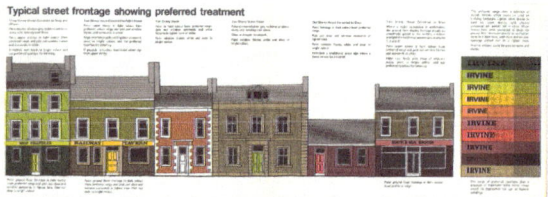

FIGURE 5.6 Proposals for the refurbishment of historic buildings in the central area: a counterpart to the modernity of the new town centre (© Ayrshire Archives/North Ayrshire Council).

FIGURE 5.7 Glasgow Vennel, as restored (© Crown Copyright: HES).

FIGURE 5.8 Towerlands, Bourtreehill, following restoration work (© North Ayrshire Council).

Leisure

Irvine was designated at a time when many people were becoming better-off and had a growing amount of free time. Average weekly earnings grew by 130 per cent between 1955 and 1969,[71] while recent increases in people's leisure time were predicted to continue. The idea of leisure as a vital component of social life and something which the state might encourage was increasingly recognized.[72] At Billingham in north-east England, for example, leisure facilities were integral to the new town centre, being considered by the local authority to be 'essential to the community's well-being'.[73] Recent historians including Otto Saumarez Smith and Guy Ortolano have seen the way in which the public sector sought to encourage an ever-greater range of leisure activities during the late 1960s and 1970s as evidence of social democracy's ability to adapt to new ideas.[74] 'Fun' was increasingly the keynote. At a time of growing international travel, leisure centres often offered pseudo-Mediterranean settings with palm trees and free-form pools in which to splash about, as opposed to earlier rectilinear swimming pools intended for more serious exercise. There were shifts in the awarding of performing arts subsidy, too, away from an earlier focus on professional excellence towards support for more diverse, participatory forms.[75] The plan for Irvine – with its images of a leisured population having a good time, enabled and supported by the state – essentially sought to apply these ideas at an urban scale. IDC was acutely aware that evidence from earlier new towns had proved that recreational facilities were a 'necessity'.[76] Where possible, land unsuitable for other uses would be allocated to sporting, social and religious groups.[77] Many would be accommodated in a central 'town club' in the harbour area, as will be discussed below.[78] Meanwhile the development corporation hoped that private investment in tourism would attract investment; they aimed to create 'one of the most modern holiday resort and recreational centres in Europe'.[79] Inspiration came from the successful Aviemore ski resort, which had opened in 1966.[80] As Aviemore had attracted visitors to its ski slopes, Irvine hoped it could draw tourists to its coastline.[81] The area already boasted several activities, such as golfing, salmon fishing and water sports, and had the recently built Harbour Arts Centre.[82] With good rail and road connections and proximity to Prestwick Airport, the Scottish Tourist Board in 1968 highlighted the Ayrshire coast as a potential growth area.[83] It was hoped that visitors would come from across Britain and that they could even be enticed from North America.[84]

The Gosling plans for the harbourside and foreshore were highly optimistic. The harbour area had long been a popular site for local leisure, with golfing and boating common despite the presence of large areas of contaminated industrial land.[85] It seemed clear to IDC that the site had unrealized potential.[86] IDC's plans thus anticipated the construction of hotels, housing, holiday homes, pubs, casinos, nightclubs, an oceanarium, hovercraft terminal, ski slope and even a funfair (Figure 5.9).[87] The first phase of these plans created a substantial leisure centre at what would have been the western end of the megastructure to act as a 'catalyst for development'; it was named the Magnum when it opened in 1976.[88] Whilst living in Brazil in the early 1960s, Gosling became aware that many families spent their weekends attending sporting clubs, swimming., and playing football and tennis. His new 'town club' – terminology that echoed contemporaneous 'city club' proposals for Milton Keynes – was for all residents, regardless of income.[89] It was hoped that it would provide an opportunity for social interaction; it was also intended to encourage residents to try new things. Although echoing what had been built in Billingham a decade before and similar in conception to Stevenage's contemporaneous Arts and Leisure Centre, it also reflected a longer architectural tradition in which, as discussed in Chapter 1, the term 'centre' was understood to refer to a type of building that would bring people together and would empower them as individual citizens as well as members of the community.[90] While the Magnum's exterior design was an inconspicuous 'plain metal clad box', the interior housed activities for the whole family under one roof, including a pool, ice rink, sports hall, squash courts, multi-use theatre, art studios, crèche, exhibitions spaces and accommodation for local

FIGURE 5.9 Plans for the Harbour-Foreshore area, c. 1971. The MGB coupe was David Gosling's own and featured in many drawings of what was proposed for Irvine; it and the Mini represent the emerging leisured/consumer society (© Ayrshire Archives/North Ayrshire Council).

social clubs (Figure 5.10).[91] Those who did not wish to participate could observe the activities from a raised central corridor with viewing galleries, a café, bars and restaurants,[92] a feature which recalled the emphasis on transparency as a spur to action in the *ur*-centre, the Pioneer Health Centre, Peckham, of the 1930s.[93] Upon its opening in 1976, the Magnum was Europe's largest leisure centre.[94] Although it was therefore a notable development and was novel in its multifunctional character, as a single building it also suggests a more conventional view of recreation than was perhaps implied by the earlier proposals for the new town, in which leisure was seamlessly integrated throughout. Nonetheless, it was hugely popular, with visitors in the late 1970s ranging from 15,000 a week in the winter to 25,000 in the summer, and attendance reaching 14,000 one Easter Monday.[95]

Ambitions that the centre would be a catalyst for further harbourside development were short-lived. In June 1974, a deadly explosion at a chemical works in Flixborough, North Lincolnshire, prompted a re-think of Irvine's harbour development. Since the 1870s, an explosives factory had been situated directly across the harbour from the Magnum, with the site owned by ICI from the 1950s. The factory regularly shipped out unexploded ordnance through the harbour, and so Flixborough resulted in the enforcement of a safeguarding zone.[96] The initial restrictions were severe, with development banned in a half-kilometre radius, the risk of the Magnum being forced

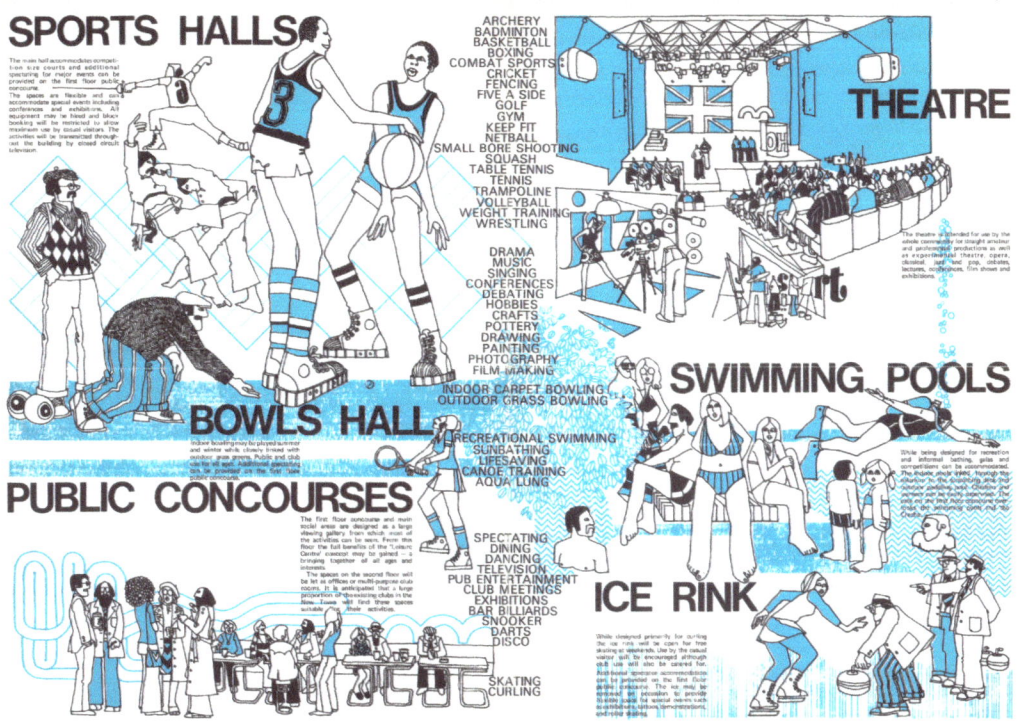

FIGURE 5.10 IDC's vision of the Magnum: a multi-functional spur to action (© Ayrshire Archives/North Ayrshire Council).

to close and much of the town centre threatened.[97] It was eventually agreed that an area of single-storey industrial units would be permitted along with the renovation of a few harbourside houses.[98]

Much like the ICI land across the harbour, the planned Beach Park area was once home to explosives and chemical factories.[99] The decontamination of this land was a crucial ambition for IDC in the early 1970s. Without the Beach Park, they feared there would be insufficient pull from the town centre to the harbour.[100] A 1963 Industry Act allowing for the reclamation of derelict land permitted the development corporation to proceed with their plans from 1975 to 1980.[101] Intended initially as home for an extensive tourism complex, the plans were significantly impacted by Flixborough. With the expansion of the town centre towards the shore hampered, a simpler approach was pursued, with graded hills, areas of marram grass and a boating pond. The site also featured the 1985 Seaworld Centre by the architects Page and Park and a red sandstone dragon atop a hill, described by Rob Close as 'the sort of light-hearted architecture that the park and sea demand'.[102]

Tourism remained a significant element of development corporation policy.[103] First proposed in the 1983 *Development Profile*, a Maritime Museum was to act as a 'vehicle for harbour action' and to combat the problems of the previous decade.[104] The aim was to acquire a series of boats to act as floating exhibits based at an area of restored wharves on the river Irvine.[105] By 1990, plans for the museum had been further expanded, with plans to relocate, re-erect and re-clad the 1872

Engineering Works of Alexander Stephen & Sons from Linthouse, Glasgow. The project involved close partnership with conservation bodies, including Historic Scotland, to re-erect sensitively the building's cast-iron columns and timber trusses. The museum was opened in 1991 and received category 'A' listed status the same year.[106] However, despite the best efforts of the planners, Irvine never truly became a substantial tourist destination.[107] The harbourside with the Magnum, Beach Park and Maritime Museum was popular with locals, and thanks to the electrification of the railways in the 1980s, journey times from Glasgow halved, allowing Irvine to become a popular day trip destination.[108] However, much of the coastal frontage was never developed. The problems were compounded by IDC, which, Read argued, focused solely on advertising industry and housing and put little effort into promoting tourism.[109]

Housing

From 1969, IDC aimed to build as many as 2000 homes a year, split between private enterprise, local authorities, the Scottish Special Housing Association and the development corporation itself.[110] In planning the housing areas, Gosling's team avoided the Radburn system, where cars were strictly separated from pedestrians; this decision reflected a growing critique of Radburn planning which in Runcorn had already resulted in the decision to apply to the Halton Brow area the Dutch 'Woonerf' principle, in which cars are subordinate to but not segregated from pedestrians,[111] and would in time also inform the plans for Glenrothes. Gosling argued that while the flow of pedestrians would be towards the public transport routes and the flow of cars towards the distributor roads, both forms of movement should be integrated under controlled conditions adjacent to homes.[112] It would be apparent to cars entering these zones that they were predominantly pedestrian spaces, and individual garages attached to homes would minimize parking on the street. Read described the areas as feeling like courtyards and claimed that Irvine 'was possibly the first place in Scotland where the concept was developed'.[113]

At the centre of each zone was the public transport route, or 'community route' (Figure 5.11).[114] This system replaced Wilson's proposed transport spine with a network of simpler, though still

FIGURE 5.11 Transport route and recently completed housing, late 1970s (© Architectural Press Archive/RIBA Collections).

segregated, bus routes.[115] The 1971 plan explained how the route would link housing communities 'in a way which was not achieved in previous new towns' – something true in a Scottish sense, at least.[116] It can most closely be compared to Runcorn's network of exclusive bus tracks,[117] but while Runcorn's system was specifically built at high cost, Irvine's used existing routes instead.[118] It was expected that most people would have cars, but that those on a lower income living in higher-density, lower-cost flats would be housed closer to public transport routes.[119] Such housing could then be designed to include covered pedestrian pathways and bus waiting areas.[120] Stylistically, it was proposed that buildings inspired by the 'architecture of the traditional Scottish High Street', with bright colour washes used along the routes while lower density housing behind, would be increasingly monochromatic, 'reflecting the vernacular architecture of the farmhouses'.[121]

An ambition to reflect 'traditional' and 'vernacular' Scottish architectural styles is a theme that runs throughout Irvine's design history, complementing the avant-garde modernity of the town centre and IDC's visual image (Figure 5.12). The 'modern vernacular' movement began in the early 1950s, with projects including Wheeler & Sproson's work in Burntisland,[122] and was elaborated by practices including Baxter Clark & Paul, Sinclair Macdonald & Son, and Basil Spence & Partners. As noted in Chapter 3, an abstracted vernacular was a key influence on the design of Cumbernauld's early housing areas. IDC's interpretation of this idea was characterized by the bold use of colour,

FIGURE 5.12 Housing at Girdle Toll: Scottish vernacular reinterpreted (© Charles McKean).

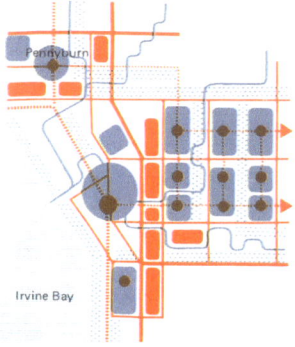

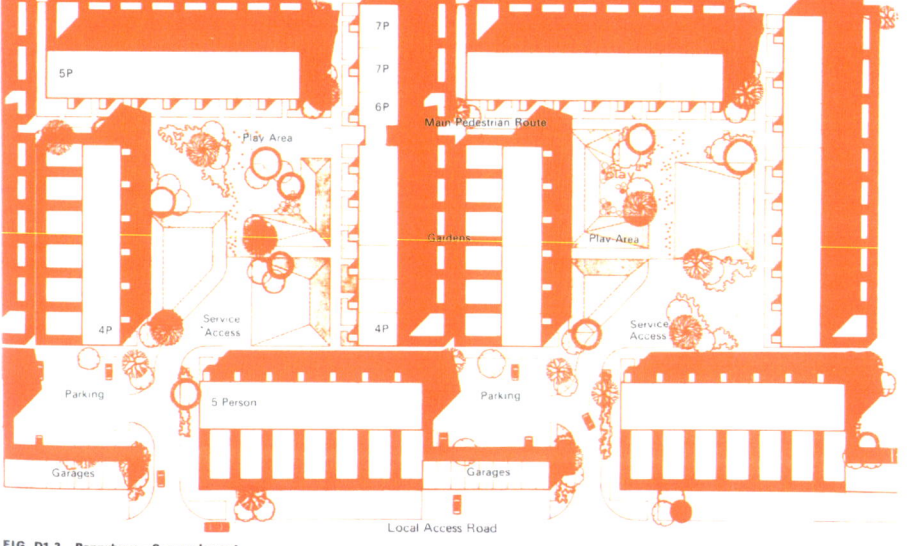

FIGURE 5.13 Pennyburn 1, as illustrated in the *Irvine New Town Plan*. The use of the Microgramma typeface for the house numbers echoed its all-pervasive use in IDC's publications and documentation (© Ayrshire Archives/North Ayrshire Council).

dual-pitched roofs, stone margins to windows, extensive use of harl (render) and the use of small-scale courtyard design.[123]

Gosling explained in a 1995 paper that 'visible construction was [considered] an urgent necessity'.[124] Before the 1971 plan had even been published, there was pressure for work to commence, particularly from the local burgh councils, who had been resistant to the creation of the development corporation.[125] Further pressure came from Dennis Kirby, IDC's general manager, who was keen to hand over design work to private contractors.[126] The first development was at Pennyburn. The site was allocated to housing in both the Wilson plan and Gosling's revised proposals, so work could begin before the latter's publication.[127] Gosling began work on Pennyburn 1 before he even had a full-sized department at his disposal.[128] Work was completed by December 1969.[129] The scheme involved eight landscaped squares with parking at entrances, each surrounded by thirty houses (Figure 5.13).[130] The courtyard layout was intended to create the kind of 'neighbourliness' which the architects believed was found in the traditional street frontage layout.[131] The houses were rendered white to contrast with dark stained timber and mono-pitch roofs. In a move seen as 'communist' by some IDC board members, Gosling moved to a house in Pennyburn with his pregnant wife and two children to better understand the impact of his design.[132] Several colleagues followed suit.[133] During the two and a half years Gosling lived there, he learnt what worked and applied this knowledge to his later work. While he had assumed that families would want to interact socially around his community squares, he discovered that 'impoverished families, with little or no mobility, valued above all else privacy'.[134] A greater emphasis on privacy can be seen in the later phases of Pennyburn and throughout the rest of the town.[135]

Once the 1971 plan had been published, IDC was able to begin work on the Bourtreehill and Broomlands neighbourhoods. These areas were described in the *New Towns Record* as the most representative of Gosling's design philosophy, with work commencing in Bourtreehill just after the publication of the 1971 plan.[136] The two areas were situated around the Broomlands Busway 'community route' and shared a local centre at Bourtreehill. It was envisaged that footpaths along community routes could be protected from the weather by the projecting upper storeys of high-density housing, but the plans were scaled back to comprise a simple segregated pathway alongside the bus route. While the core design principles remained consistent, topographical features provided each site with a sense of individuality.[137] In Bourtreehill, in particular, variety was formed by creating enclosed spaces in some areas, while in other sections long terraces opened up (Figure 5.14). The Towerlands area was rigidly geometrical, with blocks positioned at right angles.[138] In contrast, Bourtreehill North reflects the compact 'hill town' concept previously seen in Cumbernauld, refined by the adoption of Gosling's 'traffic-calmed' squares.[139] The Bourtreehill and Broomlands areas are characterized by their bold use of colour on window surrounds and sometimes also entire facades. In particular, shops in Broomlands were painted dark terracotta, and Bourtreehill featured the occasional dramatic black house.[140] Varied roof shapes and angles provided interest to the skylines of both areas.[141] The restoration of old farm buildings in Bourtreehill into a community centre added to the varied nature of the areas.[142] Described by Close as 'the apogee of Irvine development corporation residential design', these areas represent the early 1970s vision of Irvine new town at its best.[143]

FIGURE 5.14 Housing at Bourtreehill and Broomlands (© Architectural Press Archive/ RIBA Collections).

Unfortunately, Irvine's rapid expansion soon came to an end. The dramatic economic decline of the 1970s hampered the town's development, as did the policy shift to urban regeneration.[144] Irvine's population target was reduced in 1981 from 116,000 to 95,000, and again to 63,000 in the 1990s.[145] By 1983, the town was experiencing high unemployment, substantially higher than the rest of Strathclyde.[146] The town was also suffering from an increasingly poor-quality environment. Areas built before designation were thought to be 'drab and unattractive'.[147] Numerous gap sites and decaying buildings indicated a lack of economic buoyancy, impacting the confidence of industrialists and other investors.[148] In 1983, the development corporation produced a *Development Profile*, which altered the approach they would take.[149] Instead of large-scale development, the focus shifted to knitting together the existing town through infill, renewal and restoration.[150] Small sites, in particular, were allocated for experimental housing.[151] Development corporation architect Roan Rutherford spearheaded much of this work, with conspicuously successful results; he made a fundamental contribution to Irvine's architecture during the 1980s and early 1990s. Rutherford began working in Irvine after winning a competition to design housing in East Kilbride in 1976. His early projects in Irvine included well-received housing at Braehead (completed 1978), featuring double-height living areas and pine-clad mezzanines. Between 1984 and 1996, IDC received forty-six awards and commendations, thirty-seven of which were for projects overseen by Rutherford.[152] Caley House – the Kilwinning YMCA/YWCA hostel – was widely recognized; completed in the mid-1980s, it comprises a long, low building with a glazed street frontage that culminates in a glazed conservatory, crowned by a blockwork pinnacle and with chunky blockwork bays to a rear garden. Meanwhile Rutherford's 1983 Heathfield House demonstrated the growing necessity to accommodate the town's ageing population. Winner of a 1988 Civic Trust award, it provided twenty-one corridor-linked cottages in new single-storey ranges set around a courtyard, connected to communal space in a restored listed building.[153] A further sheltered housing scheme by Rutherford at Bryce Knox Court achieved four awards and commendations, including a RIBA Regional Award in 1992 (Figure 5.15). The scheme consisted of a low block, harled in pale colours and topped in a pitched pantile roof, with a top-lit communal area featuring robust blockwork, exposed timbers and extensive glazing.[154] The most significant

FIGURE 5.15 Bryce Knox Court (© North Ayrshire Council).

of the award-winning schemes, however, was Rutherford and Allan Stewart's Red Cross House (1987–92). The scheme's purpose was to enable those who had experienced extended hospital stays to reintegrate into the community and to provide services for disabled adults and young people.[155] With a series of connected buildings containing accessible accommodation, social spaces and facilities such as a pool, it adopts its contemporaries' pale harling, exposed blockwork and tiled roof plus top-lit communal spaces featuring ample glazing and lots of well-detailed, exposed timber. It won seven awards and commendations, including an Eric Lyons Housing Award (European) and a RIAS/Scottish Enterprise Regeneration Award.

During the early 1990s, IDC was once again able to construct general needs housing. Linkwood Court, Lawthorn (1992) echoed the forms of Bryce Knox Court. Lawthorn 1A of 1991 was planned with 1.5-storey houses laid out in staggered terraces arranged to take advantage of a sloping site. Finished in harl, with small windows to the street for privacy and larger windows to the rear gardens, plus generous projecting eaves to shield the buildings, the houses were provided with insulation above the required level. The harbour area also became a particular focus at the time. The shipping of explosives from the ICI factory had reduced, and the restrictions on the construction of housing which had previously applied were eased in 1993. A Harbourside Masterplan of that year proposed a combination of restoration and new building, the latter taking an increasingly distinctive approach which creatively developed the contextual modernism of the 1980s.[156] New buildings on the Harbourside (1995), Peter Street, Gottries Crescent and Cochrane Street (all 1996) were intended to have an urban quality, defining the street edge through their mass and scale. Visually, their design suggested an original fusion and development of influences including the Arts and Crafts, the 'Amsterdam school' of the early twentieth century, and the vernacular, with harled walls, sculptural curved and angled bay windows, and deep eaves, evoking a feeling of continuity without revivalism.

Conclusion

By 1994, the population of the designated area had reached just 56,000, only 19,600 more than the new town contained upon its conception in 1966,[157] and much of the vision set out in the *Irvine New Town Plan* remained on paper. Yet the architecture of Irvine as developed should not be written off as a shadow of the original plan. IDC, despite overseeing the loss of the town's historic bridge, quickly demonstrated its skill in sensitive conservation, a field in which by the 1990s it excelled. Its work – especially that by Roan Rutherford – also reveals the innovative character of Scottish architecture and the dynamism of the Scottish new towns well into the 1990s. This is a period rarely associated with vibrant public-sector design, yet IDC's output, especially its housing and its work in the harbour area, suggests otherwise. It confirms the need for a broader perspective on late-twentieth-century architecture and the history of the public sector, at least within the Scottish context, and suggests a potentially fruitful avenue for further research.

Notes

1. Irvine Development Corporation [IDC], *Irvine New Town Plan* (Irvine: IDC, 1971).
2. Guy Ortolano, *Thatcher's Progress: From Social Democracy to Market Liberalism through an English New Town* (Cambridge: Cambridge University Press, 2018), 17.
3. Rob Close, *Ayrshire & Arran: An Illustrated Architectural Guide* (Edinburgh: RIAS, 1992), 55.
4. IDC, *Development Profile Irvine New Town* (Irvine: IDC, 1983), 3.
5. IDC, *Interim Revised Outline Plan* (Irvine: IDC, 1969), 5.
6. The National Archives (London) [TNA], T224/1388, 'Hugh Wilson & Lewis Womersley, Interim Report on Planning Proposals: Irvine Growth Area', 1965, 2.
7. TNA, T224/1388, 'Central Scotland Study – Expansion of Irvine', n.d.
8. IDC, *Irvine New Town Plan*, 298.
9. IDC, *Development Profile*, 3.
10. TNA, T224/1388 'Central Scotland White Paper', n.d.
11. TNA, T224/1388, 'Central Scotland Study'.
12. Ibid.
13. TNA, T224/1388, 'Proposal for New Town at Irvine', 8 June 1964.
14. TNA, T224/1388, Wilson & Womersley Interim Report, 1.
15. 'Lewis Hugh Wilson', Dictionary of Scottish Architects, online at www.scottisharchitects.org.uk (accessed on 1 February 2024).
16. Worcester, The Hive, 499.4 BA10300 Parcel 91, Redditch Development Corporation, Minutes, 14 July 1964.
17. TNA, T224/1388, Wilson & Womersley Interim Report, May 1965.
18. IDC, *Irvine New Town Plan*, 20.
19. Hugh Wilson and Lewis Womersley, *Irvine New Town: Final Report on Planning Proposals; A Report to the Secretary of State for Scotland* (Edinburgh: Scottish Development Department, 1967).
20. IDC, *Interim Revised Outline Plan*, 1.

21 Wilson and Womersley, *Final Report*, 3.
22 TNA, T224/1388, Wilson & Womersley Interim Report.
23 Ibid., 37–9.
24 IDC, *Irvine New Town Plan*, 298.
25 For broader discussion of this: Terence Bendixson, *The Peterborough Effect: Reshaping a City* (Peterborough: Peterborough Development Corporation, 1988), 69–73.
26 R.E. Nicholl, 'Reviewed Works: Irvine New Town Plan', *Urban Studies* 9, no. 3 (1972): 389–91; TNA, T224/1388, Wilson & Womersley Interim Report, 38.
27 TNA, T224/1388, Wilson & Womersley Interim Report, 37.
28 Guy Ortolano, 'Planning the Urban Future in 1960s Britain', *Historical Journal* 54, no. 2 (2011): 477–507.
29 Arthur Ling, *Runcorn New Town: Master Plan* (Runcorn: Runcorn Development Corporation, 1967); 'A Town Called Alcan: Alcan Broadsheet', *Architectural Review* 136, no. 811 (September 1964): 69–72; University of Edinburgh, Centre for Research Collections, Percy Johnson-Marshall uncat. folders FR37, FR52, FR76.
30 Otto Saumarez Smith, 'Landscapes of Hope and Crisis: Dereliction, Environment, and Leisure in Britain during the Long 1970s', *Journal of British Studies* 62, no. 4 (2023): 988–1010.
31 'Irvine', *New Towns Record* (Planning Exchange CD-ROM set, 1996) [*NTR*].
32 'Lewis Hugh Wilson', Dictionary of Scottish Architects.
33 'Irvine', *NTR*.
34 Ibid.
35 Nicholl, 'Reviewed Works', 389–91.
36 'Irvine', *NTR*.
37 IDC, *Interim Revised Outline Plan*, 5.
38 National Records of Scotland, SEP15/589, F.M.M. Gray to W.D.C. Lyddon (1971).
39 Nicholl, 'Reviewed Works', 389–91.
40 Philip Opher and Clinton Bird, *Cumbernauld, Irvine, East Kilbride: An Illustrated Guide* (Headington: Oxford Polytechnic, 1980), Irvine 2–3.
41 IDC, *Interim Revised Outline Plan*, 7–8.
42 Ibid. At least two IDC publications set out a plan for the Gailes housing, with clusters of houses set around a tree-lined spine route, but the proposals were scrapped.
43 'Irvine', *NTR*.
44 IDC, *Development Profile*, 3.
45 Nicholl, 'Reviewed Works', 389–91.
46 IDC, *Irvine Town Centre Preliminary Proposals* (Irvine: IDC, 1969).
47 'Irvine', *NTR*.
48 IDC, *Town Centre*.
49 IDC, 'Irvine New Town Commercial Centre', in *Irvine New Town: Broadsheets* (Irvine: IDC, 1972).
50 IDC, *Town Centre*; IDC, *Irvine New Town Plan*, 119.
51 IDC, 'Irvine New Town Burgh Centre', in *Irvine New Town: Broadsheets* (Irvine: IDC, 1972).
52 IDC, *Town Centre*, 9.
53 IDC, 'Irvine New Town Commercial Centre'.
54 IDC, *Irvine New Town Plan*, 113.

55 IDC, *Irvine New Town Plan*, 81.
56 IDC, 'Irvine New Town Commercial Centre'.
57 IDC, *Irvine New Town Plan*, 113.
58 Ibid., 236.
59 Close, *Ayrshire & Arran*, 55–6.
60 Janina Gosseye, '"Uneasy Bedfellows" Conceiving Urban Megastructures Precarious Public Private Partnerships in Post-War British New Towns', *Planning Perspectives* 34, no. 6 (2019): 935–57 (pp. 954–5).
61 'Irvine', *NTR*.
62 Ibid.
63 Ibid.
64 Gosseye, 'Uneasy Bedfellows', 955.
65 Opher and Bird, *Cumbernauld, Irvine, East Kilbride*, Irvine 8.
66 IDC, 'Irvine New Town: Irvine Facelift', in *Irvine New Town: Broadsheets* (Irvine: IDC, 1972).
67 IDC, 'Irvine New Town: Kilwinning Facelift', in *Irvine New Town: Broadsheets* (Irvine: IDC, 1972).
68 'Henry Roan Rutherford', Dictionary of Scottish Architects, online at www.scottisharchitects.org.uk (accessed on 1 February 2024).
69 IDC, *Irvine New Town 1966–1996* (Irvine: IDC, 1996).
70 Close, *Ayrshire & Arran*, 58–62; 'Irvine', *NTR*.
71 Alistair Fair, *Modern Playhouses: An Architectural History of Britain's New Theatres, 1945–1985* (Oxford: Oxford University Press, 2018), 17–18.
72 Michael Dower, 'Fourth Wave: The Challenge of Leisure, a Civic Trust Survey', *Architects' Journal* 141, no. 3 (1965): 122–5.
73 Fair, *Modern Playhouses*, 18.
74 Ortolano, *Thatcher's Progress*, 254–7; Otto Saumarez Smith, 'The Lost World of the British Leisure Centre', *History Workshop Journal* 88 (2019): 180–203.
75 Fair, *Modern Playhouses*, 239–43.
76 IDC, *Irvine New Town Plan*, 139.
77 Ibid.
78 IDC, *Interim Revised Outline Plan*, 79.
79 IDC, *Development Profile*, 8.
80 'Aviemore: Remembering the Alpine-style holiday resort in the Highlands', *Scotsman*, March 2019.
81 IDC, *Development Profile*, 77–8.
82 Ibid.
83 IDC, *Interim Revised Outline Plan*, 77–8; IDC, 'Irvine New Town Harbour-Foreshore Development', in *Irvine New Town: Broadsheets* (Irvine: IDC, 1972).
84 Ibid.
85 IDC, *Irvine New Town Plan*, 136.
86 Ibid.
87 Opher and Bird, *Cumbernauld, Irvine, East Kilbride*, Irvine 10.
88 'Irvine', *NTR*.
89 IDC, *Interim Revised Outline Plan*, 78–9; 'Irvine', *NTR*.

90 Elizabeth Darling and Alistair Fair, '"The Core": The Centre as a Concept in Twentieth-Century British Planning and Architecture. Part One: The Emergence of the Idea', *Planning Perspectives* 31, no. 1 (2023): 69–98.
91 Opher and Bird, *Cumbernauld, Irvine, East Kilbride*, Irvine 10.
92 Ibid.
93 Elizabeth Darling and Alistair Fair, '"The Core": The Centre as a Concept in Twentieth-Century British Planning and Architecture. Part Two: The Realisation of the Idea', *Planning Perspectives* 38, no. 3 (2023): 525–57 (p. 555).
94 Ciaran Shanks, 'Magnum at 40: Revisit the Golden Era of Irvine's Iconic Leisure Centre', *Irvine Times*, 14 September 2006; Close, *Ayrshire & Arran*, 60.
95 Clement James, '"The Cole View": Kenneth Cole at The Magnum Leisure Centre, Irvine', *British Journal of Photography* 127, no. 6281 (1980): 1255.
96 'Irvine', *NTR*.
97 Ibid.
98 Ibid.
99 Ibid.
100 Ibid.
101 'Irvine', *NTR*; 'Roger Read', Dictionary of Scottish Architects, online at www.scottisharchitects.org.uk (accessed on 1 February 2024).
102 Close, *Ayrshire & Arran*, 60–1.
103 IDC, *Development Profile*, 8.
104 'Irvine', *NTR*.
105 Ibid.
106 Ibid.
107 'Irvine', *NTR*.
108 Ibid.
109 Ibid.
110 IDC, *Interim Revised Outline Plan*, 3.
111 'Runcorn', *NTR*.
112 'Irvine', *NTR*.
113 Ibid.
114 IDC, *Irvine New Town Plan*, 86.
115 Opher and Bird, *Cumbernauld, Irvine, East Kilbride*, Irvine 2.
116 Ibid.
117 Terence Bendixson, 'It Will Be Quicker by Bus in Runcorn New Town: Special Road Will Ensure No Jams', *Guardian*, 26 January 1966.
118 'Irvine', *NTR*.
119 Ibid.
120 IDC, *Irvine New Town Plan*, 86.
121 'Irvine', *NTR*.
122 Kat Breen, 'New Life in an Old Town. Wheeler & Sproson and the Post War Reconstruction of Burntisland and Dysart' (PhD dissertation, University of Edinburgh, 2021).
123 Close, *Ayrshire & Arran*, 55–6.

124 'Irvine', *NTR*.

125 Ibid.

126 Ibid.

127 IDC, *Irvine New Town Plan*, 20–2.

128 'Irvine', *NTR*.

129 IDC, *Irvine New Town Plan*, 248.

130 Ibid.

131 Ibid., 123.

132 'Irvine', *NTR*.

133 Ibid.

134 Ibid.

135 Alistair Fair, 'Privacy, the Housing Research Unit at the University of Edinburgh and the Courtyard House, 1959–70', *Architectural History* 65 (2022): 327–58 (pp. 335–7).

136 'Irvine Development Corporation 4th Annual Report', *Reports of the Cumbernauld, East Kilbride, Glenrothes, Irvine and Livingston Development Corporation for the year ended 31st of March 1971* (1971): 149.

137 IDC, *Irvine New Town Plan*, 220–3.

138 Opher and Bird, *Cumbernauld, Irvine, East Kilbride*, Irvine 114.

139 Ibid., Irvine 114.

140 Ibid., Irvine 12.

141 Ibid.

142 Ibid., Irvine 15.

143 Close, *Ayrshire & Arran*, 63.

144 'Irvine', *NTR*.

145 Town and Country Planning Association, *'Mark Two' New Town – Designated 7 November 1966*, https://tcpa.org.uk/new-town/irvine/ (accessed on 1 February 2024).

146 IDC, *Development Profile*, 3.

147 Ibid.

148 Ibid.

149 'Irvine', *NTR*.

150 Ibid.

151 IDC, *Development Profile*, 11.

152 IDC, *Irvine New Town 1966–1996*.

153 'Irvine', *NTR*.

154 IDC, *Irvine New Town 1966–1996*.

155 'Irvine', *NTR*.

156 Close, *Ayrshire & Arran*, 389; also '68 to 108 Harbour Street', typescript of *c.* 1995 by Roan Rutherford in the possession of Miles Glendinning.

157 'Irvine', *NTR*.

PART TWO

Life

6

Homes

The promise of brand-new, good-quality homes was the main attraction for most of the pioneers who relocated to the new towns in Scotland. For this generation, especially those moving from Glasgow where rented homes in the council sector often comprised flats, the opportunity of a house with its own front door and garden, in particular, was an attractive proposition. This specific and originally English definition of the word 'house' (a term hitherto used more broadly in Scotland and applied also to flats) increasingly represented the hopes and dreams of those with aspirations to 'better themselves': a higher standard of living and a more optimistic future for the next generation. What is notable, however, is that housing remained important to subsequent generations. As the towns expanded and began to offer a wider range of homes, including housing for purchase, they continued to meet the aspirations of those who had settled there and their descendants.

The Introduction to this book outlined the policy objectives of the Scottish Office as far as housing was concerned. The new towns presented an opportunity to showcase a view of 'best practice' in neighbourhood and housing design; new town rents, meanwhile, were a challenge to low municipal rents. Having then looked in more detail at the planning and design of the towns themselves in Part 1 of this book, this chapter focuses on individual housing stories in the context of people's lives and pulls the lens outwards to situate those decisions within the broader context of local and national housing policy and provision. We argue that housing journeys were shaped in distinctive ways by development corporation priorities, especially in terms of the provision of high-quality rental housing for all (a goal which in turn was informed by the Scottish Office's drive to improve standards), as well as the encouragement of private-sector housing construction, the sale of corporation housing prior to the enactment during the 1980s of the broader 'Right to Buy', and the construction of owner-occupied housing estates in the 1990s. In parallel, this chapter pays attention to people's emotional and material responses to new town environments, focusing on housing mobility, social stratification and spatial segregation. It argues that the desire for security in the form of a home of one's own, a greater degree of privacy and comfort, and choice in respect of type of tenure – rented or purchased – informed people's decisions to leave communities and families behind in order to make a new future for themselves and their children. The new home was the key to the new town dream.

Housing histories

The history of housing in Britain and especially in Scotland in the twentieth century has largely focused on the mass provision of municipal housing as a response to overcrowding and poor housing conditions.[1] Alongside this scholarship, there has developed a literature on urban reconstruction, rehousing and relocation, again emphasizing council housing. This focus recognizes the dominance in twentieth-century Scotland of the rented sector and, in particular, the significant role of the public sector as housing provider after 1918 – not least in Glasgow.[2] Hitherto, with a few exceptions, new towns have been a small part of this story, included in more general accounts of relocation to new estates, depicted as a policy failure by those who seek to understand Glasgow's travails, and rarely considered as distinctive in terms of housing policy or the experience of those who moved there.[3] Even works on housing design rarely address how that design impacted on the ways that people lived in their modern homes.[4] Given the central importance of housing in people's decisions to move to the new towns and to stay there, and the significance of the home as a place of refuge, privacy and family life in the post-war decades, it is surprising that scholars have given so little attention to the relationships between the built environment, the family, and social life centred on the home in towns which were expressly designed and planned to nurture these needs.

By contrast, social scientists and commentators in the late 1950s and 1960s were fascinated by the experience of elective relocation to expanding suburbs, the new towns and the expanded towns in England.[5] In places like Stevenage, Luton and Cumbernauld, improved housing and material standards of living were seen as fundamental to changing class identities, especially for the working classes. For researchers such as Ferdynand Zweig, Mark Abrams and Raphael Samuel, the process of creating new lives and lifestyles in new settlements was, for the skilled working classes, a form of emulation of their middle-class counterparts in older suburban areas.[6] This so-called 'embourgeoisement thesis' was further explored in the late 1960s 'affluent worker' study of factory workers in Luton, in which sociologist John Goldthorpe and his colleagues explored how relocation to an expanding town and work in a modern manufacturing industry changed the expectations and tastes of skilled working-class men and their wives.[7] For these workers and their families, the home was key to new family-focused lifestyles, providing a comfortable space for home-based leisure and the consumption of material goods such as televisions, cocktail cabinets, gramophones and refrigerators. Meanwhile Michael Young and Peter Willmott set out to understand the impact on community ties when people chose to leave the inner-city 'traditional' areas in London and relocate to new suburbs.[8] For all that was gained in terms of improved living conditions, it was suggested a great deal was lost in terms of social connections and support, especially for women. In all of these studies, social scientists sought to understand the impact of social and cultural change on people's lives and their sense of self; housing was a crucial element of that change.

More recently, housing has been situated at the heart of interpretations of post-war Britain. The provision of both public- and private-sector housing has long been understood by all shades of government as a key means of meeting people's aspirations, initially as one plank of the building of a post-war social democratic consensus and, by the 1980s, as an equally vital element of market liberalism.[9] In the Scottish context where, traditionally, the balance between rented and owner-occupied housing was particularly skewed towards the former, the 'property-owning democracy' narrative, whereby home ownership and especially the post-1980 sale of public-sector houses facilitated by the 'Right to Buy' takes centre stage, may appear less convincing. But the new towns, Guy Ortolano argues, represented 'the purest version' of the trajectory of housing policy in Britain: meeting need via access to rented housing at the same time as facilitating ownership in a context in which many people wanted to buy.[10] There is much in the Scottish experience, including a desire to own one's home, that mirrors developments south of the border and which perhaps anticipates what was to come in more established small towns across the country.

Building upon this literature, the following chapter seeks to shed light on the lived experiences of those who relocated to a new town in pursuit of improved living conditions. Our oral history interviews with former and current residents explored the meaning of securing a house, the decisions people made regarding location and tenancy (rented or owner-occupation), and their 'housing pathway' over the longer term.[11] The concept of the 'housing pathway' surveys successive stages of housing occupancy over the life of a household and offers a way of analysing the process by which households are affected by the intersection of life cycle events in relation to changes in housing provision and occupancy. We also consider how people's aspirations and choices in terms of where they wanted to live over their life course were shaped by national and local housing policy, and, in particular, the development corporations' policies on housing provision. By exploring individual housing pathways, we ask what was possible for aspirational people in the new towns in Scotland. What does this tell us about the building of a 'modern' Scotland in the immediate post-war decades and beyond?

Moving for a house: The 'pioneer' generation

In a 1970 survey, 40 per cent of East Kilbride respondents reported that a new house was the key factor in deciding to move to the town.[12] Although those living in the very worst slums only rarely were able to take advantage of the opportunity offered by the new towns, for many others, living in cramped or shared accommodation of slightly higher though frequently still poor quality, the new towns presented the chance of something better. After the Second World War, housing shortages resulted in many young married couples living with parents or other relatives, or sharing accommodation with other families. Only a quarter of couples married in the 1950s were able to begin married life living independently.[13] In this context, a house (especially in the more specific 'English' use of the term) was 'an expression of independence, autonomy, control of life'.[14] As Langhamer argues, this period is characterized by a powerful sense of generational change with post-war homemaking for women offering something other than the maternal drudgery of their mothers' lives, although promises of an easy-to-run modern home were overblown.[15] The same is true in terms of their aspirations for their children – a desire for progress manifested in a new start in a healthier environment, providing children with their own bedroom and space to play safely both indoors and outside (Figure 6.1).

FIGURE 6.1 Children playing in Cumbernauld, 1970s (© Architectural Press Archive / RIBA Collections).

Susan's recollection of her parents' decision to leave a flat in Glasgow for a house in Cumbernauld in 1964 is typical of stories told by the pioneer generation. She described the living conditions of her childhood in a run-down tenement:

Well, it was a slum really, with a lot of social problems. We lived in a flat which was right at the top and it was two rooms with a small corridor that joined them. One was the kitchen and the other was the living area. There were box bed spaces in both of the rooms. The coal bunker was in the hallway. So, that was it really. There was no indoor bathroom. There was a toilet that was a flight down and that was it. My sister and I slept in the kitchen in the box bed. We had bunk beds and my parents they turned the box bed area into a studio because they both liked to paint and there was tools and things, things like that. So that was their tiny bit for themselves. And they had a fold-down couch. […] So that was folded down at night. But by day it was the living room. So in that sense, although there was essentially no bedrooms. It didn't feel … We weren't all lying on the floor. You know, in one room or anything like that.[16]

Susan recalled her parents desiring more for themselves and for their daughters. The Townhead area, to the north-east of Glasgow city centre, was 'emptying out'; they had 'to kind of campaign to get out', setting their sights not on a flat in one of Glasgow's new peripheral 'schemes' nor a high-rise city centre development, but on a house in a new town with a garden. In this respect, both space and privacy were important. Susan's family's tenement flat lacked hot water. It was therefore necessary to use the facilities of the 'steamie', the local self-service washhouse, but Susan's mother, being shy, found the steamie to be 'really intimidating because you really had to be, sort of, fast to get all the different bits of equipment and so on'. Although there is a great deal of nostalgia for this era in the city's history, with the steamie holding a particularly notable place in the communal memory of tenement life and women's sociability, the enforced communality of this mode of living was not for everyone.[17] Indeed, it is worth underlining the point that Susan's parents were not unusual in desiring a house with their own front door and a garden rather than even a modern tenement flat (which would still feature a shared staircase and back green). People wanted their own space, indoors and outdoors.[18] Planners and designers recognized and even encouraged this wish. While the 'neighbourhood units' of the early new towns were intended to foster neighbourliness and community, privacy was also an important consideration in post-war housing design, though one which historians have not hitherto emphasized to the same extent.[19] Official reports stressed the value of privacy, understood in terms of freedom within the home and garden from overlooking, good soundproofing, and the arrangement of houses to avoid unwanted contact; moreover, residents' surveys showed that they 'evidently enjoyed the opportunity to withdraw offered by their new surroundings'.[20]

Eventually Susan's parents decided on Cumbernauld because 'it was in the country' and was 'sort of greener'. Like many early residents, they were interviewed by the development corporation housing department ostensibly to ensure they 'would pay the rent and look after the corporation houses'.[21] Linda, whose family moved to Cumbernauld in 1964, similarly recalled how 'they came to vet you'; they asked what her parents' aspirations were 'and they obviously said, we want a better life, at that point, for the three kids that they had'.[22]

In 1968, 75 per cent of residents surveyed by Cumbernauld Development Corporation stated that they had 'bettered themselves' by moving to the new town.[23] This view was shared by Polish sociologist Ferdynand Zweig who, a year later, was commissioned to produce a study of the town. Zweig suggested that 'self-selection goes a long way towards explaining many of the basic attitudes of the Cumbernauld residents' who considered themselves 'higher-class people'.[24] Describing Cumbernauld as a 'fitted carpet town', Zweig noted that 'keeping up with the Joneses' was a 'widespread phenomenon of great significance' and that material comfort and the desire for all the 'latest gadgets' including fitted kitchens was accompanied by a feeling among residents that their move to the town has been 'a step up socially, on the first rung of the ladder of self-improvement'.[25] Zweig's description of the working classes struck a somewhat condescending tone towards people who had legitimate aspirations to leave behind poor housing and a limiting environment; he underestimated the contribution of consumer goods to feelings of well-being and comfort. But, liking 'nice things' did not necessarily add up to competitive materialism.[26] For Susan's mother, her experiences of childhood poverty ensured that 'she was all about looking forward'. She wanted 'a new life'; she did not 'want to even talk about the past'.[27] These working-class pioneers were 'socially highly ambitious'; they had sacrificed a lot to meet the higher costs of this aspirational post-war world. In Cumbernauld, it was said that 'they have created not just a new physical environment, they've created the idea of a new lifestyle and altogether new future for the people who come there' (Figure 6.2).[28]

From the inception of the new towns programme, the aim was to create 'balanced communities', ensuring that these were not just one-class, one-industry towns. This goal meant attracting and retaining the middle classes, as, echoing long-established thinking, it was assumed that this group would take the lead in forming and leading local organizations, and would act as a model of good citizenship. Glenrothes Development Corporation (GDC) in 1966 suggested that the retention of middle-class families would 'instil considerable confidence in the working population', which was 'essential for the well-being of the town'.[29] Over time, however, the new towns abandoned the selectivity experienced by Susan's and Linda's parents, and began to look like any other small urban settlement in respect of their social make-up, incorporating financially precarious families as well as professionals, managers and executives. This development was partly in response to Glasgow's formalized 'overspill' policy after 1957, which saw the city actively encourage migration to the new towns among those on its housing list, as well as the drive from

FIGURE 6.2 Kitchen in a Livingston home, *c.* 1970 (© West Lothian Archives and Records Centre).

the late 1970s to accommodate more vulnerable families in public-sector housing. The result was spatial segregation, a situation writ large in Cumbernauld where the modern Scandinavian-style houses overlooking the park (inhabited by architects and other professionals) contrasted with the high-density accommodation in Carbrain. While the early new towns may have been popularly understood as utopian in their beginnings, especially in relation to the built environment, class distinctions related to housing policy and provision were planned into their development and became increasingly evident over time.

For the first wave of new residents though, the marked contrast between their previous homes and the facilities provided as standard in their new houses ensured that they were excited about relocating. Annie's parents, who moved to Glenrothes in 1954 from a prefab outside Edinburgh, 'must've thought they'd died and gone to heaven' when offered a house 'with two bedrooms and running water'; it was 'just like hitting the jackpot'.[30] Cathy used similar language to describe her delight at her house in East Kilbride:

> We went to see the house in Junipers and it was amazing, up and down the stairs and a massive big cupboard in the hall, your sitting room, kitchen, wee toilet downstairs and then when you went up the stairs we had a smaller bedroom and two big bedrooms, another cupboard here and a big bathroom. It was heaven, it was just so different, back and front door … it was the first time ever in a brand-new house, we thought we'd won the lottery and gone to heaven.[31]

Shirley, who moved to East Kilbride as a young mother in the 1960s was clear that the house was the attraction, especially as the alternative was a high-rise flat in Castlemilk, one of Glasgow's peripheral estates. Shirley's account draws attention to not only the aspirational quality of the new town but also the importance of chain migration in encouraging relocation:

> I went through this thing about how lovely it would be to have a garden – to hang your nappies out in a garden, I'd never had that … My husband at the time, he was a tailor's cutter … ended up he was working for Levi's … they had a sort of factory up here. We got word that we could get a house up here, back and front door, they were just getting built out in Greenhills … and

I thought back and front door how lucky am I! We never really thought about moving ... but, there was really a lot of flats in Castlemilk, there really wasn't a back and front door as such ... so I never would have thought of moving out of this high rise flat except we'd heard you could get a house in East Kilbride, and at that time East Kilbride was the place to live. I mean as my mother used to describe it, 'you'd need to wear a hat when you were going to East Kilbride' ... Aye, because it was really lovely then. And my sister lived up here at the time and my mother-in-law ... From her house we used to see them building Greenhills and she used to say 'be great if you could get a wee house up here' and as I say, my sister already lived up here and I used to come and visit her and I used to think it would be lovely to live up here, it's beautiful, it was in those days, it was so nice.[32]

But professionals, too, were attracted by the offer of better housing. Beryl moved to Cumbernauld in 1965 with her architect husband who had secured a job with the development corporation. Their former home had been a flat in a sub-divided Victorian house in Oldham. While this was 'very grand, kind of big windows and high ceilings', moving to 'a nice, modern, manageable house' with three bedrooms in Carbrain was 'very nice' – and much warmer.[33] A couple of years later, with a baby on the way, the family moved to Kildrum to what was termed a patio house, an L-shaped type of home planned around a walled garden which evoked fond memories from Beryl and her daughter Jenni:

I remember it being L-shaped. You know, because we were round the courtyard, and all the bedrooms were on one side of the L, and then the other side, you came up, and there was a bathroom, and cupboards, and then you were into the living room, and the kitchen, which was, you know, I liked that.[34]

Notwithstanding their large windows and open plan layout, patio houses offered a particularly high degree of privacy, a critical factor in people's assessments.[35] It was a 'very private house' recalled Beryl; 'you could be in your garden space, as it were, without being overlooked by anybody, it was very private ... designed for the people who live in them, not for people walking by'.

The house in the new town brought increased material comfort, privacy and opportunities, but at a price. Many families were willing to incur a higher cost of living in order to gain access to these opportunities for their children, which comprised 'fresh air', access to the countryside and leisure amenities, an education in modern school buildings and eventually work in the new industries or public sector. In addition to the costs of furnishing a new home, development corporation rents were generally higher than those charged by the nearby local authority. For some, the rents proved to be unaffordable. In East Kilbride, Glenrothes and Cumbernauld, graduated rent schemes were introduced which offered means-tested rents related to household income.[36] In 1966 in Cumbernauld, a man employed by Burrough's machine manufacturers explained that his rent was based on his pay, 'but if I was sacked and couldn't get a new job my rent would automatically come down'.[37] This was a controversial scheme in Cumbernauld and not all residents were 'keen on subsidizing others'. There is also evidence of a minority of tenants accumulating rent arrears. As early as 1960, GDC recorded an increase in the number of people requiring 'guidance and help regarding the payment of rent'.[38] Assistance had been obtained from 'local organisations and others for gifts of money, clothing, food etc in hardship cases'. Five years later, GDC was one

FIGURE 6.3 Housing at Dreghorn, Irvine, 1971 (© Architectural Press Archive / RIBA Collections).

of the first authorities to appoint a Housing Welfare Officer to assist 'the very small proportion of tenancies where difficulties occur'. Despite this support, rent arrears continued to grow, even though the graduated rent scheme benefitted 1062 tenants or 14.33 per cent of all tenants by 1969.[39] The problem was less pronounced in East Kilbride, with, from the early 1970s, close cooperation with the social work department to support families with financial difficulties,[40] but even then, the official Residents' Handbook in the early 1970s contained an advertisement for the 'Secret Loans Company'.[41]

Notwithstanding their expense, the new towns continued to attract residents keen for a fresh start. Housing provision adapted to meet demand. By 1970 in Cumbernauld there were fifty-seven different types of house to cater to all needs with five standards of finish.[42] But one consequence of both growth and the development of new neighbourhoods was what Zweig had already noted as 'Neighbourhood Divisions', observing residents' ambitions to live in areas with more 'prestige value and social standing' or simply 'better class' with 'nice people living there'.[43] Cumbernauld was not exceptional. There were similar levels of variation and choice in all of the new towns (Figure 6.3). Initially, a small amount of 'executive' housing was built by the corporation for rent in areas that then became 'desirable'. From the 1960s, owner-occupation levels began to increase. By providing for the aspirations of residents, the new towns began to replicate the spatial segregation evident in established settlements.

Moving on? Home ownership and providing for the second generation

The aspiration that brought families to the new towns ensured that they continued to want more in terms of housing. Some families such as Linda's have remained in their original home to the present day, often becoming homeowners along the way. However, a more common housing trajectory described by our interviewees was for families to accept the first rented home they were offered (sometimes in flats or maisonettes), remaining there for a relatively short period of time before applying to the development corporation for a bigger house, often in an area of the town they perceived to be more desirable or 'better class'. In some instances, families decided to buy a house in the town, either from a private developer or the corporation. An even smaller minority took the decision to buy a plot of land from the corporation and to commission their own house.[44]

Susan's family initially moved to Carbrain in Cumbernauld, one of the earliest neighbourhoods. But problems with water ingress, the lack of central heating and limited green space around the estate prompted Susan's parents to join the housing waiting list for something better. They eventually accepted a house in a new area built to extend Cumbernauld village in 1969. 'It was a better house,' recalled Susan. 'It had central heating and it was in a different kind of environment'.[45] Like many others in new towns, Susan's parents' ambitions for a better quality of life in terms of housing, the environment and quality of the neighbourhood continued beyond the initial move; they only settled when they were satisfied (Figure 6.4).

For others, the aspiration for better quality housing, and perhaps also prestige and social standing, involved buying their own home.[46] Well before the 'Right to Buy' of the 1980s, pent-up demand for ownership was evident in the new towns, challenging the dominant narrative of Scottish housing which emphasizes renting among all social classes. From the late 1950s, as post-war austerity eased and with Scottish rates reform making owner-occupation more financially advantageous than hitherto, the new towns began setting aside land for private developers and for individuals to build their own homes, whilst also building some housing for sale themselves.[47] By the mid-1960s, a target of 25 per cent owner-occupation had been set for the Scottish new towns, and 50 per cent in England and Wales, in part to reduce public-sector expenditure. In the later new towns, Livingston and Irvine, owner-occupation was provided for from the outset. In the earlier new towns, however, with substantial amounts of corporation rented housing already built, it was realized that it would be necessary to sell some homes in order to achieve the target. As a result, from the mid-1960s, the sale to tenants of corporation housing was actively promoted, with varying degrees of success.[48] Among East Kilbride residents surveyed in 1970, while only a small percentage were then owner-occupiers, 17 per cent were interested in purchasing, with a house built by a private developer (and thus potentially 'different' in style and location from corporation-

FIGURE 6.4 Housing at Broomlands, Irvine, 1979 (© Architectural Press Archive / RIBA Collections).

rented housing) being the most popular option.⁴⁹ Relatively few did buy at this stage, however: the discovery of the likely cost of buying and running housing built to a high specification tended to be off-putting. Nonetheless, some did take the plunge. For example, Moira and Tom, both teachers, relocated to Carbrain in Cumbernauld from Glasgow in 1966 'deliberately to get a house'. The couple had a young child and had been subletting a basement flat. The move to the new town was the only way to obtain 'a modern house, initially rented, with all the conveniences of the bathroom and a nice kitchen and good play areas as the children were going to be growing up'. But soon this couple aspired to buy their own home. Just five years later, they purchased a 'chalet-bungalow' in the Kildrum area. They stayed there for twenty years.

Even the modest increase in owner-occupation potentially exacerbated existing distinctions between neighbourhoods in the towns in the 1970s. Jim M described how the Glenrothes housing office allocated corporation housing according to a hierarchy of suitability based on perceived social status. Jim moved to Glenrothes in 1972 to work for General Instruments as a manager where he was considered a key worker. On this basis he presumed he would be entitled to a 'nice house' to rent in the town. Yet, on choosing to settle in the area overlooking the town park the housing officer informed Jim that these were reserved for executives. The housing officer was 'quite clear that I would not get one of these houses I had picked'.⁵⁰ The family did eventually rent a similar house nearby in the desirable area of South Parks, a house they purchased in the 1980s. The notion of the balanced community, so prominent in planners' conceptions of the new towns, was not necessarily a socially mixed community at the level of the neighbourhoods. Although the 'all in it together' myth is often uttered by pioneers and their children to suggest there was little sense of class distinction, in part because almost 'everybody was in a council [i.e. corporation] house', over time class differences increasingly became spatial as those who could afford it moved to larger and better quality houses or became owner-occupiers.⁵¹

At the end of the 1970s East Kilbride and Glenrothes had reached some 20 per cent owner-occupied, and Cumbernauld nearly 30 per cent.⁵² The subsidies which accompanied 'Right to Buy' after 1980 allowed a much greater number of people to buy. Bill's housing journey illustrates this trend. He and his wife moved into a two-bedroom, flat-roofed house in Tanshall in Glenrothes when they married in 1974. When their second son was born, they applied for a larger house and moved to a brand new home at Pitcoudie. As the children grew, they moved again in 1986, but this time they decided on South Parks as it 'was always seen as the place to be in Glenrothes for a long, long time, and we bought a house'.⁵³ Similarly, Audrey moved to Glenrothes from Glasgow with her first husband in 1966 when she was only eighteen years old. She married for a second time in 1988, and after renting a flat in Leslie for five years the couple bought a house in South Parks in 1991 as 'I always wanted a house in South Parks'; 'everybody wanted to have a house in South Parks'.⁵⁴ Although a fairly ordinary neighbourhood of semi-detached houses, perhaps it was the ordinariness that made the area desirable. There was no experimental architecture here; rather it contained the kind of houses that would later become ubiquitous when built by private developers in estates on the periphery of most towns and cities.

The flipside of the growth in owner-occupation coupled with a 'virtual embargo' on the construction of 'general needs' rented housing developments during the 1980s was a shortage of homes to rent.⁵⁵ The development corporations in the early new towns became concerned about providing housing for the second generation from the late 1960s onwards. Indeed, East Kilbride increasingly debated the merits of further overspill agreements with Glasgow in favour of providing housing for young families already resident in the town, though in the 1970s the Greenhills neighbourhood was designed to provide housing capacity for both groups. The fear was that young people who had grown up in the new towns would have to leave to find suitable accommodation when starting families of their own.[56] In the end, the building of general needs housing was resumed in the mid-1980s, albeit in much reduced numbers.[57] Despite the new-build programme, young families struggled to find housing in East Kilbride and by 1989 there were 4,300 names on the housing waiting list.[58] The problem was not confined to East Kilbride. By the early 1990s Angie, whose parents moved to Cumbernauld in 1975, found it 'really hard to get a flat' and her name 'had been on the housing list for years' as the waiting list was 'absolutely huge'.[59]

The growing shortage of corporation-rented accommodation was compounded in the 1980s by a serious increase in rent arrears and of bad debts written off by the development corporations thereby restricting their ability to build. In Glenrothes, unemployment resulted in 'increased social difficulties' and it was argued that 'more has to be done' in 'trying to help tenants avoid building up large rent arrears and then, if arrears do build up, trying to recover them'. By 1981, rent arrears had doubled in a year; one-fifth of all tenants were in arrears with over 500 families seriously behind in their rent and rate payments owing sums varying from £100 to £500.[60] Even those who had decided to buy their own homes could find themselves struggling with the burden of mortgage payments as interest rates rose. In 1985, GDC recorded that 16 per cent of all applicants housed during the year were formerly owner-occupiers; a year later in Cumbernauld 'mortgage repayment difficulties' were becoming more prominent in the figures for homelessness nominations.[61]

At the same time as the new towns were struggling to house their growing populations in a diminishing supply of homes, the earlier housing stock was beginning to require serious refurbishment, especially in areas where houses were of unconventional construction. The use of prefabricated systems for some buildings proved to be especially problematic in terms of water ingress and damp. For the most part, such housing was not situated in the more desirable areas of the towns. Indeed, the fact that these homes had often already required substantial ongoing maintenance prior to refurbishment had contributed to the negative reputations of some areas. These neighbourhoods were also those where 'social and welfare problems' were more readily apparent, as a result of lower incomes and unemployment. In Cumbernauld, the flat-roofed housing in Carbrain suffered from ineffective heating and was among the first to be comprehensively refurbished in 1979.[62] As Susan suggested, 'really by the early seventies, Carbrain had begun to go down the slide and people didn't want to live there'.[63] The same was true of specific areas in the other new towns, such as Craigshill in Livingston, discussed in Chapter 4. Some areas were modified or even demolished, such as the area known as Deans South in Livingston which was controversially declared uninhabitable in 2004.

Expansion through private development

Builders began constructing housing for sale in East Kilbride from the late 1950s, and other new towns followed suit, partly in recognition of the mid-1960s target for 25 per cent owner-occupation, but the scale of private-sector provision in all the new towns dramatically expanded during the 1980s. Built by national house-building companies, with some exceptions these new housing estates were rarely in keeping with or sympathetic to earlier public-sector designs, landscaping or layouts (Figure 1.9). Yet such housing was instrumental to the expansion of the towns in the lead up to the wind-up of their development corporations in the mid-1990s. It was popular with younger generations of residents wishing to set up home. Living in these areas became and remains aspirational; these were the new desirable places for the second and subsequent generations. Elizabeth Henderson purchased a newly built 'Barratt Solo' flat in 1982 designed for single living and unusual in that it was 'pre-furnished', 'so all your carpets and your curtains and your white goods and the actual furniture was already there. You had a sort of a bed that became a settee and you'd get your bedding in the box underneath … it was very small and you couldn't really have anyone to stay – well, I suppose you could sleep on the floor if you had a party or something'.[64] Vicky, whose parents moved to Cumbernauld in 1976, has friends who live in 'these newer estates', built privately from the 1980s onwards and including Eastfield, Balloch and Westerwood. It was her view that '[d]efinitely the town has been instrumental in that pathway' in terms of younger generations having similar residential trajectories of their parents. She identified the 'Right to Buy' as crucial in aiding the social mobility of her generation.[65] While this is true in other urban and rural areas in Scotland, arguably this pathway and its intergenerational benefits were available earlier and on a larger scale in the new towns

The 'Right to Buy' not only increased the demand for owner-occupation but in some ways also drove the dramatic expansion of the new towns. In Cumbernauld, Vicky notes that some people bought their development corporation house and then sold it on at a profit, enabling them to move to newer privately developed areas of the town. The development corporations, keen to complete the towns in terms of population, encouraged large-scale developments, such as Stewartfield in East Kilbride and Westerwood in Cumbernauld, before other similarly sized towns in Scotland. Yet, whilst owner-occupation has certainly been embraced by the pioneers and their children, residents with historic connections to the pioneers are at best ambivalent and more often are highly critical of the private housing boom. Andy, whose family moved to Cumbernauld in 1966, still lives in the town and is a homeowner. He argued that the 'over-development of the town' in terms of private housing estates, especially to the north of the town, 'has been its downfall', exacerbating distinctions between the haves and the have-nots.[66] For him, 'the town was never intended to be as big as this' and the newer housing estates are 'designed for commuters' with 'no facilities, just houses'. As Moira stated, referring to the new neighbourhoods sited the other side of the motorway, 'you felt that that wasn't Cumbernauld over there, it was so different' and 'you just felt it was nothing to do with us really'.[67]

Meanwhile the distinction between some of the older areas of the towns and the original and newer prosperous areas has become increasingly obvious in terms of the maintenance of the housing stock. Vicky's experience of living in Carbrain after buying a house in 2003 was that 'the houses could feel quite dilapidated because there were more bought houses with fewer people with the means to maintain it'.[68] Her neighbours were 'people like us on relatively low incomes with big families, so not a lot of spare cash'. Those who took advantage of the 'Right to Buy' were often unprepared for the cost of maintaining a home after previously depending on the development corporation for repairs. From a heritage perspective, the privatization of corporation housing stock has, through external modification, led to a diminution of the integrity and quality of the original architecture and design of corporation housing and landscaping in some areas. As Susan explained, 'the communal areas in Cumbernauld were set up in a way that assumed it would be social housing for ever and a day' and 'development corporations were taking responsibility for maintaining those areas' including 'car ports, communal car ports, communal parking, green areas and so on'.[69] Following the winding up of the development corporations in the mid-1990s and the growth of the buy-to-let sector, the issue of responsibility for maintenance became more acute with collective action by residents to improve the external appearance constrained by the unwillingness of some absentee landlords to invest. Those houses which remain in what is now known as the 'social' rented sector, i.e. under local-authority or housing association management, are comparatively well-maintained.

Conclusion

The way in which the quality and availability of housing informed both the material experience and retrospective memory of the new towns is significant in the light of recent changes in tenure. Our interviewees look back on a period when a new town house, whether rented or owned, was a sign of aspiration, respectability, the willingness to work hard to improve one's family's life chances and a conduit to a different kind of lifestyle – more private, more family focused. We will return to this theme in Chapter 7. Some still appreciate the distinctive built environment of the new towns. For Susan, living in Cumbernauld has meant that she has lived 'from the age of five in houses that are absolutely drenched in light. That I feel quite oppressed going into semi-detached Victorian houses frankly. The kind of housing that middle-class people are supposed to aspire to.'[70] The modern architecture and features that first drew people to the new towns remain attractive for some residents today. For others though, while the house might still meet their needs, changes in tenure have had a marked effect on people's sense of well-being. Bill's father remained in the house in Glenrothes where he brought up his young children. Bill describes the area where his father lived as having become 'totally different', describing it as lacking friendliness in part owing to the impact of 'a lot of buy-to-lets', which has 'changed the feel of the area'.[71] 'It doesn't feel as safe as it did but it doesn't feel unsafe, if that makes any sense' commented Bill: 'but there's something about it, and I think it's because nobody knows anybody, you know'. This perceived loss of neighbourliness or the closeness of community is not unique to the new towns but is perhaps more obvious to people who vividly remember moving to and establishing new communities with their parents.

The housing available in the new towns symbolized social mobility and security, at least until the 1980s. Moving to a better home, one with its own front door and garden, was the material representation of bettering oneself. The opportunity to purchase a home was, for many, the natural extension of that aspirational mentality. Yet, for some, the social mobility afforded by home ownership was counterbalanced by concern over the impact of 'Right to Buy' over the long term. Bridget suggested that 'it probably wasn't the best thing that the houses got sold off'. Meanwhile Beryl even expressed guilt in the context of the current shortage of affordable rental accommodation:

> Well, erm ... well, to buy a house meant that there was, in a sense, there was a house less for people who were coming out who needed a house, who couldn't afford to buy a house. That's what I'm meaning.[...] but at the time, it seemed the right thing for us to do. But we were thinking about ourselves, our family ... I feel now, I feel aggrieved, people's inability to have somewhere decent to live.[72]

By providing decent homes, the new towns enabled individuals and families to improve their quality of life whilst, at the same time contributing to a more general project of state improvement by enabling people to feel they were beneficiaries of investment in their lives and their children's lives.[73] While some interpreted the new town project – and in particular residents' desire to improve themselves in material ways, including buying one's own home – as an indicator of consumerist individualism and a decline of community, Lawrence has suggested that these places allowed people to 'reconcile personal ambition with collective progress'.[74] These two themes were to play out within families with consequences that could not have been predicted by the planners, as the next chapter explores.

Notes

1. See e.g. Lynn Abrams, Barry Hazley, Ade Kearns and Valerie Wright, *Glasgow: High-Rise Homes, Estates and Communities* (London: Routledge, 2019); Tom Begg, *50 Special Years: A Study in Scottish Housing* (London: Henry Melland, 1987); John Boughton, *Municipal Dreams: The Rise and Fall of Council Housing* (London: Verso, 2018); Sean Damer, *Scheming: A Social History of Glasgow Council Housing* (Edinburgh: Edinburgh University Press, 2019); Miles Glendinning and Stefan Muthesius, *Tower Block: Modern Public Housing in England, Scotland, Wales, and Northern Ireland* (New Haven and London: Yale University Press, 1994); Lynsey Hanley, *Estates: An Intimate History* (London: Granta, 2012); Pearl Jephcott with Hilary Robinson, *Homes in High Flats: Some of the Human Problems Involved in Multi-Storey Housing* (Edinburgh: Oliver and Boyd, 1971); Alison Ravetz, *Council Housing and Culture: The History of a Social Experiment* (London: Routledge, 2003).

2. Examples include: Ade Kearns, Valerie Wright, Lynn Abrams and Barry Hazley, 'Slum Clearance and Relocation: A Reassessment of Social Outcomes Combining Short-Term and Long-Term Perspectives', *Housing Studies* 34, no. 2 (2019): 201–25; Michael Keating, *The City That Refused to Die: Glasgow: The Politics of Urban Regeneration* (Aberdeen: Aberdeen University Press, 1988); Chik Collins and Ian Levitt, 'The Modernisation of Scotland and Its Impact on Glasgow, 1955–1979: Unwanted Side Effects and Vulnerabilities', *Scottish Affairs* 25, no. 3 (2016): 294–316; Ian Levitt, 'New Towns, New Scotland, New Ideology, 1937–57', *Scottish Historical Review* 76, no. 2 (1997): 222–38.

3. The main exception being Clapson's work on Milton Keynes: Mark Clapson, *Invincible Green Suburbs, Brave New Towns: Social Change and Urban Dispersal in Post-War England* (Manchester: Manchester University Press, 1998) and Mark Clapson, *A Social History of Milton Keynes: Middle England/Edge City* (Portland: Frank Cass, 2004). More generally in an English context, see Ben Jones, 'Slum Clearance, Privatization and Residualization: The Practices and Politics of Council Housing in Mid-Twentieth-Century England', *Twentieth Century British History* 21, no. 4 (2010): 510–39; Jon Lawrence, *Me, Me, Me: The Search for Community in Post-War England* (Cambridge: Cambridge University Press, 2019); Lynn Abrams, Barry Hazley, Valerie Wright and Ade Kearns, 'Aspiration, Agency and the Production of New Selves in a Scottish New Town, c.1947–c.2016', *Twentieth Century British History* 29, no. 4 (2018): 576–604.

4. The exception is Judith Attfield, 'Inside Pram Town: A Case-Study of Harlow House Interiors', in *A View from the Interior: Feminism, Women and Design*, ed. Judith Attfield and Pat Kirkham (London: Women's Press, 1995). For an earlier period, see Deborah Sugg Ryan, *Ideal Homes, 1918–39: Domestic Design and Suburban Modernism* (Manchester: Manchester University Press, 2018).

5   Raphael Samuel conducted a study of Stevenage which is discussed in Lawrence, *Me, Me, Me*. See also Peter Wilmott, 'East Kilbride and Stevenage. Some Social Characteristics of a Scottish and an English New Town', *Town Planning Review* 34, no. 4 (1964): 307–16; Peter Wilmott, 'Housing in Cumbernauld: Some Residents' Opinions', *Town Planning Institute Journal* 50 (1964): 195–200.

6   Ben Jones, *The Working Class in Mid-Twentieth-Century England: Community, Identity and Social Memory* (Manchester: Manchester University Press, 2012), 156–7, 181.

7   John H. Goldthorpe, David Lockwood, Frank Bechhofer and Jennifer Platt, *The Affluent Worker in the Class Structure* (orig. 1969; reissued Cambridge: Cambridge University Press, 2010).

8   Michael Young and Peter Wilmott, *Family and Kinship in East London* (Harmondsworth: Penguin, 1957).

9   See Guy Ortolano *Thatcher's Progress: From Social Democracy to Market Liberalism through an English Town* (Cambridge: Cambridge University Press, 2019), 213–16.

10 Ibid., 227–9.

11 David Clapham, 'Housing Pathways: A Post-Modern Analytical Framework', *Housing, Theory and Society* 19 (2002): 57–68.

12 James M. Livingstone and Andrew J.M. Sykes, *East Kilbride 70: An Economic and Social History* (Glasgow: University of Strathclyde, 1971).

13 Rachel M. Pierce, 'Marriage in the Fifties', *The Sociological Review* 11, no. 2 (March 1963): 233.

14 Claire Langhamer, *The English in Love: The Intimate Story of an Emotional Revolution* (Oxford: Oxford University Press, 2013), 180.

15 Ibid., 183. See also Claire Langhamer, 'The Meanings of Home in Postwar Britain', *Journal of Contemporary History* 40, no. 2 (2005): 341–62.

16 Interview with Susan, Cumbernauld, 1 June 2022.

17 On tenement living see Miles Horsey, *Tenements and Towers: Glasgow Working-class Housing 1890–1990* (Edinburgh: RCAHMS, 1990); Ernest Reoch, *Farewell to the Single End* (Glasgow: Glasgow District Council, 1976).

18 Abrams et al., *Glasgow*.

19 This argument draws on Alistair Fair, 'Privacy, the Housing Research Unit at the University of Edinburgh, and the Courtyard House, 1959–70', *Architectural History* 65 (2022): 327–58.

20 Ibid., 329.

21 Interview with Urlan Wannop, *New Towns Record* (Planning Exchange CD-ROM set, 1996).

22 Interview with Linda, Cumbernauld, 15 June 2022.

23 Cumbernauld Development Corporation [CDC], Annual Report 1968.

24 Ferdynand Zweig, *The Cumbernauld Study* (London: Urban Research Bureau, 1970), 46.

25 Ibid., 31 and 46. See also Samuel's work on Stevenage which similarly explored whether people felt pressured to keep up with the Jones's. Discussed in Lawrence, *Me, Me Me!*, 98–9.

26 Lawrence, *Me, Me, Me*, 98–9.

27 Interview with Susan, Cumbernauld, 1 June 2022. See also Carolyn Steedman, *Landscape for a Good Woman* (London: Virago, 1986).

28 Interview with Urlan Wannop, *New Towns Record*.

29 Glenrothes Development Corporation [GDC], Annual Report 1966.

30 Interview with Annie (and Alison), Glenrothes, 21 October 2021.

31 Interview with Cathy, East Kilbride, 2011.

32 Interview with Shirley, East Kilbride, 2011.
33 Interview with Beryl (and Jenni), Auchtermuchty, 30 June 2022.
34 Interview with Jenni (and Beryl), Auchtermuchty, 30 June 2022.
35 Fair, 'Privacy', 343–5.
36 Rent was means tested with CDC stating that 'tenants are left free to decide whether to disclose their earnings or otherwise but disclosure is necessary in order to obtain the benefit of a graduated rent'. CDC, Annual Report 1963; East Kilbride Development Corporation [EKDC], Annual Report 1965; GDC, Annual Report 1967.
37 Jack House, 'Cumbernauld', *Evening Times*, 9 November 1966.
38 GDC, Annual Report 1960.
39 GDC, Annual Report 1969.
40 EKDC, Annual Report 1971.
41 EKDC, Residents' Handbook, *c.* 1970 [copy at EK Central Library].
42 Zweig, *Cumbernauld*, 26.
43 Ibid., 39–40. Zweig developed his own classifications of the neighbourhoods according to what residents told him as well as his observations on the housing density and size of cars parked outside.
44 Among the individuals interviewed for this book, self-building was more common in Cumbernauld in the 1960s. See Valerie Wright and Alistair Fair, 'The Opportunity and Desire to Buy: Owner-Occupation in Scotland's New Towns, c. 1950–1980', *Contemporary British History* 38, no. 2 (2024): 219–44.
45 Interview with Susan, Cumbernauld, 1 June 2022.
46 See J.B. Cullingworth and V.A. Karn, *The Ownership and Management of Housing in the New Towns: Report Submitted to the Minister of Housing and Local Government* (London: HMSO, 1968).
47 See Wright and Fair, 'Opportunity and Desire'. 'Owners' rates' were abolished after 1956 (Begg, *50 Special Years*, 180).
48 Wright and Fair, 'Opportunity and Desire'.
49 Livingstone and Sykes, *East Kilbride 70*, 17–18.
50 Interview with Jim M, conducted online, 28 October 2021.
51 Interview with Iain, Kirkcaldy, November 2021.
52 Wright and Fair, 'Opportunity and Desire', table 1.
53 Interview with Bill, Glenrothes, December 2021.
54 Interview with Audrey, Glasgow, November 2021.
55 Robina Goodlad and Suzie Scott, 'Polo Mint Planning: A Review of Strategies for Housing in the Scottish New Towns', Discussion Paper 33, Centre for Housing Research, University of Glasgow, 1989, 19 and 48. See also Ortolano, *Thatcher's Progress*, 245.
56 EKDC, Annual Reports, 1966 and 1988. The needs of the second generation in terms of housing are first mentioned in 1966 with shortages and growing waiting lists noted for the first time in 1988.
57 The government allocated resources for a three-year new-building programme of 1,400 houses across the five new towns. Goodlad and Scott, 'Polo Mint Planning', 48.
58 Ibid., 49.
59 Interview with Angie, Cumbernauld, 17 June 2022.

60 GDC, Annual Report 1981. A year later, 25 per cent of tenants were in arrears with 500 each owing over £200. See also GDC, Annual Report 1982.
61 GDC, Annual Report 1985; CDC, Annual Report 1986.
62 North Lanarkshire Record Centre, CDC Archive, UT-015-4, 'Rehabilitation in Carbrain: The Planning Study', September 1979.
63 Interview with Susan, Cumbernauld, 1 June 2022.
64 Elizabeth Henderson in *Life Is for Livingston: Our Story* (West Lothian Council, n.d.), 19.
65 Interview with Vicky, Glasgow, 5 August 2022.
66 Interview with Andy, Cumbernauld, 31 May 2022.
67 Interview with Moira, Doune, 12 August 2022.
68 Interview with Vicky, Glasgow, 5 August 2022.
69 Interview with Susan, Cumbernauld, 1 June 2022.
70 Ibid.
71 Interview with Bill, Glenrothes, 26 November 2021.
72 Interview with Beryl (and Jenni) Auchtermuchty, 30 June 2022.
73 Lawrence, *Me, Me, Me*, 100–101.
74 Ibid., 102.

7

Families

New towns offered the opportunity to live family life differently. The post-war period in Britain has been characterized by the retreat to the home. Influenced by Michael Young and Peter Willmott's study of the impact of relocation from inner-city London to an out-of-town estate in 1957, a work that suggested the disappearance of extended family networks and which included a chapter on 'house-centred couples', the post-war narrative of aspiration for a home-focused lifestyle has endured.[1] Family life for all social classes, it has been argued, became more private, more intimate and more focused on the domestic, contrasting in its relations with kin and community with the apparent porosity of earlier periods.[2] From the 1960s, families became smaller, while intergenerational and proximal living became less common as the post-war housebuilding programme rehoused many of those living in overcrowded and unsanitary homes. Home improvement, television-viewing and home entertaining took the place of the gender-segregated leisure that was commonplace in more established and especially working-class communities.[3] While elements of this picture have recently been challenged, it is incontrovertible that a new model of family life became established on the new housing estates and in the new towns of post-war Britain. This change was perhaps especially pronounced in central Scotland, given the contrast between new town housing and the predominant pre-1919 urban housing form: the tenement flat, with its shared stairways, drying greens, back courts and, often, toilets, all requiring negotiation between neighbours and, in many cases, rotas relating to use and cleaning duties.[4]

The desire for increased familial privacy was anticipated and guided by new town planners, architects and policymakers who cleaved to the view that town planning shaped behaviour. Although ideals of 'community' were central to the conception and planning of the new towns, these places were also the fulcrum of the new privatized family model, albeit a model which was based on ideas about divided gender roles and race that were beginning to be outmoded.[5] Thus, as we saw in Chapter 6, they offered desirable, relatively spacious single-family homes, no shared facilities and a degree of privacy unusual for residents who had been used to overcrowded accommodation in Glasgow or indeed substandard housing in other urban centres or in some cases rural communities. Guiding the design of the new towns and the houses within them in Scotland, as was the case in England, was the idea that the home would be the centre of (nuclear) family life, providing a welcoming, warm and spacious environment for the family and its constituent members to thrive. Advertisements and architects' plans invariably portrayed a family inhabiting the space and family members fulfilling stereotypically gendered roles.[6] Certainly many

FIGURE 7.1 At home in 1970s Livingston (© West Lothian Archives and Records Centre).

of those who moved to the new towns, at least the first and second generations, aspired to this lifestyle, based on a tripartite model of work, consumption and family.[7] The desire for a home of one's own cannot be underestimated in people choosing to move to a new town, as we saw in Chapter 6, but just as important was the aspiration for a way of life that was more family-focused, reflective of post-war affluence, and which delivered benefits for children (Figure 7.1).

In what follows we argue that although many amongst the pioneer generations did achieve the family-focused lifestyle they desired, over the longer term a more complex picture emerges. New town living produced unintended and unanticipated outcomes for family life which are rarely articulated, so strong is the 'aspiration and success' narrative in both contemporary and retrospective accounts. New homes and new towns did not necessarily make new families, and sometimes when they did it was not in the forms anticipated by those who planned these towns or moved to them. Several factors created an environment which exerted strains on families: the pressure of high rents and the expenses incurred in home-making; the increased propensity of women to undertake paid work to afford the new lifestyle or to achieve some independence; the absence of ready-made support networks; the home as a pressure cooker; and the opportunities for new kinds of relationships through work and leisure. The freedom of living away from established communities also provided a significant chance for new forms of intimacy. By the 1970s, the development corporations were expressing concerns about marriage breakdown, poverty, lone motherhood and domestic abuse. These were social problems exacerbated by growing male unemployment, inflation and changing social attitudes towards personal relationships. The new towns were not unusual in this regard, mirroring broader social trends. Yet it remains striking that places designed to enable the nuclear private family to thrive often contained the very factors that undermined it.

Achieving the 'new town dream'

Bill recalled that his Glaswegian parents decided to move to Glenrothes in 1958 because of 'the offer of a house, work and the new town dream, I suppose'.[8] The 'new town dream' is the dominant narrative used by former and continuing residents to account for their active choice to achieve a better quality of life for their families. The meanings attached to this idea varied enormously.

Material improvements, discussed in Chapter 6, were but part of it.[9] Far more significant in retrospective memory stories was the sense that relocating to a new town represented aspiration, the opportunity to get on, and for children to get on, freed from the constraints and expectations that limited ambition and opportunity in their native communities. Alongside a new home, the new town encompassed other more intangible elements of the post-war settlement. Expanding employment and education opportunities, and government investment in the welfare state at a national and local level in a context of unparalleled economic growth in the 1950s and 1960s, evinced narratives of social mobility, benefitting not just the pioneers but, crucially, their children too.[10] New towns were the spatial and material embodiment of this ambition. And those children recognize the sacrifices made by their parents: their determination to make a new life for themselves and their family. Linda described her mother, who moved to Cumbernauld in 1964 from Glasgow's east end, as an independent person who 'just wanted to get on with her life and have her own family, and that was it. She really didn't worry too much about leaving her sisters or friends or anything. She really, really was determined.' Furthermore, Linda was grateful to her parents 'for giving us the life that we got ... it was pioneering ... I do think it was like moving abroad, it was like ... we've got this new life, new homes, new way of doing things.'[11]

Linda's story is replicated many times by our respondents from the pioneer generations. This is not surprising. It was a message conveyed by the development corporations, keen to portray their towns as places that worked for families across generations. Take Cumbernauld Development Corporation's (CDC) case study of the Fergus family, published in its 1990 Annual Report as an exemplar of the town's success:

> In 1956 Mr Alec Walker and his family uprooted themselves from the busy city of Glasgow to the newly established Cumbernauld new town when the factory he worked for was relocated. Today, over 30 years on, four generations of the family are enjoying life in the new town. In March this year, his great grand-daughter, Rebecca Fergus was born to Jean and William Fergus of Barbeth Road, Condorrat. Great-great grandmother, Helen Shanks (93), great-grandmother Jean Walker and grandmother, Helen McAuley are all delighted with the new member of the family. Jean is determined that her daughter will grow up in the town. She comments: 'As far as I am concerned, Cumbernauld is a great place to bring kids up.' Like his wife, William Fergus was born in Cumbernauld and is self-employed as a tree surgeon. His father lived in the old village before the new town was established. Before she had her baby, Jean studied at Cumbernauld College evening classes while working during the day in the town centre. She plans to continue her studies when Rebecca is a little older. Says Jean, 'I can't see us moving from Cumbernauld, we have everything we need here !'[12]

For many of our interviewees, the gamble on a new life in the new town paid off. They found what they were looking for: the chance to raise a family in a decent house with a garden, the opportunity to create a family life characterized by shared pursuits in contrast with the gender-segregated social world of the city. People appreciated the new towns as family-focused with their pedestrian-friendly and safe environment, provision of leisure facilities and plentiful work in the early years (Figure 7.2). Memories tend to recall how the dream was achieved in this context. It is easy to tell a story about the benefits of moving to a new town when personal experience and dominant or popular representations align.[13] But relocation did not turn out to fulfil the dream for

FIGURE 7.2 Children's play area in Cumbernauld, *c.* 1970 (© Architectural Press Archive / RIBA Collections).

all. Marriage breakdown, economic hardship and loneliness were evident in the stories told to us, particularly by women. These stories reveal much about the interplay between individual aspiration and the effect on individuals and families of the social and economic changes that new town living brought about. Without downplaying the success stories, which were many, we suggest that individual narratives are often most illuminating when complicating or challenging the dominant 'new town dream' trope, as they highlight some of the distinctive and less known features of new town life and help to situate the new towns within the broader trajectory of modern Britain. When we delve more deeply into people's stories, we discover that the agency of individuals exerted pressures on families. The ambition for social mobility, a better life, getting on, sometimes came at an economic and personal cost. The new lives forged in the new towns were not always the lives that had been envisaged by those who moved there.

Taking a wider view, moreover, it is clear that social trends that were to characterize the 1970s and 1980s in Britain were writ large in the new towns. Opportunities in education and employment for women and men created as many strains as contentment. By the mid-1970s the honeymoon of the pioneers was over and life in the new towns replicated and, in some cases, anticipated economic and social trends evident elsewhere as the nuclear family of the 1950s and 1960s transmogrified into a range of possible household formations incorporating lone parents, singletons, cohabiting couples and blended families. In the rest of this chapter, we focus on the reality of trying to make the dream work and the ways it could go wrong for families. Assessments of the new towns hitherto have tended to take a short-term perspective. Accessing retrospective life story narratives from three generations of residents paints a more complex picture that acknowledges the tenacity and drive of the pioneers but also recognizes that over the longer term the making of new lives sometimes had unanticipated consequences, especially for women. And new town families soon came to resemble families everywhere else.

Faltering dreams

Audrey moved from Glasgow to Glenrothes with her husband in 1966. As archetypal pioneers they fitted the model of family envisaged by architects, planners and administrators. Audrey's husband's job at a hydraulics factory guaranteed them a house but they had to get married before they were eligible. Audrey immediately set about looking for work to be able to meet the high rent but she only lasted three months in Woolworths before having her baby. In moving, Audrey was separated from her kinship network. 'I don't think there was that then, the support, you know, you became friends with people but I don't think it was supporting me. I don't know if I needed support.'[14] Though her mother visited, 'when she went home I was crying, but that was me, you know, when somebody goes away you have a wee tear'. Audrey had to make do with writing long letters in the absence of a telephone.

While Audrey is able to reflect on this time in her life by recounting this episode with humour and stoicism, her memory of being lonely challenges the popular narrative of community-making in the new towns which either celebrates the ease with which new residents, especially young mothers, got along with one another despite their differences or recalls the propensity of those from Glasgow to stick together. For example, Janice Scott Long, writing for *The Guardian* in 1965, described her experience of settling into life in Cumbernauld, emphasizing that social life in the town was thriving regardless of an absence of amenities such as cinemas, dancehalls and tea shops. According to the journalist, 'the young women, housebound by young families are intellectually starved' and as a result lecture courses in almost any subject were over-subscribed, women's organizations had 'enormous memberships' while further education classes received an 'overwhelming response'.[15] In East Kilbride, it was similarly reported that afternoon lectures run by the Workers' Education Association were popular amongst young mothers, though no doubt in part because of the free crèche provided.[16]

Yet not everyone wanted to attend formal classes as a form of socializing or relaxation. Regardless of Scott Long's suggestion that 'a new class system is being born' and that 'friendship is offered and accepted on the basis of equality', alternative accounts offer a more complicated picture. In the absence of community facilities and ready-made networks, loneliness was very real, perhaps especially in Glenrothes which was more isolated from major centres of population than the other new towns and harder to reach by public transport. Alexander moved to the new town with his young family in the 1950s and was conscious of the 'quite different problems' in Glenrothes:

> In East Kilbride you got a sick child and you want help from your mother or that, all you did was you got on a bus and went into Glasgow or your mother came out and helped you. East Kilbride was commutable distance, Glenrothes not a commutable distance from anywhere. So we had a problem for a while of the wife saying to the husband, 'I'm not staying here, I'm going back to my mammie' [laugh], so yeah aye.'[17]

'No wonder they've got the New Town blues', opined Cumbernauld resident Mrs Moira Winter in an interview for the *Daily Record* in 1957, referring to the post-war variant of so-called 'suburban neurosis', an alleged manifestation of poor mental health amongst female residents of new housing estates.[18] 'What we don't have is a place for women to meet and have a cup of coffee and a blether. A lot of women can't stomach church clubs and since we are all skint we can't go to the pubs. It's pathetic the number of women you see out pushing their prams, killing time slowly and painfully.'[19] Mrs Winter put her finger on the problem. This generation of women was not suffering from neurosis. Rather they no longer looked to traditional organizations like Young Wives or the Townswomen's Guild to provide social contact, and with nowhere to park small children they were trapped.[20]

One response was the provision of housing suitable for older couples, in order to encourage some of the 'Glasgow grannies' to move to help their daughters; CDC even celebrated the arrival of the first 'Glasgow granny' in 1960.[21] Parents and sons and daughters of residents were positioned quite high up on the list of groups waiting for homes.[22] By 1979 in Glenrothes, for example, retired parents and offspring of residents accounted for around 30 per cent of all housing allocations.[23] There were also formal and informal attempts to encourage the formation of new social networks. In East Kilbride, new female residents were welcomed into the area by the 'Welcome Waggoners', a group of 'housewife' volunteers inspired by the welcome offered to the pioneers of the 'wild west' in the United States. Newcomers were greeted with a basket of gifts and a 'pamphlet on what goes on in the town'.[24] In addition, as Chapter 8 demonstrates, women began to help themselves, establishing preschool playgroups and other 'do-it-yourself' initiatives in line with a UK-wide self-help movement to plug a gap in provision of child care and opportunities for social contact that were not allied to religious or traditional women's groups.[25]

Women's retrospective accounts stressed their own or their mothers' resilience, drawing on modern concepts to articulate a positive response to adversity whilst at the same time acknowledging some of the more uncomfortable features of new town life. In Cumbernauld, Linda emphasized her parents' strength – 'they always had hope, which is something you cannot buy [...] it's not what happens to you, it's how you deal with it'.[26] Her mother attended evening cookery classes at Cumbernauld High School and was involved in volunteering in the town. However, she was aware that some others responded differently, recalling that 'a lot of my mum's friends, we didn't know at the time, but now when I look back, they did have alcohol problems, they drank'. Linda ascribed this to depression, isolation and 'people trying to fill a void' as 'I think a lot of women didn't just want to be at home'. We have glimpses here of a different reality in which the pioneers struggled to realize the dream.

Residents often found that rents and the cost of living were higher than they had been in Glasgow and in other urban centres, the consequences of the Scottish Office's desire to drive up public-sector rents as well as, in the early years, the lack of much choice when it came to the provision of shops. 'We came out here from a room-and-kitchen in Townhead because we thought there was a bright future and we wanted to give our kids a chance,' explained Cumbernauld resident Moira Winter in 1966. 'We didn't want them to be brought up in a tenement sharing a lavatory with every other family on the stairhead.'[27] Yet the dream was already 'becoming a nightmare, our rents have risen 100 per cent in two years. They will have risen another 50 per cent by 1970 [...] A recent survey showed we pay 4 per cent more on £2 worth of groceries here than we would in Glasgow.'[28] Meanwhile in Glenrothes, Audrey remembered thinking 'oh my god that's dear' when she found out the rent on her new flat in Glenrothes was £4-16-8, which was high compared with Lanarkshire, and 'that was just rent, you'd still rates to pay'.[29] Residents' surveys and those undertaken by social scientists in the early years of the new towns came to similar conclusions. In 1967, the cost of living was the second most significant complaint after the lack of entertainment in Cumbernauld (Figure 7.3).[30]

Setting up home was a financial strain for some couples. Audrey was excited about her new flat but had 'next to nothing'. She and her husband bought a convertible 'three-piece suite' that they used for a month before they bought a bed. But Audrey rejected being described as poor because 'everybody was like that'. After moving into a bigger house just after her husband lost his job, she bought dining furniture using her husband's redundancy package. She was able to make

FIGURE 7.3 Cumbernauld women protesting against an increase in rents (© The Scotsman Publications Ltd).

the house 'comfortable', with white furniture and an orange carpet, as she could decorate, tile, fit carpets, dig gardens and build furniture. She taught herself these skills as well as building a 'stereo thing to put the stereo on, a television shelf' at night school.[31] Such ingenuity was required when family finances were limited and retrospective memories tend to emphasize the positive, stressing individual and collective self-help. Linda remembered that in Cumbernauld neighbours would borrow 'tea, sugar, milk' from each other as well as money.[32] She also recalled a new neighbour borrowing 'a rug and a lamp because she had relatives coming, and they were ashamed of the linoleum', just one example of the pressure felt by some occupants of new housing to furnish their new homes in a fashion that aligned with their new status as new town residents. However, purchasing on credit was the most common strategy to achieve the 'look' as well as essentials. Donna who grew up in Irvine recalled her mother using the Provident, a loan agency, to purchase school uniforms: 'And I remember the first day at school going in with all my old stuff on and being mortified thinking folk are going to realize that ... and then we went on the Saturday and got new stuff to wear.'[33]

First-generation residents were relatively open at the time and in retrospect about the financial stretch incurred by moving, but later generations kept their financial difficulties closer to their chest, perhaps explained by cultural changes encompassing family privacy as well as the prevailing political climate which emphasized individual success.[34] By the 1980s, people were less transparent about financial problems and stories about privations and cultures of reciprocity are less prominent in personal accounts of that time. Angie, whose parents had moved to Cumbernauld in 1975 from the Red Road high flats in Glasgow, instinctively knew not to tell any of her friends that she had pocket money as 'I think it is because I knew they didn't'. 'I think I did realize that other people didn't have as much but it wasn't really spoken about.'[35]

The new towns were intended to encourage growth in the Scottish economy, and were, especially following the Toothill Report of 1961, understood as 'growth points' in the central belt of Scotland (as discussed in the Introduction). However, they were not completely insulated from the impacts of global economic change and especially deindustrialization. From the mid-1970s onwards and especially in the 1980s, many families struggled financially as a result of unemployment. In 1974 in East Kilbride, for example, around 900 workers, the vast majority women, were made redundant upon the closure of British Sound Recording, which manufactured parts for record players.[36] In Cumbernauld in 1979, discount vouchers were given to over 2,000 tenants 'receiving rent or rates rebates' to help with electricity bills.[37] In Glenrothes, rent arrears increased steeply from 1981, and though they levelled off in 1984, in 1987 31 per cent of tenants were still in arrears and 55 per cent qualified for housing benefit.[38] Indeed Glenrothes had the highest number of termination of tenancies in 1987 of all the new towns with just over 8 per cent (compared with 3 per cent for East Kilbride and 4 per cent for Cumbernauld).[39] While the majority reflected people moving for work or buying their own homes, the number who gave up their tenancies for domestic reasons or because the rent was too high grew over the period between the 1960s and the early 1980s.[40] By the early 1990s when mortgage rates were high, in Glenrothes 16 per cent of all new lets were to former owner-occupiers of whom 46 per cent had financial difficulties; marital breakdown accounted for 30 per cent.[41] The new town dream became increasingly hard work in such circumstances.

Gender roles

The new towns deliberately fostered family life through housing provision, town planning, provision of work for men and women, and family-focused leisure facilities. But it was precisely these conditions that facilitated the kinds of new lifestyles, expectations and opportunities which could place existing relationships under pressure and enable new kinds of intimacies. The new towns were not exceptional in this regard and it would be wrong to exaggerate the speed and depth of change. There was, for example, a great deal of continuity in women's everyday experiences of the double burden of combining paid work and unpaid caring plus emotional labour in the home, especially in Glenrothes where the legacy of traditional industry militated against more equal gender roles, at least in the early years. But a convergence of pressures and opportunities (especially for women) against a background of more widespread social change conspired, by the 1970s, to produce a rather different landscape to that envisaged by the original planners. Social problems such as alcoholism, domestic violence and gambling alongside the growth of more liberal social mores sometimes translated into broken marriages, lone parents and homelessness. New towns were not unusual in this regard but may have sown the seeds earlier than more established settlements.

For the majority of families, financial pressures were more corrosive of the new town dream than the liberalization of attitudes to sex and relationships. 'Problem families' became increasingly visible with the 'rediscovery' of poverty by social scientists during the 1960s and then as a product of perceived economic and societal 'decline' in Britain in the 1970s.[42] Like local authorities elsewhere in Scotland, the development corporations increasingly had to provide 'for the care of young folk of working age who lack suitable home backgrounds, and for certain classes of families with problems'.[43] Yet, from the mid-1970s onwards, the development corporations in Glenrothes, Cumbernauld and Livingston began reporting 'social problems'. In 1983 even Livingston Development Corporation, whose annual reports otherwise were relentlessly optimistic, acknowledged the effect of unemployment in the town which required 'a great deal of supportive effort from area management staff in order to maintain family stability'. One manifestation of this effort was the Craigs Farm Community Centre which housed a training workshop as well as a community cafe, printing services, a craft shop and toy library, addressing 'the problems of poverty, family breakdown, alcoholism and support to children's groups … '[44] Poverty did exist here, albeit rarely acknowledged, and its consequences – food insecurity, drinking, violence and the shame these produced – were manifested behind closed doors. Few of our interviewees spoke about such experiences unprompted, but those who did offer memories of gambling and drinking provide a glimpse of the pressures. It can be difficult for individuals to compose settled narratives around such experiences in the context of the new towns, but uncomfortable memories were produced in interviews which intimated an alternative and often concealed reality of families blighted by alcohol, insecurity and in some cases, violence.

The confluence of the social relaxation of norms and practices around sex and relationships from the mid-1960s, the arrival of lots of young couples and the opportunities to meet people in new kinds of spaces such as the Cumbernauld Cottage Theatre, evening classes and social clubs, created an environment in which more liberal attitudes to marriage and monogamy could flourish. Stories about 'car keys on the table' were not apocryphal.[45] Moira recalled 'a lot of unrest in marriages' which she ascribed to the falling away of 'family constraints' which meant that 'suddenly they could do what they liked'. She became aware of wife-swapping and extra-marital affairs through her job and in her social life at the Cottage Theatre. The folk club at the theatre was a crucible for more liberal sexual morals and gossip about those who participated, though Moira found it 'totally, totally beyond my comprehension. I couldn't get a handle on this kind of life at all.'[46]

There is some evidence for Cumbernauld being in the vanguard of change in this regard, perhaps on account of its proximity to Glasgow and its significant middle-class community whose lifestyles were more akin to those who frequented the more bohemian parts of the city.[47] Susan and Michael's egalitarian marriage in Cumbernauld whereby they shared childcare enabling Susan to launch her career is another indication of Cumbernauld's status as a place where change was happening.[48] Yet coexisting with the liberalization of personal relationships were more conventional attitudes to sexual behaviour and public morality as is evident in accounts from residents of Glenrothes, a town defined more by its proximity to traditional mining towns. Alison's maternal grandparents moved to Glenrothes from Edinburgh in the 1950s. They were one of the original families to move into the first development corporation houses in Woodside; they made friends with neighbours, joined the church and all sorts of civic society organizations in the town. Like many of their generation, they were very conscious of respectability and worried about perceptions of their family and they were keen to be well regarded by neighbours and the community at large. As Annie, Alison's aunt, remarked: 'I think the constrictions of my parents, you know, round here about always be seen to be doing the right thing and, you know, keep it all above board.'[49] Alison's mother however had rebelled against the confines of her upbringing – she did go to college – but she left after a term to get married with Alison being born the following year. She would tell Alison, 'education's really, really, important, do not get pregnant, do not get married, it's the worst thing you can ever do'.[50] Three generations of one family encapsulate the shifts in moral attitudes from the 1950s to the 1990s that were not unique to the new towns. Yet people had taken such a risk to move there and had such high expectations of what the new town could offer their children that they placed such great emphasis on not wasting the opportunity they had strived to give them.

Alison grew up in a troubled household; her parents eventually separated but only when her mother 'was financially able'. Before then women were socially and economically constrained from leaving the marital home. Annie described how 'the sort of clinging together thing that my parents had to do, that was where they got their kinda steadfastness from, was staying in your relationship, making sure the kids were sorted, you know, don't let them be too different, everyone had to stay the same'. But these efforts to maintain a semblance of stability had consequences. 'The women get a hard face, d'you know what I mean? And you see these hard-faced women, you know they've been through it'.[51] Social constraints were amplified by most women having no independent means. Most tenancies were in the husband's name though some years before the change in the law under the Matrimonial Homes (Family Protection) (Scotland) Act 1981, Glenrothes agreed that all new tenancies would be in joint names, to the benefit of the corporation and the tenants.[52]

So influential has been the communal narrative of the new town dream that stories like Alison's, and Bill's and Audrey's related below are rarely articulated. Yet Claire Langhamer has shown for the immediate post-war decades how changing expectations of intimate relationships and especially marriage centred on individual fulfilment had resulted in increased separations and demands for divorce law reform.[53] The growing numbers of women participating in further and higher education, their increasing propensity to work outside the home, and a gradual questioning of separate and unequal gender roles underpinned this trend. In the new towns, where higher proportions of married women worked than the national average, those social changes combined with economic pressures and new venues and opportunities for intimacy sometimes resulted in the end of the dream (Figure 7.4).

Bill married young as his future wife was pregnant with their first child. She was sixteen; he was two years older and had been working for two years. Both sets of parents 'weren't convinced' but 'they just let it happen and it worked'. This was mainly because throughout their marriage for 'the best part of twenty years' they had both attained their respective goals professionally. They had worked hard to combine paid work with raising a family, his wife working part-time on a 'swing shift' when the children were young. Bill is proud of both of their achievements, he was becoming established in his career and his wife 'went full time', 'built her career' and 'it was great'. Their combined striving allowed them to move from a rented house to owner-occupation in South Parks, a desirable area of Glenrothes. The couple were by this point a busy dual-income family in their early thirties. While they had 'built up a good life', were financially comfortable and took holidays abroad,

FIGURE 7.4 Crusader Insurance Company, Livingston, *c.* 1979 (© West Lothian Archives and Records Centre).

they would go on to separate six years later. Bill remembered other couples separating around the same time and people leaving the town.[54] Audrey was one of them. Another young bride, Audrey bowed to expectations to marry when she became pregnant at seventeen, but by the time her daughters had grown up Audrey reassessed her life and future, recalling: 'so, I mean, you just think, "what am I doing here?" kinda thing'.[55] She was thirty-eight years old. At this point she met someone else while on a night out with friends, which helped her decide to leave her husband and the family home: 'I don't know how I had the courage to do it really, I just packed everything up and I moved out.' She divorced her first husband and remarried two years later in 1988.

Audrey and Bill were part of a trend in rising divorce rates in Scotland, which increased steadily throughout the second half of the twentieth century rising from a peak of 4,803 in 1968 to an all-time high of 13,365 in 1985.[56] While Audrey reiterated that the upturn in divorces among people she knew was because 'a lot of people got married young', she also described tensions in her marriage over her return to college as her husband was 'a bit jealous because I think I was a wee bit more educated than he was sort of thing and I think that's what it was really'.[57] Audrey was not alone in wanting more from life. She was part of an upsurge in women returning to education, and for some this resulted in a reassessment of their life goals. This trajectory was not unique to Scotland or the UK with women around the Global North seeking independence and fulfilment through education and careers.[58]

In both Bill and Audrey's accounts, there are intimations of the impact of much larger social changes: the rise in women's participation in the labour force, especially part-time and shift work; the growth of women returners to education and their entry into the health and social care professions; and the loosening of the norms around heterosexual relationships.[59] The new towns were distinctive in providing increased and new opportunities for married women to work. Indeed, the economic strategy employed in each new town was dependent on attracting sufficient female labour and much of this was part-time and shift work to enable married women with children to re-enter the labour force.[60] Some factories even offered childcare. A BBC film on working wives made in East Kilbride in 1966 featured a modern factory with a 'well-run crèche … [which] had absolutely first class conditions for mothers who want to work'.[61] Figures for 1971 show the percentage of women engaged in paid work outside the home in East Kilbride (45 per cent) and Cumbernauld (43 per cent) exceeding the UK average of 38 per cent, the higher participation in East Kilbride in particular reflective of the flexible opportunities available.[62] Working-class women in Scotland had for generations combined paid work with their work in the home through financial necessity. This did not challenge the division of labour in the home or gender stereotypes; men remained breadwinners and women's wages were seen as supplementary. However, in the new towns, as elsewhere in urban Scotland and beyond, women chose to work, not only because they needed the money but because they wanted a degree of autonomy. Such work, while not always empowering, did lead to an increased sense of independence which could impact on marriages.

New family forms

By the late 1970s, then, the new town dream that sustained the pioneers was being refashioned. The provision of homes for separated spouses and the need to provide accommodation for those who had become homeless, many of them via marriage breakdown, was a response to changing family forms and lifestyles. The profile of families was beginning to look rather different from the nuclear model. The national rise in unmarried and/or single mothers commented on widely in the popular press was no different in the new towns. Annie remembered her parents being 'terrified of us getting pregnant unmarried'.[63] She described there being 'an occasional unmarried pregnancy and it would be seen as, like, scandal of the century'. But it was not so much unmarried mothers that challenged the conformity of community in the new towns but the growth of lone parents resulting from marriage breakdown. Recognizing the problem of marriage breakdown, in 1977 Cumbernauld provided four 'housing units' for 'spouses with marital problems'.[64] By the 1980s in Glenrothes, more than 20 per cent of total lets were to single parents and they were the largest group amongst those designated as Special Needs Households requesting accommodation.[65] In 1986–7, of 129 single parent households accommodated, 38 were unmarried mothers and 85 were 'separated or divorced wives and family' indicating that women were leaving marriages and the family home. By 1989 around 10 per cent of housing allocations were in response to marital breakdown.[66]

Vicky, who grew up in Cumbernauld in the 1980s, remarked that to remain married was 'seen as the achievement'.[67] Despite the financial pressures experienced by many couples, staying together was often easier than separating owing to the need for two incomes. Lone parents and especially lone mothers did endure financial hardship. Vicky recalled the 'food instability' in her household centred on an anecdote in which she was offered an extra fish finger at a friend's house. When she asked for extra at home her mother 'slammed the plate on the table' stating that she got more at her friend's house because her friend had a dad at home. Vicky's mother oscillated between part- and full-time work depending on the levels of state support she received. But despite her mother's efforts and maintenance payments from her father, Vicky recalled the stigma of being a child in a one-parent family, especially when it impacted on her own self-esteem, such as when her mother could not afford her school uniform from the school's supplier or feeling 'that there were trends and cultures and sort of stuff that I was always on the periphery of'. But Vicky understood that 'things just weren't as easy for her [mother]'. As a solution, Vicky got a part-time job when she was twelve years old 'so that I had my own money' and 'you know, I paid my own way towards school lunches and stuff like that' and 'just to, you know, make sure I kept up with that sort of stuff'. That sense of the new town as an aspirational place where people had all the consumer goods that were new, the signifiers of a 'good life' endured with Vicky also feeling the need to 'keep up' with her peers as a child and young teenager.

The absence of nursery provision was a particular problem for lone parents with young children. In East Kilbride there had been calls for the establishment of day nurseries as early as 1969 to respond to the growing numbers of mothers in work. When Scottish Development Department funding was not forthcoming campaigners were left to lobby major employers to invest in childcare, a call which was taken up by the Laird Portch clothing factory.[68] Maggie moved back to Glenrothes in 1982 from Dundee where she had benefitted from the historically generous provision of nurseries owing to the comparatively high proportion of married women in paid work in that city. In the new town, on the other hand, Maggie continued working with a patchwork of childcare; her daughter attended nursery in the morning and was looked after by her cousin, a registered childminder, in the afternoon. As a graduate with a career, Maggie accepted she was 'not your average single parent'; her economic and social capital as well as a strong family support network and ties in the community in which she had grown up enabled her to manage as a single parent when many others struggled.⁶⁹ Lone parents like Vicky's mother and Maggie may have been assisted by the local Gingerbread group (an association for one-parent families) which organized activities and provided information about benefits and fundraising through its Newsletter. But the Glenrothes group only had eight members in 1987 and there is limited evidence of Gingerbread's presence in the other new towns.⁷⁰

Whilst there is no evidence that the new towns were particular incubators of social problems, neither were they insulated from them. This chapter has alluded to the use of alcohol as an aid to loneliness and Vicky referred to the normality of 'deeply entrenched problematic drinking behaviour that radiated out amongst their families and into the community'.⁷¹ Linda recalled that growing up in Cumbernauld 'you knew the people, the dad that drank, and there was a bit of domestic violence and things like that. But we were more accepting then, because it was part of life'.⁷² Alison's account of her parents' marriage breakdown encapsulates the facade hiding a more troubling reality. Her parents were 'violent to each other' but sometimes they would take out their frustration and anger on their daughter, holding her accountable for her perceived loyalty to the other. While she would sometimes attend school visibly upset, no one in authority ever intervened to ask her directly what was going on at home or offer help or support. For Alison the story of Glenrothes cannot be told without addressing domestic abuse. 'We were totally hiding in plain sight'; her family did not come to the attention of social workers because we were 'well dressed, we had new shoes, we got fed three times a day, we lived in a semi-detached house […], no one was ever going to touch us with a bargepole. Good schools, we worked hard.'⁷³ For Alison, the silence concealed a normality of family tensions manifested in violence and excessive alcohol consumption. 'Why would you talk about something that's so … it's like, it's just life'. By the 1990s Women's Aid was active in or nearby all of the new towns with East Kilbride's refuge established in 1992 and in Glenrothes, Gingerbread similarly provided accommodation for women who were forced to leave the family home with a Women's Aid branch nearby in Kirkcaldy.

Conclusion

In most respects families in the new towns experienced the same pressures as families elsewhere. The process of moving away from extended family and taking on the financial commitments of a new home was a commonplace experience up and down the British Isles. Financial difficulties, marriage breakdown, the rise of lone parents and a loosening of traditional attitudes towards relationships were, however, writ large in the new towns precisely because they militated against the dominant image of the new town dream that centred on the nuclear family. This meant that when families experienced difficulties, at least until the early 1980s, it could be hard to find support. Notwithstanding the fact that composing a settled narrative around such experiences is difficult for narrators when they challenge the myth of the new town dream, these stories demonstrate how the modern environment, encompassing private homes (albeit in close proximity), opportunities for women to work, distance from family and former community norms and even unfamiliar mixed-sex socializing, enabled a break from traditional patterns of behaviour. It would be stretching the argument too far to say that the new towns were petri-dishes, growing the culture that would come to be normalized across the country. But here we do see elements of social and economic life – rising rates of married women in work, growing incidence of marriage breakdown and the emergence of more complex family forms – which anticipated national trends. The new towns were built as family towns but designed to sustain a family model that was already beginning to change in the 1960s. By the 1980s, modern Scotland in the guise of the new towns no longer represented the planners' ideals.

Notes

1 Michael Young and Peter Willmott, *Family and Kinship in East London* (London: Routledge & Kegan Paul, 1957).
2 Claire Langhamer, 'The Meanings of Home in Post-war Britain', *Journal of Contemporary History* 40, no. 2 (2005): 341–62; David Kynaston, *Family Britain 1951–57* (London: Bloomsbury, 2009).
3 Lynn Abrams, Barry Hazley, Ade Kearns and Valerie Wrught, 'Aspiration, Agency and the Production of New Selves in a Scottish New Town, c.1947–c.2016', *Twentieth Century British History* 29, no. 4 (2018): 576–604; Jon Lawrence, *Me, Me, Me: The Search for Community in Post-War England* (Oxford: Oxford University Press, 2019), 127–31.
4 See Alistair Fair, 'Privacy, the Housing Research Unit at the University of Edinburgh and the Courtyard House, 1959–70', *Architectural History* 65 (2022): 327–58.
5 Guy Ortolano, *Thatcher's Progress: From Social Democracy to Market Liberalism through an English New Town* (Cambridge: Cambridge University Press, 2019), 5–6, 14–15.
6 See e.g. the Dudley Report on post-war housing in England: *Design of Dwellings* (London: HMSO, 1944), 34, 36, 38; See also Elizabeth Darling, *Re-forming Britain: Narratives of Modernity before Reconstruction* (Abingdon: Routledge, 2007), 143–55.
7 Tripartite model: Alistair Kefford, *The Life and Death of the Shopping City: Public Planning and Private Redevelopment in Britain since 1945* (Cambridge: Cambridge University Press, 2022).
8 Interview with Bill, Glenrothes, 26 November 2021.
9 See Lynn Abrams and Linda Fleming, *Long Term Experiences of Tenants in Social Housing in East Kilbride: An Oral History Study* (Glasgow: University of Glasgow, 2011).
10 On education see Peter Mandler, *The Crisis of the Meritocracy: Britain's Transition to Mass Education since the Second World War* (Cambridge: Cambridge University Press, 2022).
11 Interview with Linda, Cumbernauld, 15 June 2022.
12 Cumbernauld Development Corporation [CDC], Annual Report 1990.
13 This is referred to by oral historians as the theory of composure. See Lynn Abrams, *Oral History Theory* (London: Routledge, 2016), 66–70.
14 Interview with Audrey, Glasgow, 5 November 2021.
15 Janice Scott Long, 'The Gum Boot Society', *The Guardian*, 8 December 1965.
16 'Clubs Foster Community Spirit', *Glasgow Herald*, 28 August 1968.
17 Interview with Alexander, Glenrothes, 9 November 2021.
18 S.D. Coleman, *Mental Health and Social Adjustment in a New Town: An Exploratory Study in East Kilbride* (Glasgow: University of Glasgow, 1965). More generally see Ali Haggett, *Desperate Housewives: Neuroses and the Domestic Environment 1945–1970* (London: Routledge, 2012); Mark Clapson, 'Working-Class Women's Experiences of Moving to New Housing Estates in England since 1919', *Twentieth Century British History* 10, no. 3 (1999): 345–65.
19 *Daily Record*, 10 April 1957 (as quoted in Derek Lyddon, Cumbernauld Overview: *New Towns Record* [Planning Exchange CD-ROM set, 1996]).

20 Traditional women's organizations such as the Townswomen's Guild were active early on in Glenrothes, but it is likely their presence declined in the 1960s and 1970s. National Library of Scotland: *Glenrothes Bulletin,* July 1955 vol. 2. See Lynn Abrams, *Feminist Lives: Women, Feelings and the Self in Post-War Britain* (Oxford: Oxford University Press, 2023), 198–200.

21 CDC, *Annual Report*, 1960.

22 Glenrothes Development Corporation [GDC], Housing Management Report 1979. It was not until 1988 that a new points-based system was introduced, taking more account of housing need and less of employment status. GDC, *Housing Management Report*, 1989, 3.

23 GDC, Housing Management Report, 1979, 4.

24 'Chance for Housewives to join Free Gift Bandwagon', *Hamilton Advertiser*, 17 October 1969.

25 Lynn Abrams, 'The Self and Self-Help: Women Pursuing Autonomy in Post-War Britain', *Transactions of the Royal Historical Society* 29 (2019): 201–21.

26 Interview with Linda, Cumbernauld, 15 June 2022.

27 *Daily Record*, 10 April 1957.

28 Ibid.

29 Interview with Audrey, Glasgow, 5 November 2021.

30 Andrew J.M. Sykes et al., *Cumbernauld: A Household Survey and Report* (University of Strathclyde, Department of Sociology, 1967).

31 Interview with Audrey, Glasgow, 5 November 2021. See also 'Clubs Foster Community Spirit' [*Glasgow Herald*, 28 August 1968] which mentions carpentry evening classes for women in East Kilbride.

32 Interview with Linda, Cumbernauld, 15 June 2022.

33 Interview with Donna, Irvine, 12 June 2023.

34 On privacy and secrecy, see Deborah Cohen, *Family Secrets: The Things We Tried to Hide* (London: Viking, 2013).

35 Interview with Angie, Cumbernauld, 17 June 2022.

36 '900 Jobs Lost as BSR Retreat', *Scotsman*, 3 December 1974; 'Wives Face the Axe in 900-job Cutback', *Daily Express*, 3 December 1974.

37 CDC, Annual Report 1979.

38 GDC, Housing Management Report 1987, 10.

39 Ibid., 3.

40 GDC, Housing Management Reports 1960–1990.

41 GDC, Housing Management Committee 1992, 17.

42 On the 'problem family', see John Welshman, 'The Emergence of a Discourse Concerning the Rise of the "Problem Family"', *Social Policy & Society* 16, no. 1 (2017): 109–17; Ben Rogaly and Becky Taylor, *Moving Histories of Class and Community: Identity, Place and Belonging in Contemporary England* (Basingstoke: Palgrave Macmillan, 2009).

43 CDC, Annual Report 1976.

44 Livingston Development Corporation [LDC], Annual Report 1983.

45 Interview with Rhonda, Glenrothes, 21 October 2021.

46 Interview with Moira, Doune, 12 August 2022.

47 See Charlie Lynch, 'Scotland and the Sexual Revolution c. 1957–1975: Religion, Intimacy and Popular Culture', PhD dissertation, University of Glasgow, 2019.

48 Interview with Susan, Cumbernauld, 1 June 2022. See also Chapter 9 of this book for an extended discussion of Susan and Michael.
49 Interview with Annie (and Alison), Glenrothes, 22 October 2021.
50 Interview with Alison (and Annie), Glenrothes, 22 October 2021.
51 Interview with Annie (and Alison), Glenrothes, 22 October 2021.
52 GDC, Housing Management Report 1979, 19.
53 Claire Langhamer, 'Love, Selfhood and Authenticity in Post-War Britain', *Cultural and Social History*, 9, no. 2 (2012): 277–97.
54 Interview with Bill, Glenrothes, 26 November 2021.
55 Interview with Audrey, Glasgow, 5 November 2021.
56 Divorce law reform had occurred with the Divorce (Scotland) Act 1976, which included the provision for divorce by mutual consent. In addition, from 1984, Sheriff Courts could hear divorce cases rather than at the High Court in Edinburgh. See https://www.nrscotland.gov.uk/statistics-and-data/statistics/statistics-by-theme/vital-events/vital-events-divorces-and-dissolutions/divorces-time-series-data (accessed on 29 April 2024).
57 Interview with Audrey, Glasgow, 5 November 2021.
58 Lynn Abrams, 'Heroes of Their Own Life Stories: Narrating the Female Self in the Feminist Age', *Cultural and Social History*, 16, no. 2 (2019): 205–24.
59 See Eve Worth, *The Welfare State Generation: Women, Agency and Class in Britain since 1945* (London: Bloomsbury, 2021); Abrams, *Feminist Lives*.
60 See Laura Paterson, 'Women and Paid Work in Industrial Britain', PhD dissertation, University of Dundee, 2014. In 1951, slightly over a quarter of all married women worked, almost doubling by 1971. By 1981, almost two-thirds of married women worked, 70.
61 Scottish Marriage Guidance Council, *News and Views*, 5, March 1966 (National Library of Scotland).
62 Jo Foord, 'Conflicting Lives: Women's Work in Planned Communities', PhD dissertation, University of Kent, 1990, 350. However, there were significant differences in part-time working. In East Kilbride, 28 per cent of women worked part-time; the equivalent figure for Cumbernauld was 10 per cent (pp. 115–16).
63 Interview with Annie (and Alison), Glenrothes, 22 October 2021.
64 CDC, Annual Report 1977.
65 GDC, Housing Management Annual Report 1988, 4; 1987, 8. In 1986–7, of 129 single-parent households accommodated, 38 included unmarried mothers and 85 separated or divorced wives and family (Ibid., 9).
66 GDC, Housing Management Committee 1989, 5.
67 Interview with Vicky, Glasgow, 5 August 2022.
68 'Day Nurseries Call by Councillor', *Hamilton Advertiser* 11 July 1969; 'Delay for Nursery', *East Kilbride News* 18 July 1969.
69 Interview with Maggie, conducted online, 1 February 2022.
70 NLS, *Gingerbread Newsletter*: Fife Federation, December/January 1987.
71 Interview with Vicky, Glasgow, 5 August 2022.
72 Interview with Linda, Cumbernauld, 15 June 2022.
73 Interview with Alison (and Annie) Glenrothes, 22 October 2021.

8

Community

New towns have been seen as exemplars of the alleged decline of community in the post-war era, with the aspirational desire to better oneself supposedly reflecting an individualist position which manifested itself in consumerism, a wish for privacy and a rejection of the claims of the collective.[1] More recently, however, historians have rejected the binary framework of the 'competing claims of community and individualism', demonstrating that the desire to better oneself was a shared project, that self-improvement was seen as a collective endeavour, enjoyed not just by one's neighbours but also by 'people like us' sharing in the Welfare State project.[2] The new towns occupy a significant place in this debate, partly because they were a focus for sociological research in the 1960s. They were regarded by scholars as laboratories in which to investigate the relationship between self and society at a time when traditional social networks seemed to be eroding.[3] Indeed, Cumbernauld's landscape consultant argued in 1957 that if the town could embody the qualities of older settlements then:

> it will have character and personality. Only then its inhabitants will feel that there is their own town, there is their home, the place to which they belong. From that may more readily grow their sense both of community and individuality, two values our present world is so rapidly destroying.[4]

But communities needed to be nurtured. The new towns more than anywhere else were emblematic of state-sponsored community-building in the post-war decades. Planners, architects and development corporation personnel alike believed that they had a role, through physical and policy interventions, in creating 'balanced and self-sufficient' communities, as described in the earlier chapters of this book.[5] They also envisaged new towns as cohesive and stable communities, spatialized through planning and design, and fostered by means of active community-building, incorporating both top-down (state-led) and bottom-up (popular) initiatives.[6] This practice was sometimes formalized under the name 'social development'. Social development built on established ideas of 'active citizenship', understood as something participatory and communal. It emerged as a partnership between the public and voluntary sectors in some of the English new towns during the 1950s and especially the 1960s, being taken up in Scotland in Livingston, in particular, as was noted in Chapter 4 of this book. Social development encouraged connections between people in order to build new communities, but was also concerned with encouraging individuals to fulfil their own aspirations and ambitions, and to find satisfaction not just within the home but also at the broader urban scale.[7]

In what follows, we focus predominantly on community in the Scottish new towns as lived experience rather than outcome of policy, planning or state-sponsored intervention, though all impacted on peoples' experience. We understand community as active, grassroots and elective, subject to change in response to a range of local and national variables including population demographics, local initiatives, national trends in leisure consumption, and shifts in the economy and employment which impacted in different ways on each of the new towns. The model community envisaged by those who planned, built and governed the new towns was never achieved or even achievable, modelled as it often was on some idealistic Scottish small town, but other forms of community, built from the grassroots and better aligned to wider social and economic developments, did emerge in the early years.[8] To take on board Lawrence's argument, community existed in two forms: an imagined form of social relations and the lived version manifested in 'the micro-level interactions which people experienced in their everyday lives'.[9] The imagined community and the lived community rarely aligned, though they were probably at their closest in the pioneer years when people were thrown together on new housing estates with few points of contact apart from their neighbours and work colleagues.

This chapter charts the ways in which community was experienced using three models which roughly align with the stages of new town development. We begin with the community of necessity or circumstance, which emerged organically amongst the pioneers in a relatively short period of ten to fifteen years. This was followed by a form of elective community, forged out of choice rather than need and cohering around the interests and needs of specific groups rather than being focused on the neighbourhood.[10] By the late 1970s, while there was still much evidence of collective activity in a plethora of clubs and community groups, population mobility, the growth of owner-occupation, the decline of organized religion, the increase of married women in paid work, and the provision of commercial leisure and entertainment all meant that the distinctiveness of the new town community was progressively diminished. The idea of community still carried meaning for people – why else would so many of our interviewees speak so warmly of the community spirit of the pioneer years? – but their own ways of doing community were practised through friendships, and what Spencer and Pahl described as 'hidden solidarities', less rooted to place or to kin.[11]

Balanced, self-sufficient and all-in-it-together

'One of the main tasks facing managers of new towns is the inculcation and development of a "community spirit"', remarked *The Manchester Guardian*'s Special Correspondent on visiting Glenrothes in 1958, 'an aim which seems naïve and perhaps impossible to the cynical'.[12] The town was described as 'antiseptic'. Yet considerable effort was expended by the authorities to foster community and a feeling of belonging. New town development corporations mobilized to assist, support and facilitate social connection, inspired by a model of active, participatory citizenship which drew on the ideas of the interwar voluntary sector and a longer tradition of liberal thought.[13] The new town was to be a participatory community in which everyone had a stake through involvement in activities beyond their immediate neighbourhood or family group, thus ensuring vitality and stability. Especially in Livingston, the particular commitment of the development corporation to the practice of social development meant that newcomers there were visited and given a 'helping hand' by 'lady Housing Visitors' (former social workers not dissimilar from Glasgow's feared 'Green Ladies', who monitored hygiene and household management amongst municipal tenants). In addition to providing information on the town's amenities, Livingston's visitors persuaded families to take part in activities, as well as assessing whether a family was likely to need ongoing support; a kind of surreptitious monitoring familiar to newcomers from Glasgow, who were perhaps keen to leave it behind.[14] By 1968, a Welcoming Committee consisting of residents involved in community work called on newcomers to stimulate engagement in clubs and inform them of social and educational facilities in the town.[15] In the first residential area of Livingston, Craigshill, the development corporation staffed a caravan to act as a one-stop-shop for queries.[16] Communities were built by people in this world view, but it was believed that people required interventions to achieve the desired outcomes. And those interventions were never really benign. The kind of community imagined by new town officers bore little resemblance to the urban communities from where many of the first residents hailed. Whilst endeavouring to break down the 'Them and Us' complex and to create a functioning, cohesive community where everyone played their part, residents and officials alike, it was clear that at least some of those who were unwilling to buy in to this ideology were unwelcome, at least in the early years. The minority 'who by the very nature of their environmental upbringing just would not fit into a new community' were seen to be a disruptive element.[17]

James moved with his wife and children to East Kilbride in 1975. His description of the kind of community that emerged in Greenhills is reminiscent of the aims of the planners for a self-sufficient, balanced community, where class was unimportant, where everyone shared an aspirational mindset and where sociability was centred on the church:

> The good thing was, there were a lot of young families moved in at the same time and we all became very friendly … that was the bond between us the children were young and they played together … there was a good community spirit … it was a good environment for the children to grow up … We were all working-class people. Naebody was better than anybody else. We all had jobs, they weren't high flying jobs, they were just jobs … We went to the church down the road eventually and made a lot of friendships. They came from all over East Kilbride … There was folk had fancier houses than us but they didn't treat us any different.[18]

James' retrospective account mirrors the positive picture of new town community painted by officials in all the new settlements, whilst also recognizing the challenges. In the case of Livingston, the housing and social development manager acknowledged the need for 'newcomers to accept a community responsibility at an early stage', otherwise 'sooner or later each family will inevitably become its own social desert; an oasis in isolation, that in some cases could be dangerously introspective, possibly anti-social', but he observed amongst the pioneers at the grassroots level a 'real spirit of involvement'.[19] The 1961 issue of the *Cumbernauld News* proclaimed that 'community spirit is being developed'. The people who had moved to the town 'have the spirit of adventure' and 'regard living in the new town as a challenge'. Given that most had come from Glasgow where, it was said, people were 'naturally friendly' and were 'all in the same predicament', it was believed that community would grow organically, assisted by the churches and youth organizations which had already laid foundations.[20] Yet church-going and associated clubs were not singled out by many respondents as aids to social integration, a finding evident in community studies elsewhere.[21] And when Ferdynand Zweig investigated Cumbernauld almost ten years later, he described it as a place where people developed only transient relationships with others and preferred to 'keep oneself to oneself', at home watching television. He suggested its 'impressive list of social clubs' was a façade with 'most of them leading a shadowy existence'.[22]

In these representations of community, we see two sides of the same coin. The pioneers' spirit of adventure which is alluded to by so many of our interviewees from that generation did not exclude (and indeed often incorporated) a desire for privacy and the choice to engage (or not) with manifestations of community, be they evening classes, sports clubs or church groups; this is what Savage calls 'elective community'.[23] Nicky, who grew up as a new town child in East Kilbride, encapsulates this dichotomy in his memories of family life in the early years, aligning his account with two dominant narratives about post-war Britain: the privatized family which allowed individual family members to pursue their own interests, and the striving for a better life which was conceptualized within a broader appreciation of community:

> Yeah, you know, I mean, my mum … I can't actually remember my mum doing anything. You know, family would come round, maybe we'd go and visit my gran. You know. My dad [slater and plasterer] played the classical guitar, that was his release. He played, he studied sheet music and he sat with his guitar … I don't know if it was just my parents, but they weren't ones for going out and partying. They had me and they had a wee kid on the way, or just been born. Plus they're doing night shift and day shift jobs, trying to make as much money as they can, paying for this three-bedroom house and trying to bring up two little ones. I do remember us going out to events and stuff. But it was work-related dos and stuff, with my mum. But I remember … people often talk about community spirit of places and stuff like that. And I just remember it was a really strong feeling. And where I came from … And all the neighbours were talking to each other and going into each other's houses and all that. I can totally remember that. And it's a really strong feeling that everybody knew everybody.[24]

Nicky's account appears contradictory but in fact combines what most people wanted from the new town: the chance to be an individual, supported by the knowledge that one lived among like-minded souls. The neighbourliness recalled by Nicky is a common trope amongst former residents, employed not so much to describe but to conjure up the spirit of the place whilst saying little about the real levels of engagement. Sarah, whose family moved to Cumbernauld from another new town, Harlow, recalled:

> [I]t was quite a close community then because a lot of people were in the same boat. They'd all come to the new place and there were a lot of young children there. So, I think … they'd a really good social life, social scene they had because they were all in the same boat. So, they didn't have established family networks there. So, they were all new and had come from a lot of different places. Probably the majority were Scottish … but with us being kind of Irish and English we didn't have any other family in Scotland. So that became like a big family.[25]

And Bill who moved from Glasgow to Glenrothes repeated a common refrain: 'it was a community where you did know everyone'.[26]

Bill's and Sarah's memories are replicated repeatedly by our first-generation respondents, yet closer analysis of these narratives reveals a more complex picture, without seeking to deny the genuine sentiments of the pioneers. The cross-class mixing that pervades these stories was not all that it seemed. In all of the new towns, as Chapter 6 explained, the style of housing and its location distinguished the better-off residents from those with lesser means. Lucile moved to Glenrothes when her father obtained a job with the development corporation. She described the area her family moved to as mixed but conceded that there was 'a slight mix, [...] yes there was doctors, architects, solicitors, surveyors and then you had people who owned their own business'.[27] Beryl, on the other hand, described her Cumbernauld neighbourhood of Carbrain as containing people who hailed from Glasgow's tenements alongside some who worked for the development corporation because it was 'development corporation policy to have the people who designed the town, et cetera, living amongst the people they were designing for'. But Beryl's account is revealing of other ways in which the story of everyone in the same boat needs to be complicated. Beryl's family were English and her account negotiates carefully around the issue of otherness:

> Yeah, but I think being English was a bit of a barrier, until the baby was born … And we discovered that people tended to be moved from Glasgow, if people from a tenement could be moved into a street, then that was the way it seemed to be done … So as not to break up communities. [...] Yeah. And so, I used to see, the fence was very high, and I used to see this vacuum cleaner going that direction one day, and then going that way another day, and I couldn't see who was carrying it, I just could see the top of the vacuum cleaner. So I'd become pregnant, and once you've got a baby, everybody talks to you. Because, I think being English, I was a bit kind of, not one of us … Not that they were unfriendly, at all. But once a baby comes along, people feel more free to speak to you. So, we got on very well, all the neighbours, there, I think.

Our interviewees found it difficult to narrate a story that undermined the dominant and positive picture of everyone mucking in together. Beryl folded her memories of being isolated amongst a community of Glaswegians into a more positive story once she was one of the mums and became part of a female mutual support network. And towards the end of this segment of the interview, she identified the city tenements as a model, alluding to the 'myth' of tenemental life that in itself conceals tensions beneath a veneer of community reciprocity. 'I think the development corporation were keen not to destroy, that kind of, you know, because it is a support network. And you can live in a place and never know your neighbours at all.'[28] Jim, however, offered a more forthright view, recalling that his sister was affected by anti-English feeling: 'if you speak with an English accent you're almost discarded, you know, "you're not one of us". So that starts off on a negative. I know she had more problems than I did'.[29] Andy in Cumbernauld likewise recalled being bullied at primary school. His family had moved to the town from London and his accent was a giveaway: 'I think it was partly 'cause I was new but it was how I spoke, it was my accent, you know. It was my accent then. And I don't think, probably, in Cumbernauld, there maybe wasn't the same kind of mix as there might be now'.[30]

The residents of Scottish new towns were not only predominantly Scots but also overwhelmingly white. We can only surmise that structural racism – taking the form of failure to encourage and recruit Black and ethnic-minority residents, and the tendency for non-white tenants to be in private-sector rather than public-sector rented housing – contributed to the racial demographics of the towns. Official records are largely silent on race and ethnicity, an exception being Livingston's response in 1972 to the appeal to assist fleeing Ugandan Asians by supplying accommodation for two families and establishing a working party to 'encourage involvement by the local community'.[31] Our interviewees keenly remember encounters with the few non-white inhabitants in those years, recognizing that their curiosity and what would now be understood as micro-aggression were a consequence of both the rarity of Black neighbours and what one Glenrothes interviewee described as their own 'ignorance'. 'I wouldn't say it was badness', she reflects, describing her classmates' behaviour: 'it was just "I've never seen hair like this, can I touch your hair?"'[32]

But while there may have been racial homogeneity, class differences which had always been present – if papered over by the determination of new residents to identify themselves with a new aspirational class – rose to the surface during the 1960s and 1970s. The 1957 Housing and Town Development (Scotland) Act saw Glasgow begin a more deliberate policy of encouraging those on its housing list to move to the new towns, including East Kilbride. 'I know when I worked in the town centre', recalled James from East Kilbride:

> that there was a culture of 'oh they're the overspill, they're not as good as us'. I think there was a bit of snobbishness, I think there's still a bit of snobbishness in East Kilbride. People look down their nose at folk fae Glasgow but they forget that most of them came from Glasgow, it's strange. Greenhills used to get a bad name in the town. Calderwood used to have a bad name. But every area has problems … but as I say there was a kinda snobbishness, people did look down on folk who came in from Glasgow, especially overspill families.[33]

As was outlined in the Introduction to this book, the term 'overspill' was originally coined within 1940s policy and planning discourse simply to refer to the reduction of inner-city populations through relocation to other places. Thus, in one sense, the majority of East Kilbride's residents could be defined as 'overspill', whether they had arrived before or after the implementation of the 1957 Act, and whether they had come to the town of their own initiative or had been encouraged to move under the terms of a formal 'overspill' agreement.[34] But, as James' recollection shows, among Scottish new town citizens the label seems to have taken on a new, pejorative meaning during the 1960s, as a means of disparaging the more recent Glaswegian newcomers. They had not, it seemed to some, arrived entirely of their own volition; they had come to the town because they had been presented with few alternatives. They were perceived to lack the resources and the ambition to aspire to this new kind of life; it was, indeed, sometimes thought that they might tarnish the reputation of the new towns. The Greenhills area of East Kilbride was often associated with 'overspill', partly because its construction during the 1970s coincided with a period in which the town had a formal agreement with Glasgow and perhaps also partly because its houses were smaller and cheaper, suggesting that prejudice was class-based, the antithesis of the tendency to present the new towns as outside the class system.[35]

Women and men had different ways of making and participating in community in the early years. Men moved to the new towns for work and found friends this way. Women, who were less likely to be in work early on, had to try harder to make social connections when there were no rules. Tenement life at least was bounded by shared tasks, and rules of engagement around the use and cleaning of shared spaces. But in the new towns, patterns of neighbourliness could be made anew in accordance with personal preference and need, contrasting with the enforced communality of the tenement. Rhonda commented that 'you think you know people and neighbours but sometimes you don't. And then you don't really want to know sometimes cause I think when you do know you think "oh my god" but you're better keeping yourself to yourself.'[36] Sylvia enjoyed the relative anonymity in East Kilbride compared with life on a Glasgow housing estate as she 'wasn't into joining things'.[37] And Helena, who moved to East Kilbride in the 1970s, distanced herself from a model of community she implicitly associated with working-class neighbourhoods. For her visiting neighbours was by invitation. 'We weren't in the habit of running in and out of each other's homes'.[38] But as women increasingly joined the labour market, they began to participate in the sociability centred upon workplace friendships and activities. Vicky remembered her mother enjoying a 'real sense of family and community' when she worked for HMRC in Cumbernauld.[39] Like some of the other large employers in the new towns such as Rolls Royce in East Kilbride, 'community was fostered', in Vicky's words, via a workplace social club, a social committee that organized family outings and employee perks, perhaps in an attempt to retain a stable workforce. Later on in the 1990s, when Vicky also started to work for HMRC, she described it as a 'whole wee village' with a shop, delicatessen, a gym and a canteen.

It is incontrovertible that the planners' vision for community in the new towns was designed to undercut the kinds of working-class and gendered leisure culture that was seen by many to characterize static communities in the cities. The close-knit, sex-segregated model of social relations described in 1957 by Elizabeth Bott in her *Family and Social Network* exemplified this perception.[40] So, in the new towns, community halls replaced traditional pubs, many of which still excluded women until the 1970s. Late 1950s East Kilbride's two 'new style' public houses were places 'where people could meet socially while having a drink' and so were dubbed 'chummy pubs' by the press, distinguishable 'from the old type where people go merely to consume liquor', though they were still opposed by the churches.[41] And while church buildings were provided for both Christian denominations, there were initially no football stadia. Instead of the gender- and class-segregated entertainment venues found in parts of Glasgow and Edinburgh, the new towns offered, in addition to the workplace social clubs (which welcomed families), cultural venues like the Cottage Theatre in Cumbernauld and the Repertory Theatre Club in East Kilbride, plus neighbourhood halls designed for youth and other voluntary organizations, children's parties, jumble sales and other 'purposeful' activity.

It was recognized that, in order for community to develop and thrive, the building blocks needed to be put in place. Community centres were built by the local authorities, under whose remit (rather than that of the development corporation) such venues fell, though the need for the authorities to focus limited resources on providing schools and fulfilling other statutory functions meant that such infrastructure could be slow to appear; East Kilbride's Murray community hall was still incomplete in 1961 (Figure 8.1).[42] But, drawing on the voluntarist origins of social development,[43] other groups also became involved in fostering community. In East Kilbride, the local authority in 1963 established a Civics Association, consisting of representatives of active clubs, to coordinate local groups and ensure civic amenities were meeting the needs of residents, a model borrowed from small burghs and villages with their traditions of galas and fetes rather than Scotland's urban

FIGURE 8.1 Murray Community Centre, East Kilbride, with the neighbourhood shops behind (© The Scotsman Publications Ltd).

communities. One of its ventures was Civic Week, a mini-festival or 'shop-window for life in the town'.[44] Likewise Cumbernauld's Civic Trust brought together all the voluntary organizations in the town – around 250 in 1970, ranging from the Cumbernauld majorettes to carpet bowls and car maintenance, along with the usual variety of sports, youth and church clubs.[45] For a time, a new kind of 'associative culture' informed by choice – of activity and with whom – did appear to thrive.[46] In Glenrothes, for example, the weekly calendar of events in the *Grapevine* community newsletter, was packed with meetings of – mainly – youth and women's groups from the judo club and the scouts to the 'Welcome-In Ladies Club', the floral art group and multiple playgroups. Clubs catering to men or mixed participants were fewer and included various bands, a rifle and pistol club, and the squadron air training corps. Only the St Ninian's Church Men's Group was explicitly men-only.[47] Livingston Development Corporation's commitment to social development meant that it was especially active in promoting local clubs and organizations. Applicants for housing were asked to provide information about their leisure-time interests. They were then matched with relevant clubs; where there was no existing group, individuals would be invited for a chat to discuss setting something up and thus 'the social relations section becomes a clearing house through which those with common interests can be put in touch with each other'.[48]

Yet, as Zweig intimated with respect to Cumbernauld, this apparent hive of community activity may be misleading. For at the time, as studies of aspirant communities elsewhere in the UK demonstrated, the home was becoming a place not just for family life, but also as a place of sociability, rather than, as hitherto, a place to escape from to other, perhaps warmer places of communal activity.[49] As recalled by Annie, whose family moved to Glenrothes in the 1950s, there was a lively social life in the local Woodside area, focused on parties with families taking turns to host the neighbours.[50] A survey of peoples' leisure activities in Glenrothes in 1971 found more than half of those who responded did not belong to any group within a year of moving to the town. The most popular leisure activity was visiting hotels and public houses with commercial leisure – cinema, dance halls and the like – a close second.[51]

Encouraging social participation was only one arm of the development corporations' attempts to create a cohesive, balanced, participatory and stable population. It is clear that community-building was regarded as a long-term exercise, requiring provision of housing as well as community facilities. Twenty years after the foundation of East Kilbride, the development corporation embarked on a programme of building homes for the sons and daughters of existing tenants to encourage the next generation to commit to the town.[52] This policy is in marked contrast to the contemporaneous management of council housing by local authorities whereby, from 1977, 'sitting tenants' had to give way to 'priority needs' cases. Whereas the development corporations actively sought to ensure the longevity and diversity (in terms of age) of the community, the logical endpoint of the central state's governance of general council housing was residential transience and community deformation.

Elective communities

Fostering community through intervention could only work while people had few alternatives and were still establishing social networks. Once the settling-in process had run its course, people began to rely less on the likes of the churches and instead began to forge their own networks, guided by their own interests and needs. In this respect, the new towns were the ideal environment for the emergence of a new kind of elective community based around choice and self-help. This was less a community of circumstance, old loyalties or residential proximity; rather it was driven by initiatives to provide resources to meet the need of certain groups who had interests and experiences in common. Shirley, who moved from Castlemilk in Glasgow to East Kilbride, encapsulated this shift:

> In Castlemilk I loved it. I absolutely loved the Young Mothers in the church … and when I came up to East Kilbride I thought it would just be a matter of joining the same things up here; no it wasn't like that. Totally different. I tried it, well there wasn't a church up in Greenhills at the time, I went to the Westwood church and it was never the same. It lost the community thing, I don't know what that would be really. I still liked East Kilbride but I don't know, there was something different from living in Castlemilk … I got a wee bit disheartened … I went to the playgroup with [daughter] so I met people through that … I think there was a Gingerbread group or something like that and that's where I went because you could take your kids and that's where I met new friends.[53]

Women, and especially mothers of preschool children, were at the forefront of this movement to provide companionship and support for those isolated from family and lacking ready-made networks. The Pre-School Playgroups Association (PPA) quickly established a presence in the new towns from the early 1960s, coinciding with changes in women's opportunities and expectations and facilitated by the provision of community amenities. In Cumbernauld, one of the first playgroups was established in a community room incorporated into a housing estate 'to benefit children in high flats and ordinary housing'.[54] By 1973, playgroups were ubiquitous in the new towns with fifteen in East Kilbride, fourteen in Livingstone and eleven in Cumbernauld.[55]

Those who started the first playgroups were not the 'housewives' praised by Patrick Dollan in East Kilbride in 1954 for their 'excellent standard of housekeeping and … the first class way in which the windows were dressed'.[56] By the 1960s, young mothers who had given up work on the birth of a child were looking for ways to escape the house, relieve their boredom and isolation, and provide their children with opportunities for play and learning. Jackie described how, as a young mother in the late 1990s, she found her community with women in the same circumstances:

> Yeah. First three years, I went to toddlers' groups. Like, I had my itinerary the first three years. I loved it. Me and Angela … three days a week, we went to the toddlers at the school … we used

to go to Langlands for the toddler group. I was the secretary and we were also fundraisers, we did the tuck shops, we knew all the teachers, we know all the parents. Loved it ... knew everybody.[57]

The PPA offered earlier generations of women like Jackie not only a ready-made community, but a stepping stone to further education and a career. Mother-helpers were encouraged to take courses run by the PPA and their involvement in managing a local group, raising funds and engaging with the local authority grew their self-confidence. Jackie returned to college part-time when her child was three years old, the beginning of a journey that ended with her becoming an educational psychologist.[58] However, as new town populations became more economically diverse and mothers of young children increasingly undertook paid work, the self-propelled character of community organizations began to falter. As early as 1966, the Scottish PPA was concerned about children living in high flats in new towns including in Cumbernauld and were awarded a government grant to establish provision in these areas.[59] By the late 1970s, playgroups were increasingly instigated by outside agencies, responding to social workers' concerns about young mothers' mental health and children at risk. Many families, it was reported, 'are suffering from the effects of ghetto living, unemployment and problems of family life'.[60]

The new towns also offered young people the opportunity to break away from the traditional sectarian and class-based structures commonplace in Scotland's cities. Although separate Catholic schooling was offered to new town residents, several of our interviewees remarked upon their ignorance about the difference between Protestant and Catholic faiths. Alison recalled:

[M]e and my friend were fourteen when we found out that she was Catholic and I was Protestant ... that didn't exist. Football exists but I don't know about that, but you'd sort of associate with being Christian 'cause you go to church but me and my friend didn't know about Catholicism and Protestants till we were, like, fourteen.[61]

And in Cumbernauld, Vicky recounted how everyone in her Protestant family:

talked about going to the Catholic church but it was because that was the only place that had anything for children. So, they would go, I think it was called, the social club was called Stairways, but they had like Saturday morning film clubs for kids and they did do family events. But it was open to all denominations, because there wasn't anything else.[62]

The development corporations had placed considerable emphasis on the presence of the two main Christian denominations in the new towns – church buildings were amongst the first to appear – but they overestimated the extent to which active faith shaped community, despite the claims of the churches themselves that they formed 'the largest voluntary caring agency in the town' with provision for all generations via youth groups, playgroups and lunch clubs for the elderly.[63]

Gang culture had a long history in the housing schemes of Glasgow and Edinburgh, and revived in the 1970s as unemployment and drug culture began to make inroads in working-class areas.[64] Although in the early days of Cumbernauld the only gang was said to be teetotal and called themselves 'the Lemonade Boys', in later years a less benign gang culture manifested here.[65] Andy knew that the local Cumbernauld gang had a presence in the Centurion bar of the Golden Eagle Hotel. However, his friendship group met at Larry's Record Bar in Cumbernauld Town Centre: 'it was all music. 'Cause maybe you couldn't get in the pubs, you certainly knew ... aye, and looking back on it, you'd made a conscious decision to avoid the kind of violence that was around'.[66] He and his friends listened to music and drank beer in his bedroom, or attended gigs at the Cottage Theatre which, as Andy recognized in retrospect, seems unusual: 'Aye, and the idea of teenagers going in a theatre, I mean, normally you'd think that's a really hard thing to get young people to do. But they had bands on.' Likewise Sarah also discovered an alternative culture from that of her middle-class parents at the Cottage Theatre where she took part in drama and folk music and discovered politics. She described herself as living in 'two different worlds'.[67]

While the coming-of-age feature film *Gregory's Girl*, set in Cumbernauld in 1980, painted a portrait of adolescent *ennui* in a relatively safe environment where teenage crushes were the most exciting happening, for some young people, the lack of excitement suggested more risky paths. Nicky grew up in East Kilbride in the 1980s where, in his words, 'nothing happened'. He vividly described how the music of a local band, The Jesus and Mary Chain, alcohol and drugs provided an escape from 'the shittiness':

> But I remember the singer said the only thing you can do in East Kilbride is just take drugs, cause it's that bad ... East Kilbride is shit, man. There's nothing to do. All the exciting things were happening in Glasgow. East Kilbride was ... nothing happened in East Kilbride, you went to the crap discos where they played crap music, and you know. You got a bottle of Thunderbird and got leathered before you're even out and then woke up in the forest outside the Dollan Baths at two in the morning ... we'd become teenagers. That's what happened. When you're doing things like that or kind of looking for something a bit more. Getting chased off of folk isn't as much of a buzz as, you know, going out and doing acid and listening to ... music. Slightly more exciting ... We were always really into music and possibly to our detriment looked towards these people as the guiding lights and heroes and wanted to do what they had done, which was take lots of drugs and listen to music and be in bands and stuff. That was our escape from the shittiness of East Kilbride. Cause it was pretty crap, I mean ... there was no doubt about it. Once you're hitting 20, 21, you're like I need to get out of this dump, man. Seriously. Cause nothing happens in East Kilbride. At all.[68]

Nicky moved to Glasgow to escape the 'small-town mentality' and vowed never to return, a sentiment shared by others for whom the new town was a constraint on exploring new identities. 'I was keen to get away,' recalled Alison, 'but also although I couldn't put it into words, I kinda recoiled against the kind of homophobia.'[69] After moving to Edinburgh to go to university she would go on to volunteer at Milestone House, a hospice for people who were HIV positive.[70] However, discussions of attitudes towards alternative sexualities or lived experience were rare in our interviewees' accounts. Just as the new towns were predominantly white spaces, so it would appear that traditional attitudes towards sexuality were also dominant.

Serviced community

The community infrastructure of the pioneer years remained in use as the new towns matured, but a combination of generational change and the increasing provision of amenities – predominantly shopping and leisure centres but also cultural facilities like the Howden Park Centre in Livingston,

Irvine's Magnum and the Dollan Baths in East Kilbride – helped to forge what we term 'serviced communities'. The emphasis increasingly became the satisfaction of individual needs, although, as noted above, elements of this idea had always been part-and-parcel of social development practices. As the new towns grew, commercially run amenities, such as cinemas, arrived, while shopping itself was increasingly seen as a leisure activity rather than a chore. In East Kilbride, evidence that people were travelling to Glasgow for shopping and entertainment challenged the authorities' desire for a self-contained, balanced community and prompted consideration of wider provision in the town.[71] Sylvia recalled how she often visited Glasgow at weekends. 'I remember one of my neighbours saying to me when I lived in St Leonards saying, "Oh I'm going into toon," and I went "oh you're going onto the town centre?" and she said "Noo I mean I'm going into Glasgow, I don't call [East Kilbride] the toon," and I thought, "oh right".'[72] As was discussed in Chapter 1, by the late 1950s there was growing demand here for social amenities as well as better retail provision.[73] In response, the new 'town centre', developed by a commercial organization on behalf of the development corporation, was opened in 1959, expanded in 1962 and again in 1971, with further extensions in 1989 and 2003.[74] The town gained its first cinema in 1968, seating almost 1,000, offering 'a new focus for family leisure in a new community', and allowing East Kilbride to compete with Glasgow for this kind of entertainment. In the same year the town's landmark swimming pool – the Dollan Baths – was opened and the corporation also announced the development of an experimental sports and leisure centre for young people – the Key Centre discussed in Chapter 1 – with a gym, sports equipment, photography studio, metal and woodworking shops and a coffee lounge.[75] 'East Kilbride breathes wellbeing' was the assessment of a reporter from the *Scottish Daily Express* on a visit in 1968 which praised the town's amenities. The Town Centre was so convenient for a mother with four children taking a break in a self-service café: 'I'd never have got it all done in Glasgow – the shopping, I mean – and still have time for a coffee before he comes in for his lunch,' while Scotland's largest swimming pool was a mecca for families.[76]

The first phase of Cumbernauld's Town Centre, opened in 1968, was conceived as the 'much needed heart' of the town, with its shopping, leisure and parking facilities. In a household survey of 1985, under-cover shopping provision in the town centre was praised, as was the Tryst Sports Centre, although the absence of facilities for teenagers was also widely commented on.[77] Meanwhile in 1976 in Glenrothes, the development corporation proudly announced that 'to the ordinary townspeople probably the most significant event in the year has been the virtual completion of the new all-enclosed Town Centre. There is little doubt that this has brought a new spirit of belonging to the town' (Figure 8.2).[78] Seven years later, there was still no town centre hall and no central library, though the 'provision of new sports facilities and a new entertainment centre incorporating two cinemas, bars, a bingo hall and discotheque had gone some way to meeting [residents'] needs'.[79] The Kingdom Centre, as it was known, continued to expand in succeeding years, incorporating a restaurant-ballroom-public house complex and community halls but mainly seeing the expansion of shopping facilities including large supermarkets, influenced by the 'the rapid spread in this country of the American and Continental phenomenon called the "hypermarket", "superstore", or "out-of-town shopping centre"'.[80] In comparison with most other Scottish towns, leisure and retail provision in the new towns was streets ahead.

By the 1970s, then, facilities were increasingly centralized in major developments, sometimes commercially financed and often seen as magnets for a much wider catchment area. Irvine's

FIGURE 8.2 Glenrothes Town Centre (© The Scotsman Publications Ltd).

Magnum Centre is the epitome of this trend. Opened in 1976, the Magnum was, as we saw in Chapter 5, a multipurpose leisure and entertainment facility, conceived as a 'focal point for recreational, cultural and leisure activities' which in its early years was the second most popular tourist attraction in Scotland.[81] Just over ten years later it was enhanced by a new maritime museum and a beach park as well as an expansion of retail space in the town.[82] We discuss the place of this development in the town's economic landscape in Chapter 9. Such emphasis on the provision of retail and leisure services from the 1970s mirrors developments elsewhere as towns and cities competed to attract visitors and their discretionary income. These were new forms of serviced sociability for different generations and interest groups, provided by a combination of public-sector and private-sector bodies, and showing the ways in which the 'dynamic social democracy' of the 1970s was able to adapt to new priorities and agendas.[83]

Conclusion

When new town residents talk about community, they are apt to hark back to a traditional notion of face-to-face social connection rooted in kinship and place, and characterized by reciprocity. Maggie from Glenrothes clearly had this model in mind when she offered a negative assessment of the present-day new town: 'I would say in as much there's a sense of community, a lot of it's pretty negative. Like, people will come together if they've got a moan. I don't think people are as inclined to help their neighbours necessarily.'[84] Whilst this form of community may well have existed for the pioneers, it soon transmogrified into elective networks based on need or shared interests, and determined by life stage or personal preference, especially amongst the second- and third-generation residents. Community-building efforts by the authorities were effective for some in the short term, but as the towns grew, people began to call for better leisure, culture and retail provision and these facilities replaced the neighbourhoods as spaces for community cohesion around specific interests such as music or sport. From the 1980s, as Liz Spencer and Ray Pahl have argued, it became increasingly difficult to reconcile the desire for personal autonomy with social connection.[85] Housing mobility and tenancy changes, commuting for work, frenetic lifestyles, and improved forms of communication enabled wider social and friendship networks, described as 'hidden solidarities', which have less rootedness in place. This shift has been described as the story of 'retreat' away from the original optimistic efforts to build community towards 'individual affirmation'. Unlike the residents of Milton Keynes who, according to Guy Ortolano, campaigned for services and housing as 'social democratic subjects', with community being created through activism, we have seen little to compare in the Scottish new towns, at least not whilst under development corporation governance.[86] Yet perhaps this absence also attests to the overall success of the new towns in satisfying their residents during the early decades.

Notes

1. See the discussion of the Stevenage Survey undertaken by Raphael Samuel, in Jon Lawrence, *Me, Me, Me: The Search for Community in Post-War England* (Oxford: Oxford University Press, 2019), 88–100. This project was undertaken under the auspices of the Institute for Community Studies, led by Michael Young and responsible for numerous publications rooted in observations of people's everyday lives. See Holly Smith, *A Historical Perspective. Michael Young's Legacy and the Work of the Institute for Community Studies*, online at https://youngfoundation.b-cdn.net/wp-content/uploads/2023/11/History-of-TYF-and-ICS-A4-draft.pdf?x59628 (accessed on 30 April 2024).
2. Lawrence, *Me, Me, Me*, 100–102. See also, for discussion of supposed binaries, Alistair Fair, 'Privacy, the Housing Research Unit at the University of Edinburgh, and the Courtyard House, 1959–70', *Architectural History* 65 (2022): 327–58 (p. 353).
3. For example, Ferdynand Zweig, *The Cumbernauld Study* (London: Urban Research Bureau, 1970); Peter Willmott, 'Some Social Characteristics of a Scottish and an English New Town', *Town Planning Review* 34, no. 4 (1964): 307–16.
4. Derek Lyddon, Cumbernauld Overview, *New Towns Record* (Planning Exchange CD-ROM set, 1996).
5. P.D. McGovern, 'The New Towns of Scotland', *Scottish Geographical Magazine* 84, no. 1 (1968): 1. See also J.B. Cullingworth, *Environmental Planning Volume III: New Towns Policy* (London: HMSO, 1979).
6. Guy Ortolano, *Thatcher's Progress: From Social Democracy to Market Liberalism through an English Town* (Cambridge: Cambridge University Press, 2019), 146–70.
7. For this argument: Alistair Fair, '"The Needs of New Communities": Social Development, the New Towns, and the Case of Milton Keynes, c. 1962–87', *Modern British History* 35, no. 4 (2024): 261–77.
8. See for an example of idealism: Elizabeth Mitchell, *The Plan That Pleased* (London: Town and Country Planning Association, 1967). On alternative forms of community to that envisaged, see the example of Milton Keynes in Ortolano, *Thatcher's Progress*, 170–82, and, on the Thamesmead estate in London, Sam Weatherell, *Foundations: How the Built Environment Made Twentieth Century Britain* (Princeton, NJ: Princeton University Press, 2020), 93–106.
9. Lawrence, *Me, Me, Me*, 66.
10. Mike Savage, 'The Politics of Elective Belonging', *Housing Theory and Society* 27, no. 2 (2010): 115–35.
11. Liz Spencer and Ray Pahl, *Rethinking Friendship. Hidden Solidarities Today* (Princeton: Princeton University Press, 2004).
12. 'The Day When a New Town Loses Its Tag', *The Manchester Guardian*, 10 September 1958.

13 See Tom Hulme, *After the Shock City: Urban Culture and the Making of Modern Citizenship* (London: Royal Historical Society, 2019), 22–3; Alistair Fair, 'Community Centre: New Housing Estates in Scotland', in *Reconstruction: Architecture, the Built Environment and the Aftermath of the First World War*, ed. Neal Shasore and Jessica Kelly (London: Bloomsbury Visual Arts, 2023), 119–42. See also Fair, 'The Needs of New Communities'.
14 Leslie Higgs, *New Town. Social Involvement in Livingston – An Account of the Formative Years* (Glasgow: Maclellan, 1977), 127.
15 Ibid., 195.
16 Ibid., 154. Similar efforts were made in East Kilbride including meetings to welcome new residents and to inform them of the aims of the new town: 'Meeting of New Residents', *Hamilton Advertiser*, 25 October 1958.
17 Higgs, *New Town,* 130. See also Ortolano, *Thatcher's Progress*, 179, on the limits of community as conceived by the development corporation when faced with activism.
18 Interview with James, East Kilbride, 2011.
19 Higgs, *New Town,* 152.
20 *Cumbernauld News*, 2 June 1961.
21 See Lawrence, *Me, Me, Me,* 65–6, which suggests that while religion may have fostered social connection it 'did not provide an instant, unproblematic sense of community'.
22 Zweig, *Cumbernauld Study,* 58.
23 Savage, 'Politics of Elective Belonging'.
24 Interview with Nicky, East Kilbride, 2016.
25 Interview with Sarah, Cumbernauld, 19 July 2022.
26 Interview with Bill, Glenrothes, 26 November 2021.
27 Interview with Lucile, Muthill, 25 November 2021.
28 Interview with Beryl (and Jenni), Auchtermuchty, 30 June 2022.
29 Interview with Jim B, Glenrothes, 4 November 2021.
30 Interview with Andy, Cumbernauld, 31 May 2022.
31 Livingston Development Corporation, Annual Report 1973.
32 Interview with Alison (and Annie), Glenrothes, 22 October 2021.
33 Interview with James, East Kilbride, 2011.
34 Elspeth Farmer and Roger Smith, 'Overspill Theory: A Metropolitan Case Study', *Urban Studies* 12, no. 2 (1975): 151–68.
35 See Lawrence, *Me, Me, Me,* 88–90 and on Crawley new town, B.J. Heraud, 'Social Class and the New Towns', *Urban Studies* 5, no. 1 (1968): 33–58.
36 Interview with Rhonda, Glenrothes, 21 October 2021.
37 Interview with Sylvia, East Kilbride, 2011.
38 Interview with Helena, East Kilbride, 2011.
39 Interview with Vicky, Glasgow, 5 August 2022.
40 See Mike Savage, 'Elizabeth Bott and the Formation of Modern British Sociology', *The Sociological Review* 56, no. 4 (2008): 579–605.
41 'East Kilbride Plans Chummy Pubs', *Evening Times*, 5 June 1959.
42 Alistair Fair, 'Citizenship, Community, and the New Towns in Post-war Scotland', in *The New Town of Edinburgh: An Architectural Celebration*, ed. Clarisse Godard-Desmarest (Edinburgh: John Donald, 2019), 193–216 (pp. 208–9).

43 Fair, 'The Needs of New Communities'.
44 'Clubs Foster Community Spirit', *Glasgow Herald*, 28 August 1968.
45 North Lanarkshire Archives [NLA], UT 059-06, Cumbernauld Development Corporation, *Activities and Societies in Cumbernauld* (1970).
46 Mark Clapson, *Invincible Green Suburbs, Brave New Towns: Social Change and Urban Dispersal in Postwar England* (Manchester: Manchester University Press, 1998), 185.
47 *Grapevine*, October 1976. Copy at National Library of Scotland.
48 Higgs, *New Town*, 164–5.
49 Lawrence, *Me, Me, Me,* 129–30.
50 Interview with Annie (and Alison), Glenrothes, 22 October 2021.
51 *Social Survey 1971: Report on Results of Social and Economic Survey Carried Out in 1971* (Glenrothes Development Corporation, 1971), 31–3.
52 'Homes for Sons and Daughters', *Glasgow Herald*, 7 November 1967.
53 Interview with Shirley, East Kilbride, 2011.
54 Institute of Education [IoE], PLA/PPA 2/9, Jennifer Overton of Scottish PPA to SED, 26 September 1966.
55 National Library of Scotland, Scottish Pre-School Playgroups Association, *Annual Report*, 1972–3.
56 *Hamilton Advertiser*, 11 December 1954.
57 Interview with Jackie, Larkhall, 22 June 2022.
58 See Lynn Abrams, *Feminist Lives: Women, Feelings and the Self in Post-War Britain* (Oxford: Oxford University Press, 2023), 206–13.
59 IoE, PLA/PPA 2/9, letter from SPPA, 26 September 1966.
60 IoE, PLA/PPA 2/28, *Playgroups in Areas of Need* (1977), produced by working party of Scottish Executive Committee of the PPA (1977).
61 Interview with Alison (and Annie) Glenrothes, 22 October 2021.
62 Interview with Vicky, Glasgow, 5 August 2022.
63 Cumbernauld Development Corporation, Annual Report 1993.
64 See Angela Bartie, 'Moral Panics and Glasgow Gangs: Exploring "The New Wave of Glasgow Hooliganism," 1965–1970', *Contemporary British History* 24, no. 3 (2010): 385–408.
65 *Daily Record*, 10 April 1957 (as quoted in Lyddon, Cumbernauld Overview, *New Towns Record*).
66 Interview with Andy, Cumbernauld, 31 May 2022.
67 Interview with Sarah, Cumbernauld, 19 July 2022.
68 Interview with Nicky, Glasgow, 2016.
69 Interview with Alison (and Annie) Glenrothes, 22 October 2021.
70 Ruth McCabe et al., 'Milestone House: The Story of a Hospice for People with HIV/AIDS', *Journal of the Royal College of Physicians of Edinburgh* 52, no. 1 (2022): 73–9.
71 'East Kilbride's Lack of Social and Business Centre', *The Manchester Guardian,* 10 September 1958.
72 Interview with Sylvia, East Kilbride, 2011.
73 'East Kilbride Amenities', *Glasgow Herald*, 12 September 1958.
74 'Prime Minister Visits "Opportunity Town"', *Hamilton Advertiser*, 2 May 1959.
75 'Take One!', *Scottish Daily Express*, 2 December 1968.
76 'Don't Get Run Over by the Prams', *Scottish Daily Express*, 5 September 1968.

77 Lyddon, Cumbernauld overview, *New Towns Record*.
78 Glenrothes Development Corporation [GDC], Annual Report 1976.
79 *Glenrothes Development Profile*, 1983, 22. Copy at National Library of Scotland.
80 GDC, Annual Report 1971.
81 'Magnum Leisure Centre', *Irvine Scotland*, online at https://irvinescotland.info/irvine_that_was/the-magnum-leisure-centre/ (accessed on 30 April 2024); 'Remembering the Legendary Magnum Leisure Centre', *Glasgow Live*, online at https://www.glasgowlive.co.uk/news/history/remembering-legendary-magnum-centre-glasgow-22776730 (accessed on 30 April 2024).
82 Irvine Development Corporation, Annual Reports 1986–9.
83 Ortolano, *Thatcher's Progress*, 17, 254–7; Otto Saumarez Smith, 'The Lost World of the British Leisure Centre', *History Workshop Journal* 88 (2019): 180–203.
84 Interview with Maggie, conducted online, 1 February 2022.
85 Spencer and Pahl, *Rethinking Friendship*.
86 Ortolano, *Thatcher's Progress,* 183.

9

Opportunity

The new towns were regarded by residents as places of opportunity, offering better jobs and education for the pioneers plus the promise of the same for future generations. Education delivered in brand new schools represented a fresh start for pupils and teachers alike, the latter often embracing innovative approaches. These schools seemed to offer a route to social mobility for children at a time of growing confidence in the importance of education.[1] In time, it was hoped that school-leavers would find jobs in the well-paid modern workplaces and skilled industries of the new towns, thereby creating a sustainable economy and society, whilst also contributing to Scotland's economic and social modernization. All of this was the manifestation of the post-war settlement, encompassing (at least in theory) equality of opportunity or meritocracy. In relocating, the pioneers were demonstrating their belief in, and desire to be part of, this revolution.

Given the centrality of jobs and education to the new town vision, it is surprising that so little attention has been paid to these aspects of their history. New towns have only a walk-on part in broader discussions of Scottish economic trends, principally as locations for the diversification of the economy.[2] Yet jobs were what enabled people to move to the new towns in the first place. The desire of new towners to 'better themselves' was not so much about the consumption of material goods *per se*, but rather meant attaining the economic and cultural resources that would underpin different lifestyle choices for themselves and, crucially, the next generation.[3] This was part-and-parcel of what Lawrence terms the ability to reconcile self and society, aligning personal betterment with general social progress. Shiny new schools and modern factories and offices were seen as the routes to this reconciliation (Figure 9.1).[4]

However, unlike other aspects of the new town experience which generate public and private narratives, people's accounts of their education and working lives offer us comparatively little to work with. The pioneers are an exception, perhaps, because moving to the new town was predicated upon a job, usually for the man in the household. The older men amongst our interviewees constructed coherent, linear accounts of working lives, ascribing their success in conventional terms with a move to a new town. For example, Bill grew up in Glenrothes. His father was a miner who relocated his family from Glasgow to the new town 'for a better life'. Bill was never going to follow in his father's footsteps. On leaving school, he took a job in a printing laboratory. This job was to be short-lived, but Bill gained qualifications at night school and graduated to work in the health and safety sector: 'The only one thing, I'll give my father his due on one thing, what he said was, "if you get a job, try and get some study with it"'.[5] Eventually,

FIGURE 9.1 Glenrothes High School (© Fife Council, John Porteous, Edinburgh).

after studying with the Open University, he became a college lecturer in Cumbernauld. Bill's career was intertwined with his life story, each change of job and qualification opening the door to more satisfying employment. Similarly coherent stories were told by male interviewees who had moved to the new towns to work for the development corporations, their working lives easily aligning with the new town narrative and being constitutive of their sense of self.[6] It was not uncommon for such men to move between the new towns across Scotland and beyond as part of their career trajectory, assisted by informal networks and a familiarity with the 'new town way' of doing things.

Yet for some of our female interviewees and the younger generations who entered the labour market in the recession years, the dominant new town narrative of opportunity made much less sense. Women who took a series of part-time, unskilled jobs in factories, retail and in domestic-related work such as cleaning have little to say about work that was often poorly rewarded and unfulfilling. Angie, who left school in Cumbernauld in 1982, told a story characterized by misstarts and dashed expectations. On leaving school:

> I wanted to look after kids. I didn't know what that meant, I wanted to look after kids. I came out of school, not really sure of anything. My dad got me a job in a furniture shop, I worked in there for a wee while and thought, no, this is not what I want to do. Left there. Got a job in R.S. McColls [newsagents] up the town centre. Worked there and that is when I met my husband. With being with him I had spoken about working with kids and all that. He is like, why don't you go to college. I am like, do you think there is a course? I did my nursery nursing.[7]

But when Angie completed her course, she 'couldn't get a job, couldn't get a job at all. Joys of Maggie Thatcher, couldn't get a job ... I ended up going to work in factories'. Angie had little to say about this work; like many of our female respondents, employment like this was instrumental and provided no insight into who she was. Similarly Audrey, who straight out of school took a job she enjoyed with a firm of chartered accountants in Glasgow, became a school dinner lady after moving to Glenrothes.[8] Both Audrey and Angie found their way back to study and employment in the education sector later in life, a nonlinear, interrupted pattern followed by many women during the 1980s and 1990s. Those who left school in the late 1970s and 1980s only to join a Youth

Training Scheme experienced narrative discomposure as their experiences failed to align not only with their own expectations but with the hopes of their parents.[9] Unlike the men we interviewed, women and later generations were often more comfortable speaking about the pioneers than their own experiences.

This chapter considers experiences of education and work against a background of changing economic fortunes. The new towns were not immune from the economic problems associated with the end of the post-war boom, although they were cushioned by their lesser reliance on traditional heavy industries and by their identification as regional 'growth points'. As adaptable and resilient communities, the new towns remained a focus of industrial and economic policy, perhaps favoured as they had attracted skilled, young, economically active households, something which was certainly used as a selling point in marketing the towns to multinational companies. Throughout the 1980s, the five new towns secured 40 per cent of all overseas investment to Scotland and 31 per cent of all jobs created.[10] Yet the reality was that with a comparatively young population and a small proportion of retired people, there was a continuing need for new jobs; in 1970 almost 40 per cent of East Kilbride's population was under the age of twenty. Each new town had economic development sections working closely with government agencies to generate employment, and there were often financial concessions for incoming firms.

We focus here on the young as it was they who encapsulated the social mobility narrative – the 'ladder of opportunity' – in the initial waves of relocation and who, in successive generations, experienced the ups and downs of the new town economies. With new towns being young places in the early decades, the fortunes of the young mirrored the fortunes of the towns.[11] But women, too, are a key part of this story. From the 1960s, women's work was central to new town economies and thus to new town narratives. As employers created part-time and shift work to attract mothers, sometimes accompanied by nurseries, and as white-collar work in public service became established, women found new social networks, a degree of autonomy and, in some case, social mobility. By the 1970s and 1980s, a period of growth in public-sector employment (especially in health and social care), the phenomenon of the woman returner to education facilitated women's career advancement at a time when the jobs that had drawn men to the new towns, predominantly in engineering and Research and Development, were beginning to diminish, raising concerns in the government. Thus in terms of life chances, the new towns held out the prospect of bettering oneself and one's children, but the window of opportunity for climbing the ladder was time-limited. For those who left school in the late 1970s and early 1980s who no longer walked straight into a job, the disappointment had added poignancy in the new towns, places freighted with hope for a better life.

First generations: Opportunity

Susan was brought up in Cumbernauld in the 1960s. She recalled: 'I think my most emotional memory is the first day at my new school because there was about 100 years of educational theory and practice between what happened in Glasgow and what happened to me on that first day.'[12] Susan's vivid memory encapsulates the modernity of educational provision in the new towns. New school buildings, new teaching methods and teachers straight out of college reflected the aspiration of the pioneers for their children, contrasting with the more traditional provision of established schools, a contrast that Susan was all too aware of when she transferred to a primary school in Cumbernauld village. She recalled:

> It was so antiquated that the children were assessed with exams at the end of every term and every subject … Then all the scores were added up. Then they were allocated a seat in class according to the position that we were in. This was in '69. So this was the very opposite of what had been going on in the new town. And just really a reminder of what the new town was achieving. That wasn't being achieved elsewhere. I absolutely hated it.

She recalled how the teachers in her first new town primary school – dressed like Mary Quant and driving their own cars – provided role models:

> But you had an example in front of you of somebody who was quite exciting and had quite an exciting car that seemed to be theirs. So, it was an example of what you could aim for and that made a difference … they had all the latest equipment for doing number work. Really Montessori style equipment and Montessori-informed learning through play and doing all of that. The sand tray, the water play. All of it and it was just night and day. And that on its own was worth moving to Cumbernauld for. Housing aside because people were moving for the housing, but they were getting this as well. They were getting a completely different education deal for their kids.

Similarly for Michael, Susan's husband, who also grew up in Cumbernauld, exposure to an education system that encouraged learning and creativity was transformative. 'I think we really benefited from that as a very working-class family. That stimulated our intelligence and I think helped us to really take to school. So, I think the education was really important for us … I think that was important for us educationally but also socially and culturally because it gave us all a certain confidence' (Figure 9.2).[13]

The 1960s was an era of educational reform.[14] These changes were arguably turbo-charged in the new towns, where new schools were designed with flexible spaces for 'child-centred' learning in informal ways and were run by new headteachers keen to embrace new teaching methods. Despite the breaking down of some barriers, as noted in Chapter 8, the continued provision of denominational segregation in primary and secondary schooling as prescribed in law in Scotland was maintained in the new towns. An education that not only provided qualifications but also offered all children the opportunity to discover their strengths and interests was manifested in the transition from the post-war bipartite secondary education model (involving 'junior secondary' and selective 'senior secondary' schools) to comprehensivization, which was introduced across Scotland after 1965 by Scottish Office Circular 600. This democratization of secondary schooling was a response to changing parental expectations as well as a new world view that prioritized equality of opportunity.[15] Parents demanded opportunities for their children, not just as a gateway to the better 'clean' jobs that were increasingly available but as a key part of the post-war settlement, and encompassing more than qualifications. Michael described school as 'a revelation because it gave us exposure to so many stimulating experiences'.[16] Yet Michael's horizons were also expanded when he accompanied his family to live overseas for four years. When he returned as a teenager, he realized that his friends, who had not ventured far from Cumbernauld, had

FIGURE 9.2 Kildrum Primary School, Cumbernauld (© Architectural Press Archive / RIBA Collections).

a 'more limited cultural experience'. 'Living in another country, having that cultural awareness, language and subsequently becoming educated. Because when I came back, I started to do well at school.' And despite leaving school at sixteen and entering the job market just as the 1970s recession hit, Michael's educational and cultural experience led him to evening classes and then university as a mature student.

The new towns sought to achieve a balance of job opportunities between white-collar and manufacturing employment. White-collar job opportunities were a particularly important part of the new town vision, designed to maintain a stable population and dissuade young people with qualifications from leaving. For example, Glenrothes in 1970 was concerned that it could not 'without assistance attract administrative and clerical jobs in sufficient numbers to cater for the increasing numbers of well-qualified late school-leavers'.[17] GDC believed that it was in the gift of central government to 'help greatly by relocating in Glenrothes jobs for these worthy young people. Otherwise they will be forced to leave the town or to take employment which does not match their abilities.' Similarly, East Kilbride Development Corporation worked to attract white-collar employment for the 'increasing number of school leavers seeking office work', and when it attracted a major civil service employer in 1978 the same impetus was cited.[18] East Kilbride, Glenrothes, Cumbernauld and Livingston all housed large white-collar employers: the Ministry of Overseas Development and the Inland Revenue (now HMRC) in East Kilbride; Fife Health Board and the regional council in Glenrothes; a Government Computer Centre at Livingston; Cumbernauld had a branch of the Inland Revenue. Employees in Cumbernauld were also offered transport to the new National Savings Bank headquarters in south Glasgow. Andy remarked that 'it wasn't unusual for you to leave school and then just start at the Savings Bank'.[19] Vicky recalled how her mother 'worked at the tax office for thirty years. But I think, it's interesting because although it's not exactly coal mines or the steel industry, it was as much a, you know, the women's industry … '.[20]

For those who moved to the new towns as adults, the job was a means to an end – a house and a different kind of family lifestyle. Ronnie set his heart on moving to East Kilbride after taking a job with Rolls Royce aero engines, one of the early employers in the town. As a single man, he could imagine family life in the new town:

> I loved it. I was single! Working Rolls Royce, doing night shift, day shift. And I'd been there about a year and Dollan Baths opened up, so every Friday after a night shift we'd go for a cup of coffee or a cup of tea and a butter toast before we went to the swimming baths … Every house I went to, all these flats, walking about and by the front door a wee bit of grass … lovely smell and fresh air, quite high up. I said to myself, if ever I get married, I'm gonna come down here to live.[21]

Once married, Ronnie imagined bringing up his children in the new town. 'So I kept thinking about East Kilbride, East Kilbride, East Kilbride.' Ronnie found new work at an engineering company, Lyle and Barclay, and began a more 'civilized' life where people socialized at home or in the Rolls Royce or Royal Air Force Club instead of the men-only pubs of Glasgow. In order to afford the higher cost of living in the new town, Ronnie took a second job in a bar while his wife also worked two jobs: as a cleaner at Rolls Royce, and in the kitchen at another of the town's major employers, Motorola.

The new towns were initially predicated on the traditional family model of a male breadwinner and stay-at-home wife but, as Ronnie's experience illustrates, women's work was often critical to achieving the lifestyle to which a family aspired.[22] New town rents could be hard to meet on a single salary. Ronnie recalled 'a lot of women taxi drivers' in East Kilbride, but this was just one of the many work opportunities taken up by married women, facilitated initially by the expansion of part-time and shift work in manufacturing industries, with electrical engineering and clothing dominating. In Glenrothes in 1969, the development corporation surmised that 'presumably, mothers who would not otherwise go out to work are having to do so under the economic pressures that afflict young couples in a new home, or have been induced to do so by the attractive conditions in the town's modern industries'.[23]

During the 1970s, women's participation in the new town labour force was consistently higher than the national figures; by 1978, 50 per cent of women were in employment in East Kilbride, with Cumbernauld only slightly lower at 45 per cent.[24] Whilst high living costs are one explanation for this pattern, women's desire to return to the workplace for their own satisfaction was also a factor.[25] In this way, the new towns anticipated the dual-income family model that was soon to become commonplace as women returned to the workplace once their children were at school.[26] But in the early 1980s, with dramatic decline in employment in manufacturing and especially in electrical engineering, women's jobs were particularly vulnerable to economic fluctuations and changes in the organization of production. Part-time workers were the first to become redundant.[27] Although the service sector was growing, with work in retail and catering as well as white-collar employment, women remained overwhelmingly in lower-grade jobs.[28] Angie's experience in Cumbernauld reflected this trend: she could only find work in factories despite having trained as a nursery nurse. Opportunities for many women continued to be constrained by not only gender but also age. While public-sector white-collar jobs were far more likely to go to young women straight out school, factory employers preferred older women who they regarded as more compliant and more likely to stay.[29] The solution for some of these women, for whom factory or other blue-collar occupations were unsatisfactory, was to return to study – as will be discussed in more detail shortly.

An education fit for the modern age and the prospect of a 'good' job for one's children were at the core of the aspiration narrative of the pioneer generation. Dual-earner families worked hard to achieve a different kind of lifestyle for themselves certainly, but they projected their aspiration onto their children in the expectation that they would have more choices than they themselves had. But the achievement of this dream was dependent on an economic landscape in which jobs with prospects were plentiful. By the 1980s this was no longer the case.

Second generation: Shrinking horizons

Ronnie had moved easily from job to job, pursuing his dream. But when his son Graham left school in 1988, the economic environment had changed. Examining the testimonies of residents of Sheppey in Kent in the 1980s, Jon Lawrence identifies 'the evaporation of the easy optimism about "progress"'.[30] Sheppey, of course, was no new town. But that easy optimism started to dissipate in the new towns, too. Following the recession of the late 1970s, the new towns lost many of their founding companies: Burroughs in Glenrothes and Cumbernauld; British Leyland (as the British Motor Corporation had become) in Bathgate, near Livingston. Irvine's manufacturing sector was concentrated in just five companies, and the town was seen as being particularly at risk. By 1987, 20.4 per cent of Irvine's population was unemployed, on a par with other former industrial areas.[31] In 1981, the Scottish *New Towns Bulletin* tried to be bullish about employment prospects, but Glenrothes had lost 1,200 jobs in the previous year; two major employers had left East Kilbride.[32] Livingston engendered hope: 800 jobs were promised in 1981 with the Nippon Electric Company's arrival.[33] Jim moved to Glenrothes in 1972. His early career had taken him from an apprenticeship in the naval dockyards to a job in the early days of computers with National Cash Registers in Dundee. But 'moving to Glenrothes, I looked around and this was the hive of electronics, there was Burroughs, Beckmans, there was Rodime which made discs for computers, the one I joined was a company called General Instruments, oh and there was Marconi, Marconi-Elliotts.'[34] With Jim's experience the 'world was your oyster'. Yet these newer employers were not necessarily open to all. School leavers, on the other hand, were confronted at this time with a bleaker employment landscape; they often lacked the skills or experience to take advantage of work in the developing electronics and computing sectors.

Concern in the early 1980s about youth unemployment contrasted with earlier optimism. All of the development corporations participated in the various government programmes – Manpower Services Commission schemes, the Community Enterprise Programme and Youth Training Schemes – as a means of providing school and college leavers with work experience as a route to full employment. Cumbernauld seems to have been especially concerned about its young people. In 1985, the development corporation noted:

> In common with the rest of Britain, Cumbernauld faces the problem of unemployment, but more acutely because of our exceptionally high proportion of young people. The Corporation has always done its utmost for the youth of the town, and recent activities include very substantial Youth Training Scheme and Community Programme Projects, the establishment of an Information Technology Centre, the development of existing space at Westfield as a group of Managed Workshops, and the planned provision of purpose built Managed Workshops at Lenziemill. Our activities range from helping young people to start their careers, to doing everything possible to assist young businessmen and entrepreneurs to develop their ideas into reality. We are now in the International Year of the Youth, and particular efforts will be made to mark it with activities of real value.[35]

Graham's career path mirrored this new environment. Graham was grateful for his education in East Kilbride – 'All brand new, big lecture theatres, fancy classrooms, a greenhouse. It was just brilliant. Fantastic. You just thought this is what the world's like, you don't realize that not every town has that.'[36] Yet in his experience, 'it was a bloody zoo'. He described the school as having 'no leadership and academic aspiration'. Graham left at seventeen:

> I managed to try and navigate a course of academia, stay on the fifth year. You stay until fifth year, teachers look at you like, 'why are you still here? Get out and get a job!' So it didn't really have any promotion of academic learning. It didn't have any system like that sort of thing that says, aspire to a thing … get out as quick as you can.[37]

While this absence of encouragement may seem surprising, schools may have become complacent in the earlier context of near full employment in the new towns. And some parents, who had moved to the new town precisely to give their children a better start in life, found it difficult to envisage alternative futures. Moreover, the expansion of higher education in the 1960s and the 1990s largely bypassed the new towns. Although during 1963–4 there was some consideration of founding a new university at Cumbernauld, none of the Scottish new towns ultimately gained such an institution, though Heriot-Watt University co-taught a digital technology course at Glenrothes Technical College while East Kilbride was the location, from 1963, of a research nuclear reactor which was ultimately used by several universities.[38] Graham's birth cohort was less upwardly mobile, measured by educational attainment, than previous generations.[39] As Mandler demonstrates, changing labour markets, a reduction in teacher-training numbers and a lack of knowledge of the higher education system amongst many working-class families placed limits on widening participation in this period.[40]

Graham's interest in computing had been nurtured at his primary school, and on leaving school he took a series of IT jobs in East Kilbride with small companies developing their computing systems – perhaps the beneficiaries of Scotland's Enterprise Trust opening a business centre in East Kilbride in 1985 to support 'small business operations' and 'create jobs'.[41] None, though, could offer him a career. A job with a pizza company in the town after 'bumming around for a year' was transformational. Graham made friends and found a new social scene in Glasgow and applied for university:

And I just didn't think I would be going, and I didn't know anyone else who was going from my school. Everyone was just dispersing this way, getting a job that way. But I didn't really have an idea, so I thought I'll do this, I'll apply to uni. Cause I wouldn't mind doing computing and I found it hard to get a job that was fulfilling … I honestly thought maybe I'd get in as a software engineer. Maybe get a degree. So I just thought I'd apply to Glasgow to do computing science … I was beginning to emerge feeling I had my own views and my own decisions to start making in life, and they weren't necessarily dovetailing [with] my dad's ideas … there comes a point when you start to diverge maybe. You know. I thought, I don't really want to do the same job my dad did. I don't necessarily want to go the same route. I've got to start picking my own. So told him I applied and he went, 'you'll not get in. Just wasting your time, when are you getting a job?' And I got the offer, he was dumbfounded. So I said, that's what I'm gonna do, I'm gonna start uni in October 1992'. And he was, yeah, he was surprised that I was gonna pursue that and I was gonna get in and all the rest of it. So I did.[42]

It took several years after leaving school, as well as a university degree, for Graham to find rewarding work with a computing firm in Edinburgh. Graham's career could only develop outside the town. As was the case elsewhere, the economic downturn punctured people's trust in the post-war promise of progress and prosperity; people fell back on personal strategies to move forward with their lives.[43] East Kilbride was no longer a guarantee of security, as it had been for Graham's parents. In 1981, in the wake of job losses in the town, East Kilbride's local welfare group, the Claimant Advisory Service, suggested that 'Scotland's oldest new town was now a problem town' with high unemployment, unaffordable rents and fuel disconnections and claiming that 'groups of people could often be seen huddled in the plaza in the town centre for warmth'.[44] Yet when asked to reflect, Graham still used the language of opportunity and aspiration to describe his relationship with the new town:

A sort of feeling of, this might sound a bit corny, but when you move out to a place like that, your sort of approach to life feels like one where you're gonna … it felt aspirational, it really did. I don't mean that in a corny way. That's what I felt. We could do things, there was opportunity. Maybe that's the better word. There was opportunities. All that felt positive to me.[45]

Although Graham's continued optimism about the new town appears to contradict his own experience, this enduring power of the 'new town dream' is not uncommon even when the reality of people's lives complicates or challenges the original optimism of that dream.

Women – Making something of themselves

As Graham and his contemporaries sought to carve out a career during the 1980s and early 1990s, women of the pioneer generation were beginning to reassess their lives. The limitations on women's career trajectories, which were felt especially acutely once children had started school, were addressed in the period by the upsurge in women returning to education. Moira recalled how she taught evening classes in Cumbernauld to adult returners taking advantage of so-called 'special recruitment' for primary school teachers as early as the 1960s to address shortages:

[T]his was aimed at mothers whose kids were well-on in school. So, I was teaching some women who were sitting their Highers at the same time as their children and that was a fabulous experience ... I had such a good time teaching those classes because the women they wanted to make something of themselves, they had left school far too early, all of them were saying.[46]

Susan similarly recalled her mother's generation who had had their children young 'developing themselves' in the 1970s by taking college courses.[47] Moira ascribed their motivation in part to living in a new town: 'So, there were all these things in the new town that I think a lot [were] inspired by the fact that you were in the new town and people really wanted to make something of themselves.'

By the 1980s, the mature woman returner to study could see her investment in herself pay dividends, fuelled by the expansion of the health and social care sector.[48] As we have already noted, Audrey left her Glasgow secondary school at the age of fifteen and walked into a clerical job. Following marriage, a move to Glenrothes and children, Audrey returned to the labour market when her youngest child was seven: 'I got a job in the school dinners because that was great hours for, you know, you could get home in time and you could get holidays and everything.'[49] As her children became less dependent, she decided to go to college:

[B]ecause I'd left school at fifteen and I thought, you know, you were looking for night schools and different things to do, and I thought 'I'm going to go to college' and they had the college in Glenrothes so I thought 'I'll apply for that' so I got in to do English and I went to do just 'O' Level English at the time and the tutor said 'you're wasting your time, do Highers' so I did Higher English at the college and Gail came with me and went into the wee crèche and it was only one day, it was a Wednesday morning and when we were finished I'd to run down the hill to where the buses went to put her on the bus to go to the nursery, the proper nursery, but she went to a crèche ... Oh I loved it, I loved it.

But when her marriage 'fizzled out' and her children became teenagers, Audrey was set on a job at the hospital: 'Aye well when I did my English I decided ... I was going to go to the tech in Kirkcaldy to do the nursery nurse course cause I wanted a job in the hospital and they were taking nursery nurses into Forthpark Hospital.' After a series of jobs in childcare and education, Audrey ended her career in educational support at the local high school.

The electronics and semi-conductor sector that had given Jim so many opportunities was also a major employer of women with Livingston at the centre of so-called 'silicon fever'.[50] The development corporation was assiduous in attempts to attract Japanese business to the town, even going so far to produce the 'Discover Livingston' brochure in Japanese.[51] By 1980, a high technology park had been established at the Kirkton campus with the anticipation of 1,000 jobs. This was shortly followed by the arrival of Integrated Power Semiconductors with the promise of 350 jobs and the much-heralded opening of Britain's first raw silicon plant (the Japanese manufacturer SEH-Europe-Ltd) in 1985. In turn, these major companies attracted smaller concerns in the electronics sector.[52] By 1988, high-tech industries accounted for 45 per cent of the town's manufacturing employment (Figure 9.3).[53] However, the majority of the jobs on offer were monotonous and at best semi-skilled. Janet, who worked in one of the semi-conductor plants recalled that the engineers and technicians were men but that

FIGURE 9.3 Mitsubishi factory, Livingston, 1984 (© The Scotsman Publications Ltd).

the operators were women, and they were ones who handled the silicon wafers. This was hazardous work, exposing workers to toxic chemicals. The workers' protective suits protected the wafers, not the operators.[54] Health issues were reported, ranging from headaches and burns to nosebleeds and, in Janet's case, eye problems. In a 'Scottish Eye' documentary, former workers including Janet recounted a raft of health and safety failings. For Janet, one of the underlying reasons for workers' complacency about conditions in the plant was the insecurity of employment:

> There aren't a lot of jobs there's … there's very few interestin' jobs if you're unskilled. A lot of the operators were very scared to speak up in case they lost their jobs and they were seen as troublemakers. But lots of them brushed aside and said, och it's … we're no workin' with anything dangerous here. But Ah felt that attitude, they were frightened. A lot of them were frightened because the management would come down on them if they were seen to be causing trouble. And there was only a few people would actually speak out.[55]

The reinvention of the new towns as hi-tech hubs brought jobs, overwhelmingly filled by women. By the 2000s, this sector of the economy was quickly contracting following the dot-com collapse and with the shift of jobs to cheaper locations elsewhere in the world. Once again, as with the economic shock that hit the more traditional manufacturing sector in the 1980s, it was women who were the victims.

Reimagined economies

In 1988 Cumbernauld launched a marketing campaign – still remembered even in the 2020s – with the call and response strapline: 'What's It Called? Cumbernauld!'. The campaign, which included television adverts, was the latest in a series of publicity efforts undertaken by all the development corporations since the 1960s which courted businesses and residents with brochures and marketing films; the latter reached a pinnacle with the surreal 1977 'thriller', *Cumbernauld Hit*. The objective of the 1988 campaign was to 'heighten the image and improve perceptions of Cumbernauld – its skills, successes and energy', though more practically it was designed to attract inward investment, taking advantage of 'the reservoir of highly skilled and adaptable labour in the area and the fact that Central Scotland has more graduates per head of population than anywhere else in Europe'.[56] Cumbernauld was beginning to reimagine itself, with leisure and shopping facilities given greater prominence than the industrial and service sector. Just two years later, an eighteen-year-old gymnast was one of the faces of a 'new generation' in Cumbernauld. Sinead Lyons was reported to have said:

> I regard myself as having grown up with Cumbernauld as well as in it. I have enjoyed watching the development of our sporting facilities, in particular the Tryst, where I practise … Like most young people in the town I am looking forward to the opening of the new Hollywood Bowl, and of other new leisure facilities which I hope will he provided in the future. Cumbernauld works as a town for me because it is young, attractive and exciting. Wherever life takes me, I will always know that I couldn't have had a better start.[57]

Cumbernauld's relentless optimism belied major changes in the town's profile, encompassing the decline of manufacturing and its replacement with the service sector. But it was in Irvine, a new town that had struggled economically almost from its inception, that this shift was most stark.

When Irvine's *New Town Plan* was published in 1971, there was optimism that ever-reducing working hours would create vast amounts of time for recreation (as was discussed in Chapter 5). The results included the Magnum for leisure and sports, along with the shopping centre, and the beach park.[58] However, storm clouds were looming. In 1976, at just the moment that the new towns programme started to be cut, Irvine Development Corporation (IDC) commented that there was 'little solace to be found' in the fact that the town's 'percentage of jobless' was lower than other industrial towns in north and central Ayrshire, as the whole region's 'situation' was 'as bad as, and in some cases much worse than, many of the deprived areas of the Central Scotland belt'.[59] Moreover, with a rapid increase in population envisaged in the town, as well as the 'increasing number of school leavers unable to obtain the white-collar jobs for which they are most suited', it was stated that the development corporation would have to 'be more active than ever in its campaign to redress the present imbalance in this field'. There were fears of social problems arising from 'a dangerous void' in the failure of the regional council to provide local community facilities 'in the new, rapidly expanding, outer housing areas' and especially 'at a time of disturbingly high levels of teenage and adult unemployment'.

Although manufacturing jobs remained – notably at the busy Ailsa-Volvo bus factory – high unemployment was an issue in Irvine and Ayrshire throughout the 1980s. While the other development corporations consistently presented a positive view of their achievements in attracting industry, IDC instead focused on the deficiencies of the Ayrshire economy, arguably to make a case for additional Scottish Office support. Irvine, like the other new towns, continued to rely on attracting manufacturing companies to locate in the town, often to offset those closing or leaving the town and relocating elsewhere. Fred, who grew up in Irvine and had been in continuous employment as an engineer, found himself being made redundant in the 1980s. Initially he was re-hired and redeployed to another department, but he knew that this was far from certain long term. As a reserve fire-fighter he decided to take the risk of going full-time and re-training. This involved working away from home during the week when his children were growing up and studying in the evenings to progress through the ranks, but allowed him and his wife to build a good life for themselves in the town.[60]

Irvine's solution to its long-term economic malaise was to embrace and diversify into the 'leisure industry' in the 1980s. The towns' coastal location ensured that it was the new town most suited to attracting tourists and day-trippers from Glasgow. Throughout the 1980s and well into the 1990s, IDC produced glossy brochures advertising the town's attractions. The Magnum's variety of uses ensured that it was popular with locals and visitors alike, attracting a million people annually in the late 1970s and 1980s.[61] Nevertheless, the leisure industry could not provide the same number of jobs as the large factories closing in this period, and Irvine never really became more than a regional destination.

Oral history evidence from Irvine highlights how residents found different ways of traversing this shifting economic landscape. When Donna left school in 1983, as the eldest of four children, she felt that further study was not an option. Money was always tight in her house as although her father was a skilled tradesman, a glazier, he 'earned a pittance', in Donna's words.[62] Her mother had worked in a variety of cleaning jobs from when Donna was young and eventually relied on Donna to help with her younger siblings, getting them ready for school in the morning when her mother was already away to work. Her parents had moved to Irvine when Donna was fourteen years old to escape the violence they had experienced living in Easterhouse in Glasgow. They worked hard to afford the increased cost of living in Irvine including the higher rent for their three-bedroomed house. Upon leaving school Donna secured a place on a youth training scheme (YTS) working for the development corporation, describing this as a happy time in which they supplemented the basic wage offered by the YTS. Everyone in her cohort was offered permanent jobs, and for Donna this was a route into a career working in the local government.

Heather, however, had a very different experience of the YTS. Her parents had bought their own house in 1958, before Irvine's new town designation, after 'living in rooms' in the town. Her father progressed from working on the railways to commuting to work in an insurance office in Glasgow. Her mother had cleaned people's houses before Heather was born but did not work afterwards. On leaving school at sixteen, Heather took a secretarial course before finding work in a dentists' office, funded by the YTS. After a year she was made redundant to be replaced by another YTS trainee; there was no opportunity to stay and progress. She soon found a job working as an administrator for the community development team at the council, where she stayed for over a decade.[63] Heather's husband Stephen also left school at sixteen, but his successful work trajectory – a first job with British Telecom, opportunities to undertake training in IT systems, and setting up his own consultancy firm whilst completing a degree with the Open University – was more common for men of his generation with opportunities for gaining qualifications offered alongside paid work, something that appears less in women's work lives.[64]

While all of these individuals reflect positively on their lives in Irvine, they do not invoke the notion of the 'new town dream' that was evident in narratives of the earlier new towns. The opportunity offered by those places was perhaps not as certain for those families relocating to Irvine in the 1970s. For example, Fred's parents were 'old Irvine' people who lived in the town before designation; Fred disputes the extent to which Irvine could even be considered a new town in the mould of the others. Similarly, Heather's parents only decided on Irvine because it was easy for her father to commute to Glasgow. Meanwhile Kenny, whose parents were also 'old Irvine' people (having bought a house in the town in 1954), had to leave his home town in order to achieve his ambitions.[65] He was supported by his physics teacher and attained a scholarship from Rolls Royce to study at university in Edinburgh.

At the turn of the 1990s, IDC finally seems to have adopted the boosterism of the other new towns, emphasizing the growth of the electronics industry in employing 15 per cent of the local workforce which had in turn accounted for the reduction of unemployment from 22 per cent to 10.6 per cent in five years.[66] This was described as a 'performance hardly equalled anywhere else in Scotland'. Such confidence involved further expansion of training and economic development organizations in the region to encourage IT training among company personnel and young people with the skills they would need for a changing workplace. Yet the development corporation was running out of time to build on this momentum and achieve its objectives before wind-up in 1996.

Arguably the Magnum has, in the popular or collective memory of the West of Scotland, come to symbolize Irvine new town. However, in the context of a life narrative approach, the Magnum is afforded little time. While it was well-used and the site of happy memories of seeing bands and enjoying a variety of sports – even Nicola Sturgeon MSP, who grew up in Irvine, fondly recalled the 'pink leg warmers and day-glo orange' at Frosty's ice-skating disco – it was a facility that was taken for granted.[67] Yet its closure in 2009 and recent demolition speaks to wider themes concerning the legacy of the new town. Arguably this is analogous with the development corporation itself. Some people mourn the loss of the Magnum, despite it being run down and needing renovation. Similarly, for some, wind-up was unremarkable: IDC had done its job and was no longer needed. For others it marked a more decisive change in the town which meant it was no longer a special place, as was the case in the other new towns.

Conclusion

For a relatively short time, the new towns largely delivered on their promises with regard to opportunity. Schools were not only designed to be fit for the late twentieth century but provided a comprehensive education in well-equipped facilities, and according to some respondents, the chance to transcend class boundaries. This was easier to achieve in an era of plentiful employment. In all the new towns, with the exception of Irvine, skilled jobs for the early new town settlers, especially men, met expectations. Opportunities of jobs with prospects for women opened up with the establishment of major white-collar employers in the towns and in the health and education sectors, which provided mature women with routes back to the workplace. By the 1980s however, the economic landscape meant the new town dream was harder to achieve, especially for the young. School leavers could no longer walk into a job in their hometown; higher qualifications were increasingly the gateway to careers but accessing that level of education meant leaving the new town and finding work elsewhere too. While the architecture and planning of the new towns, especially Irvine, adapted successfully to new contexts during the 1980s and 1990s, policymakers' vision of a balanced community in which people would live, work and remain into old age could not be sustained when people needed or wanted to leave to pursue individual lives that had outgrown the town where they had grown up.

Notes

1 Peter Mandler, *The Crisis of the Meritocracy. Britain's Transition to Mass Education since the Second World War* (Oxford: Oxford University Press, 2020). On the relationship between architecture and schooling, see Catherine Burke and William Whyte, 'The Spaces and Places of Schooling: Historical Perspectives', *Oxford Review of Education* 47 (2021): 549–55. And on England: Catherine Burke, '"Inside out": A Collaborative Approach to Designing Schools in England, 1945–1972', *Paedagogica Historica* 45, no. 3 (2009): 421–33; Geraint Franklin, '"Built-in Variety": David and Mary Medd and the Child-centred Primary School, 1944–80', *Architectural History* 55 (2012): 321–67.

2 West Central Scotland Plan Team, *West Central Scotland Plan* (Glasgow: WCS Plan Team, 1974), 120; Neil Hood and Stephen Young, *Multinationals in Retreat: The Scottish Experience* (Edinburgh: Edinburgh University Press, 1982). Also see the limited reference to new towns in Jim Phillips, Valerie Wright and Jim Tomlinson, *Deindustrialisation and the Moral Economy in Scotland since 1955* (Edinburgh: Edinburgh University Press, 2021).

3 Jon Lawrence *Me, Me, Me*: *The Search for Community in Post-War England* (Oxford: Oxford University Press, 2019), 99.

4 Lawrence, *Me, Me, Me,* 100.

5 Interview with Bill, Glenrothes, 26 November 2021.

6 Interview with William, Muthill, 3 November 2021 and interview with Alexander, Glenrothes, 9 November 2021.

7 Interview with Angie, Cumbernauld, 17 June 2022.

8 Interview with Audrey, Glasgow, 5 November 2021.

9 Interview with Janet, Livingston, 3 April 2023. Janet would also later return to education and worked in community education, primarily in youth work.

10 Robina Goodlad and Suzie Scott, 'Polo Mint Planning: A Review of Strategies for Housing in the Scottish New Towns' (Glasgow: Centre for Housing Research, University of Glasgow, 1991), 35.

11 James M. Livingstone and Andrew J.M. Sykes, *East Kilbride 70: An Economic and Social Survey* (Glasgow: University of Strathclyde, 1970), 8.

12 Interview with Susan, Cumbernauld, 1 June 2022.

13 Interview with Michael, Cumbernauld, 25 August 2022.

14 On England and Wales see Laura Tisdall, *Progressive Education? How Childhood Changed in Mid-Twentieth-Century English and Welsh Schools* (Manchester: Manchester University Press, 2019).

15 More progressive models of education had been suggested in a Scottish context from the 1940s. Although comprehensive education was officially introduced in the 1960s, there had already been experimentation in Scotland. See Lindsay Paterson, *Scottish Education and Society since 1945: Democracy and Intellect* (Edinburgh: Edinburgh University Press, 2023). Also see Cathy Howieson, Linda Croxford and Daniel Murphy, 'The Experience of 50 Years of Comprehensive Schooling in Scotland', *Education, Citizenship and Social Justice* 12, no. 1 (2017): 8–23. Mandler, *Crisis of the Meritocracy*, 50–71 emphasizes the importance of parental demand as far as comprehensivization was concerned in an English context.

16 Interview with Michael, Cumbernauld, 25 August 2022.

17 Glenrothes Development Corporation [GDC], Annual Report 1970.

18 East Kilbride Development Corporation [EKDC], Annual Reports 1961, 1978.

19 Interview with Andy, Cumbernauld, 31 May 2022.

20 Interview with Vicky, Glasgow, 5 August 2022.

21 Interview with Ronnie, East Kilbride, 2016.

22 See Jo Foord, 'Conflicting Lives: Women's Work in Planned Communities', PhD dissertation, University of Kent, 1990, 20.

23 GDC, Annual Report 1969.

24 Foord, 'Conflicting Lives', 350.

25 See Lynn Abrams, *Feminist Lives: Women, Feelings and the Self in Post-war Britain* (Oxford: Oxford University Press, 2023), 196–221.

26 On the dual income family see Helen McCarthy, *Double Lives: A History of Working Motherhood* (London: Bloomsbury, 2020).

27 Foord, 'Conflicting Lives', 369.

28 Ibid., 388–9, 395.

29 Ibid., 407.

30 Lawrence, *Me, Me, Me*, 193.

31 Goodlad and Scott, 'Polo Mint Planning', 36–7.

32 *New Towns Bulletin*, 30 October 1981.

33 Ibid.

34 Interview with Jim M, conducted online, 28 October 2021.

35 Cumbernauld Development Corporation [CDC], Annual Report 1985.

36 Interview with Graham, Glasgow, 2016.

37 Several interviewees from various new towns expressed similar sentiments about their school experience: Interview with Angie, Cumbernauld, 17 June 2022; interview with Janet, Livingston, 3 April 2023; interview with Diane, Livingston, 3 April 2023; and interview with Stephen, Kilwinning, 20 June 2023.

38 For Cumbernauld: National Archives (London), papers in UGC 7/241; for Glenrothes, National Records of Scotland, ED26/1281; East Kilbride: SUERC, online at https://www.gla.ac.uk/research/az/suerc/about/ (accessed on 2 May 2024). Cumbernauld competed with locations including Ayr and Perth but lost out to Stirling.

39 Mandler, *Crisis of the Meritocracy*, Figure 3.1, 218.

40 Ibid., 96–113.

41 EKDC, Annual Report 1985.
42 Interview with Graham, Glasgow, 2016.
43 Lawrence, *Me, Me, Me*, 193.
44 *Scotsman*, 5 September 1981.
45 Interview with Graham, Glasgow, 2016.
46 Interview with Moira, Doune, 12 August 2022.
47 Interview with Susan, Cumbernauld, 1 June 2022.
48 See Eve Worth, *The Welfare State Generation: Women, Agency and Class in Britain since 1945* (London: Bloomsbury, 2021); Abrams, Feminist Lives, 206–13.
49 Interview with Audrey, Glasgow, 5 November 2021.
50 'Silicon Fever', Channel 4 documentary, 1990, https://vimeo.com/585525943/849bec81df (accessed on 4 April 2023).
51 Livingston Development Corporation [LDC], Annual Report 1973. East Kilbride also actively courted Japanese business, and similarly produced literature in Japanese.
52 LDC, Annual Report 1984–5. Motorola established a semi-conductor plant at East Kilbride.
53 LDC, Annual Report 1988.
54 'Silicon Fever'.
55 Ibid.
56 CDC, Annual Report 1988.
57 CDC, Annual Report 1990.
58 Irvine Development Corporation [IDC], Annual Report 1976.
59 Ibid.
60 Interview with Fred, Irvine, 12 June 2023.
61 *The Herald*, 20 March 2018.
62 Interview with Donna, Irvine, 12 June 2023.
63 Interview with Heather, Kilwinning, 20 June 2023.
64 Interview with Stephen, Kilwinning, 20 June 2023.
65 Interview with Kenny, Edinburgh, 15 June 2023. (Also interview with Lucile, Muthill, 25 November 2021; interview with Fraser, Edinburgh, 7 December 2021; interview with Phyllis, conducted online, 30 May 2022).
66 IDC, Annual Report 1990.
67 *Glasgow Times*, 14 March 2018.

Conclusion: 'Out of the Ordinary'

In its 1992 Annual Report, East Kilbride Development Corporation (EKDC) reflected on its work during the previous forty-five years. Its aim since 1947, it reported, had been 'to provide new homes in pleasant surroundings', but while that goal had persisted, it had been achieved 'perhaps not in the way originally envisaged'.[1] Three years later, and with wind-up approaching, the 1995 Annual Report concluded that East Kilbride 'has survived dramatic changes in urban policy'.[2] EKDC's claims highlight two points which were at the core of Scotland's new towns programme. First, the fundamental role of these places in offering quality housing in tandem with economic and social change. As we have seen, the new towns provided opportunities for individuals and families to make new lives for themselves, centred to a greater degree than hitherto on the home. They were places of architectural creativity, whether in terms of avant-garde radicalism or, more usually, a quieter yet no less transformative 'mainstream modernism'. They contributed to (and indeed anticipated) broader shifts in housing tenure, first as places dominated by public-sector renting and then by driving owner-occupation. Second, in referring to East Kilbride's 'survival' and the extent to which housing was provided in ways 'not originally envisaged', EKDC invoked the evolving character of the new towns programme and indeed the malleable nature of the 'new town' label. The 'dramatic changes in urban policy' noted by EKDC were severalfold: the post-war agenda to refocus population and industry away from Glasgow; the refocusing of attention on Glasgow in the mid-1970s (which informed the termination of EKDC's short-lived role in developing Stonehouse new town); the planned winding-up of EKDC and the loss of the town's special status.

The new towns were the ultimate manifestation in Scotland of the post-war settlement, in which people were to be provided with good homes, jobs and opportunities to thrive (Figure 10.1). Holistically conceived to be more than simply housing estates, they were intended to be, as a 1963 film suggested of East Kilbride, 'the right kind of place in which to live a full life'.[3] In exploring the architectural and social history of these towns, this book began by stating three aims. The first was to consider how the new towns were implicated in the project to build a modern Scotland. Here a long, yet focused, view has been necessary, as the new towns did not emerge solely from post-war policies, nor were they solely the manifestation of the ideas of such late-nineteenth-century writers as Ebenezer Howard. The new towns process offered a means for policymakers and planners to advance debates about Scottish urban form, the nature of the Scottish economy, and the location of population and industry. As a result of their important role in post-war regional policy, the new towns received the funding that enabled their designers to

FIGURE 10.1 Artist's impression of an industrial estate, Stonehouse, c. 1974 (Glasgow City Archives, with permission also from South Lanarkshire Archives).

create places which attracted international attention. For as long as the new towns were thought to be central to delivering economic growth, first through industrial diversification and then as 'growth points', their special status was maintained. Although reduced in scope after 1976, with the de-designation of Stonehouse and cuts to other new towns, notably Irvine, in the light of the 1974 West Central Scotland Plan, the retention in Scotland of the new towns programme until 1996 highlights the extent to which these places remained strategically important.[4] They reveal a changing balance of public- and private-sector involvement that demonstrates the evolving character of post-war social democracy and its constituent organizations, right through to the end of the twentieth century.

Nonetheless, developments since the 1960s have also taken the idea and image of a 'modern Scotland' in other directions that have little to do with the new towns. There were comparatively well-paying jobs in post-war new town factories; the development corporations generally did well in ensuring new investment when companies left the towns during the 1960s and 1970s. However, in the light of de-industrialization and globalization, the over-reliance of the new towns on manufacturing employment was not sustainable, and other places have challenged the status and position of the new towns within Scotland. The discovery of North Sea oil not only brought wealth and new employment, but also, in its focus on the north-east of the country, created a counter-magnet to central Scotland in a way which in some ways advanced the decentralization agenda far further – geographically and indeed economically – than the new towns had done. At the same time, Glasgow's regeneration since the 1970s has been accompanied by the provision of new cultural infrastructure, a strong retail sector (at least until the early 2020s), and the effective rebranding of the city as a desirable destination for investment and tourism. In addition, Scotland's booming financial and cultural sectors in the 1990s and 2000s promoted the growth of Edinburgh, as did administrative devolution after 1999, the growth of IT-related businesses, the expansion of higher education, and rapidly increasing levels of international tourism, focused on questions of 'heritage' rather than modernity.[5]

The second focus of this book has been the architecture and planning of the new towns. The broad outlines of this story are well-known, ranging from the low-density 'Mark 1' new towns of the late 1940s via the 'urbanity' of Cumbernauld in the 1950s to the greater complexity of Livingston and Irvine in the 1960s and 1970s. We have set the new towns in the contexts of social and economic policy as well as architectural debate; we have also highlighted the need to see these places *in toto*, rather than focusing only on set-piece buildings. The new towns offered an unfolding set of answers to the question of what a 'modern Scotland' might look like: a story of multiple modernities, of mainstream practice as well as radicalism, created by a range of people and organizations. It was, at least until the late 1970s, an image intended to stem emigration and to attract investment and incomers from elsewhere. It is difficult to enumerate how many new town residents might otherwise have looked elsewhere to satisfy their ambitions, but the way in which East Kilbride's population target was repeatedly raised attests to the desirability of new town life for an aspirational section of Scotland's population, even where that life potentially came with financial and social pressures.

In terms of architectural impact, policymakers' specific ambition that the new towns might improve the standard of Scottish housing design bore some fruit. The Scottish Special Housing Association (SSHA) – itself in some ways intended to be exemplary – under Harold Buteux during the 1960s and 1970s produced developments of real design quality, including its mini 'new towns' at Tweedbank and Erskine, as well as smaller estates such as Great Junction Street in Edinburgh. Local-authority design perhaps inevitably remained more mixed, but the 'modern vernacular' of some 1960s/1970s new town design reflected broader trends, seen in places such as Burntisland and Dysart as well as parts of Edinburgh, while by the 1970s even Glasgow – long the Scottish Office's *bête noir* as far as housing design and policy was concerned – was commissioning ambitious, considered projects such as the Woodside estate. And although private-sector housebuilding largely ploughed its own furrow, some firms, such as Mactaggart and Mickel, did embrace 'modern vernacular' from the 1970s onwards; Mactaggart and Mickel also worked with the architect Roan Rutherford after the winding-up of Irvine Development Corporation.[6] Meanwhile the Scottish Office's parallel ambition that the new towns might encourage higher local-authority rents saw similarly mixed progress, with rents in fact falling in real terms during the 1950s and further pressure being applied to increase them.[7]

Third, we have focused on the interactions between the built environment and the everyday lives of individuals and communities (Figure 10.2). Our oral history interviews attempted to access not only the lived experience of moving to and living in a new town but also the meaning of those experiences. It became clear that new town narratives are embedded within the bigger story of the post-war settlement, in particular the Welfare State as enabler of opportunity. The articulation of the 'new town dream' as a collective or public history is notable, especially in the earlier new towns, resembling an emigration narrative. The children of the pioneers speak of their parents' bravery and sacrifice in moving for a new life for their children. Positive stories abound of a period – until the 1970s – when change was something to be welcomed. The exponential

FIGURE 10.2 Bespoke signage, Irvine (Photo: Miles Glendinning).

growth in married women in work and the consequential shift in gender roles, the embrace of greater privacy, and the lessening of sectarian and even class differences are all of a piece with an interpretation of post-war Britain that emphasizes the sense of collective benefit gained from post-war prosperity and investment in people. Yet for others these changes could be harder to navigate, and by highlighting these challenges we seek to nuance both the ideas of the 'new town dream' and the 'new town blues'. Furthermore, our oral history showed that it can be difficult to relate lived experience specifically to architecture and the built environment, a consequence, perhaps, of the way people relate to place. Our respondents were able to talk about place but rarely the built environment more specifically, especially everyday private spaces. One might conclude that memories are organized not around buildings but people (Figure 10.3).

The fluidity of the new town idea also emerges as a key theme with wider resonances for the study of planned urbanism in Britain and beyond. Although there was an established framework of policy and practice, the development corporations were able to adapt and survive in response to changing economic circumstances and political ideologies, whether by embracing and facilitating owner-occupation, working with the private sector, creating new kinds of business park, or innovating when it came to town centre design. It is difficult to single out one 'new town' experience. All five towns were very different places, and Stonehouse would have been different again. Furthermore, the new town 'vision' was not static, as each town changed over time.

Over the decades, the new towns have begun to feel more like other places. Some buildings have lost their distinctiveness through refurbishment and 'modernization'; others have been

FIGURE 10.3 Cumbernauld streetscape, late 1960s (© The Scotsman Publications Ltd.)

demolished. The failure to maintain the built environment and landscaping to the earlier high standards has sometimes resulted in a sense of loss for long-term residents as well as those former residents returning to visit relatives. In this respect, the winding-up of the development corporations marked a significant policy departure which had profound consequences for the built environment as well as the ways that residents experience and perceive these places, being sometimes associated in life narratives with a feeling of abandonment. As Linda stated of Cumbernauld, 'I can't understand why we've been kind of neglected. I don't understand the psyche, … it's almost like when … the North Lanarkshire Council took over in 1996, they basically said, "we're not bothered about you anymore"'.[8] This sense of neglect is perhaps all the more real given the narratives of opportunity which drew residents to the new towns in the first place, and which our interviewees invoked in articulating their own histories.

The strategies currently being employed to reimagine the new towns could take account of and celebrate what was distinctive in their heritage in developing visions for the future. Addressing how residents feel about their local history and heritage, about what matters to them in their place and celebrating these ideas in visions for the future could empower individuals and their communities to reinvigorate pride in what the new towns were, what they meant, their significance and what they could be in the future. And it is important to note, too, that the changes which these places have experienced should not be understood to mean that they have 'failed': they remain popular places to live, and it was clear in our oral history that residents care profoundly about them.

To end, we might return to East Kilbride in 1981. In that year, EKDC's chief architect commented on plans for the extension of the town centre. The aim, he concluded, was 'to produce something which was "out of the ordinary"'.[9] His turn of phrase could well be applied to the new towns programme more generally. As originally conceived, the new towns were very much 'out of the ordinary', presented to the world as and experienced by residents as such. They would be, as a 1969 film put it, 'experiments in design as well as in living',[10] places of considered planning and high-quality design. And yet, the ambition was that these places might in time become 'ordinary': they were intended to set a benchmark. In the contemporary world, with diminished public spending plus urgent social, economic and environmental challenges, the example of the new towns might similarly seem to be 'out of the ordinary', a development from another era with few useful lessons for the present. Yet the new towns offer two fundamental reminders: first, the potentially fruitful connections between socio-economic policy objectives and the careful planning of the built environment; and second, the value of good design. They also illustrate how these changes can be actively navigated by residents. These points are of lasting relevance as the project to build and rebuild 'modern Scotland' continues.

Notes

1. East Kilbride Development Corporation [EKDC], Annual Report 1992 [*New Towns Record* transcription].
2. EKDC, Annual Report 1995.
3. Scottish Moving Image Archive, *Town in the Making*, dir. Stanley Russell, 1963.
4. Industry Department for Scotland, *The Scottish New Towns: Maintaining the Momentum* (Edinburgh: Scottish Office, 1988); Industry Department for Scotland, *The Scottish New Towns: the Way Ahead* (Edinburgh: HMSO, 1989).
5. David McCrone, *Who Runs Edinburgh?* (Edinburgh: Edinburgh University Press, 2022).
6. Miles Glendinning and Diane Watters, *Home Builders: Mactaggart and Mickel and the Scottish Housebuilding Industry* (Edinburgh: RCAHMS, 2015), 167–9 and 183–6.
7. E.g. Department of Health for Scotland, *Rents of Houses Owned by Local Authorities in Scotland, 1958* (Edinburgh: HMSO, 1958); Tom Begg, *50 Special Years: A Study in Scottish Housing* (London: Henry Melland, 1987), 180–7.
8. Interview with Linda, Cumbernauld, 15 June 2022.
9. *East Kilbride News*, 20 March 1981.
10. Scottish Moving Image Archive, 1826, *New Towns*, 1969.

Interviewees

All interviews were conducted by Valerie Wright with the exception of the following:

- Interviews marked * were conducted by Lynn Abrams.
- Interviews marked ** were conducted in 2011 by Linda Fleming in collaboration with East Kilbride and District Housing Association, funded by a Scottish Government First Step Award at the University of Glasgow.
- Interviews marked *** were conducted in 2016 by Barry Hazley as part of a Leverhulme-funded project (RPG 10 2014-014).

The interviews are listed in chronological order by new town.

East Kilbride

**Cathy (anonymized), East Kilbride, 2011
**Helena (anonymized), East Kilbride, 2011
**James (anonymized), East Kilbride, 2011
**Shirley (anonymized), East Kilbride, 2011
**Sylvia (anonymized), East Kilbride, 2011
***Graham Marshall, Glasgow, 2016
***Nicky Forbes, Glasgow, 2016
***Ronnie Marshall, East Kilbride, 2016

Glenrothes

Rhonda Bissett, Glenrothes, 21 October 2021
Annie and Alison (anonymized), Glenrothes, 22 October 2021
Jim Miller, conducted online, 28 October 2021
William Rankin, Muthill, 3 November 2021
Jim Boyd, Glenrothes, 4 November 2021
Audrey Robb, Glasgow, 5 November 2021
Alexander Laird, Glenrothes, 9 November 2021
Iain Anderson, Kirkcaldy, 24 November 2021
*Lucile Black, Muthill, 25 November 2021

Bill Beckinridge, Glenrothes, 26 November 2021
Fraser Laird, Edinburgh, 7 December 2021
Maggie Murray, conducted online, 1 February 2022

Cumbernauld

Phyllis Kavannah, conducted online, 30 May 2022
Andy Locke, Cumbernauld, 31 May 2022
Susan (anonymized), Cumbernauld, 1 June 2022
Linda McCarall, Cumbernauld, 15 June 2022
Angie Docherty, Cumbernauld, 17 June 2022
Jackie Lyle, Larkhall, 22 June 2022
Beryl Cowling and Jennifer Whittle, Auchtermuchty, 30 June 2022
Sarah Breakey, Cumbernauld, 19 July 2022
Vicky (anonymized), Glasgow, 5 August 2022
*Moira Lawson, Doune, 12 August 2022
Michael (anonymized), Cumbernauld, 25 August 2022

Livingston

Diane Crompton, Livingston, 3 April 2023
Janet Wood, Livingston, 3 April 2023
Graham Menzies, Edinburgh, 24 April 2023

Irvine

Donna Hutchison, Irvine, 12 June 2023
Fred Howe, Irvine, 12 June 2023
Kenny (anonymized), Edinburgh, 15 June 2023
Heather Durnan, Kilwinning, 20 June 2023
Stephen Durnan, Kilwinning, 20 June 2023

Bibliography of Published Sources

Books and articles

Abrams, Lynn. *Oral History Theory*. London: Routledge, 2016.
Abrams, Lynn. 'Heroes of Their Own Life Stories: Narrating the Female Self in the Feminist Age'. *Cultural and Social History* 16, no. 2 (2019): 205–24.
Abrams, Lynn. 'The Self and Self-help: Women Pursuing Autonomy in Post-war Britain'. *Transactions of the Royal Historical Society* 29 (2019): 201–21.
Abrams, Lynn. *Feminist Lives: Women, Feelings and the Self in Post-war Britain*. Oxford: Oxford University Press, 2023.
Abrams, Lynn, and Linda Fleming. *Long Term Experiences of Tenants in Social Housing in East Kilbride: An Oral History Study*. Glasgow: University of Glasgow, 2011.
Abrams, Lynn, Barry Hazley, Ade Kearns and Valerie Wright. 'Aspiration, Agency and the Production of New Selves in a Scottish New Town, c.1947–c.2016'. *Twentieth Century British History* 29, no. 4 (2018): 576–604.
Abrams, Lynn, Barry Hazley, Ade Kearns and Valerie Wright. *Glasgow: High-rise Homes, Estates and Communities*. London: Routledge, 2019.
Abramson, Daniel. *Obsolescence: An Architectural History*. Chicago: University of Chicago Press, 2016.
Aldridge, Meryl. *The British New Towns: A Programme without a Policy*. London: Routledge, 1979.
Alexander, Anthony. *Britain's New Towns: Garden Cities to Sustainable Communities*. Abingdon: Routledge, 2009.
Bartie, Angela. 'Moral Panics and Glasgow Gangs: Exploring the New Wave of Glasgow Hooliganism, 1965–1970'. *Contemporary British History* 24, no. 3 (2010): 385–408.
Begg, Tom. *Fifty Special Years: A Study in Scottish Housing*. London: Henry Melland, 1987.
Bendixson, Terence. *The Peterborough Effect: Reshaping a City*. Peterborough: Peterborough Development Corporation, 1988.
Boughton, John. *Municipal Dreams: The Rise and Fall of Council Housing*. London: Verso, 2018.
Boyd, Gary A. *Architecture and the Face of Coal: Mining and Modern Britain*. London: Lund Humphries, 2023.
Bullock, Nicholas. *Building the Post-war World: Modern Architecture and Reconstruction in Britain*. London: Routledge, 2002.
Burke, Catherine. '"Inside Out": A Collaborative Approach to Designing Schools in England, 1945–1972'. *Paedagogica Historica* 45, no. 3 (2009): 421–33.
Burke, Catherine, and William Whyte. 'The Spaces and Places of Schooling: Historical Perspectives'. *Oxford Review of Education* 47 (2021): 549–55.
Cameron, Ewen. 'The Scottish Highlands as a Special Policy Area, 1886–1965'. *Rural History* 8 (1997): 195–216.
Campbell, Louise, Miles Glendinning and Jane Thomas. *Basil Spence: Buildings and Projects*. Edinburgh: RCAHMS, 2007.
Charlton, Susannah, Elain Harwood and Clare Price (eds.). *100 Churches 100 Years*. London: Batsford, 2019.

Clapham, David. 'Housing Pathways: A Post-modern Analytical Framework'. *Housing, Theory and Society* 19 (2002): 57–68.
Clapson, Mark. *Invincible Green Suburbs, Brave New Towns: Social Change and Urban Dispersal in Postwar England.* Manchester: Manchester University Press, 1998.
Clapson, Mark. 'Working-class Women's Experiences of Moving to New Housing Estates in England since 1919'. *Twentieth Century British History* 10, no. 3 (1999): 345–65.
Clapson, Mark. *A Social History of Milton Keynes: Middle England/Edge City.* Portland: Frank Cass, 2004.
Close, Rob. *Ayrshire & Arran: An Illustrated Architectural Guide.* Edinburgh: RIAS, 1992.
Close, Rob, John Gifford and Frank Arneil Walker. *Lanarkshire and Renfrewshire.* New Haven and London: Yale University Press, 2016.
Cohen, Deborah. *Family Secrets: The Things We Tried to Hide.* London: Viking, 2013.
Coleman, S.D. *Mental Health and Social Adjustment in a New Town: An Exploratory Study in East Kilbride.* Glasgow: University of Glasgow, 1965.
Collins, Chik, and Ian Levitt. 'The "Modernisation" of Scotland and Its Impact on Glasgow, 1955–1979: "Unwanted Side Effects and Vulnerabilities"'. *Scottish Affairs* 25, no. 3 (2016): 294–316.
Collins, Chik, and Ian Levitt. 'The Policy Discourses That Shaped the "Transformation" of Glasgow in the Later 20th Century: "Overspill", "Redeployment" and the "Culture of Enterprise"'. In *Transforming Glasgow: Beyond the Post-industrial City*, ed. Keith Kintrea and Rebecca Madgin, 21–38. Bristol: Bristol University Press, 2019.
Cowling, David. *An Essay for Today: The Scottish New Towns, 1947 to 1997.* Edinburgh: Rutland Press, 1997.
Crossman, Richard. *The Diaries of a Cabinet Minister*, Vol. 1. London: Book Club Associates, 1975.
Cullingworth, J.B. *Environmental Planning Volume III: New Towns Policy.* London: HMSO, 1979.
Cullingworth, J.B., and V.A. Karn. *The Ownership and Management of Housing in the New Towns: Report Submitted to the Minister of Housing and Local Government.* London: HMSO, 1968.
Damer, Sean. *Scheming: A Social History of Glasgow Council Housing.* Edinburgh: Edinburgh University Press, 2019.
Darling, Elizabeth. *Re-Forming Britain: Narratives of Modernity before Reconstruction.* Abingdon: Routledge, 2007.
Darling, Elizabeth. 'Towards Narratives of Modernity *after* Reconstruction'. In *Reconstruction: Architecture, Society and the Aftermath of the First World War*, ed. Neal Shasore and Jessica Kelly, xviii–xxv. London: Bloomsbury, 2022.
Darling, Elizabeth, and Alistair Fair. '"The Core": The Centre as a Concept in Twentieth-century British Planning and Architecture. Part One: The Emergence of the Idea'. *Planning Perspectives* 38, no. 1 (2023): 69–98.
Darling, Elizabeth, and Alistair Fair. '"The Core": The Centre as a Concept in Twentieth-century British Planning and Architecture. Part Two: The Realisation of the Idea'. *Planning Perspectives* 38, no. 3 (2023): 525–57.
Dellaria, Salvatore. 'A New Town and a Numbers Game: Runcorn, Merseyside and Liverpool'. *Planning Perspectives* 37, no. 2 (2022): 243–65.
Esher, Lionel. *A Broken Wave: The Rebuilding of England.* Harmondsworth: Penguin, 1981.
Evans, Hazel (ed.). *New Towns: The British Experience.* New York: Wiley, 1972.
Fair, Alistair. *Modern Playhouses: An Architectural History of Britain's New Theatres, 1945–1985.* Oxford: Oxford University Press, 2018.
Fair, Alistair. 'Citizenship, Community, and the New Towns in Post-war Scotland'. In *The New Town of Edinburgh: An Architectural Celebration*, ed. Clarisse Godard-Desmarest, 193–216. Edinburgh: John Donald, 2019.
Fair, Alistair. 'Privacy, the Housing Research Unit at the University of Edinburgh and the Courtyard House, 1959–70'. *Architectural History* 65 (2022): 327–58.
Fair, Alistair. 'Community Centre: New Housing Estates in Scotland'. In *Reconstruction: Architecture, the Built Environment and the Aftermath of the First World War*, ed. Neal Shasore and Jessica Kelly, 119–42. London: Bloomsbury, 2023.

Fair, Alistair. 'Stonehouse: Scotland's Last New Town, c. 1967–76'. *Urban History* 50, no. 4 (2023): 818–39.
Fair, Alistair. '"The Needs of New Communities": Social Development, the New Towns, and the Case of Milton Keynes, c. 1962–87'. *Modern British History* 35, no. 4 (2024): 261–77.
Farmer, Elspeth, and Roger Smith. 'Overspill Theory: A Metropolitan Case Study'. *Urban Studies* 12, no. 2 (1975): 151–68.
Franklin, Geraint. '"Built-in Variety": David and Mary Medd and the Child-centred Primary School, 1944–80'. *Architectural History* 55 (2012): 321–67.
Geddes, Jane, Ian Gow, Aonghus Mackechnie, Chris Tabraham and Colin Macwilliam. *Lothian*. New Haven and London: Yale University Press, 2024.
Gibb, Andrew. 'Policy and Politics in Scottish Housing since 1945'. In *Scottish Housing in the Twentieth Century*, ed. Richard Rodger, 155–83. Leicester: Leicester University Press, 1989.
Gifford, John. *Fife*. New Haven and London: Yale University Press, 1988.
Glendinning, Miles (ed.). *Rebuilding Scotland: The Postwar Vision*. East Linton: Tuckwell, 1997.
Glendinning, Miles. 'Cluster Homes: Planning and Housing in Cumbernauld New Town'. *Twentieth Century Architecture* 9, *Housing the Twentieth Century Nation* (2008): 131–46.
Glendinning, Miles. *Modern Architect: The Life and Times of Robert Matthew*. London: RIBA, 2008.
Glendinning, Miles, and Diane Watters. 'Cumbernauld New Town: Reception and Heritage Legacy'. *Architektura & Urbanizmus, Journal of Architecture and Town Planning Theory* 46 (2012): 271–87.
Glendinning, Miles, and Diane Watters. *Home Builders: Mactaggart and Mickel and the Scottish Housebuilding Industry*. Edinburgh: RCAHMS, 2015.
Glendinning, Miles, and Stefan Muthesius. *Tower Block: Modern Public Housing in England, Scotland, Wales and Northern Ireland*. New Haven and London: Yale University Press, 1994.
Glendinning, Miles, Ranald Macinnes and Aonghus Mackechnie. *A History of Scottish Architecture, from the Renaissance to the Present Day*. Edinburgh: Edinburgh University Press, 1997.
Gold, John R. *The Practice of Modernism: Modern Architects and Urban Transformation, 1954–1972*. Abingdon: Routledge, 2007.
Goldthorpe, John H., David Lockwood, Frank Bechhofer and Jennifer Platt. *The Affluent Worker in the Class Structure*. Orig. 1969, reissued Cambridge: Cambridge University Press, 2010.
Goodlad, R., and S. Scott. 'Polo Mint Planning: A Review of Strategies for Housing in the Scottish New Towns'. Discussion Paper 33, Centre for Housing Research, University of Glasgow, 1989.
Gosling, David. *Gordon Cullen: Visions of Urban Design*. London: Academy Editions, 1996.
Gosseye, Janina. '"Uneasy Bedfellows" Conceiving Urban Megastructures: Precarious Public–private Partnerships in Post-war British New Towns'. *Planning Perspectives* 34, no. 6 (2019): 937–57.
Haggett, Ali. *Desperate Housewives: Neuroses and the Domestic Environment 1945–1970*. London: Pickering & Chatto, 2012.
Hanley, Lynsey. *Estates: An Intimate History*. Granta: London, 2012.
Hendrie, William F. *The History of Livingston*. Livingston: Livingston Development Corporation, 1988.
Heraud, B.J. 'Social Class and the New Towns'. *Urban Studies* 5, no. 1 (1968): 33–58.
Higgs, Leslie. *New Town: Social Involvement in Livingston – An Account of the Formative Years*. Glasgow: Maclellan, 1977.
Hood, N., and S. Young. *Multinationals in Retreat: The Scottish Experience*. Edinburgh: Edinburgh University Press, 1982.
Horsey, Miles. *Tenements and Towers: Glasgow Working-class Housing 1890–1990*. Edinburgh: RCAHMS, 1990.
Howieson, C., L. Croxford and D. Murphy. 'The Experience of 50 Years of Comprehensive Schooling in Scotland'. *Education, Citizenship and Social Justice* 12, no. 1 (2017): 8–23.
Hulme, Tom. *After the Shock City: Urban Culture and the Making of Modern Citizenship*. London: Royal Historical Society, 2019.
Irvine Development Corporation. *Interim Revised Outline Plan*. Irvine: IDC, 1969.
Irvine Development Corporation. *Irvine Town Centre Preliminary Proposals*. Irvine: IDC, 1969.
Irvine Development Corporation. *Irvine New Town Plan*. Irvine: IDC, 1971.

Irvine Development Corporation. *Irvine New Town: Broadsheets*. Irvine: IDC, 1972.
Irvine Development Corporation. *Development Profile Irvine New Town*. Irvine: IDC, 1983.
Irvine Development Corporation. *Irvine New Town 1966–1996*. Irvine: IDC, 1996.
James, Clement. '"The Cole View": Kenneth Cole at The Magnum Leisure Centre, Irvine'. *British Journal of Photography* 127, no. 6281 (1980): 1255.
Jaques, Richard, and Charles McKean. *West Lothian: An Illustrated Guide*. Edinburgh: Rutland Press, 1994.
Jephcott, Pearl, and Hilary Robinson. *Homes in High Flats: Some of the Human Problems Involved in Multi-storey Housing*. Edinburgh: Oliver & Boyd, 1971.
Jones, Ben. 'Slum Clearance, Privatization and Residualization: The Practices and Politics of Council Housing in Mid-twentieth-century England'. *Twentieth Century British History* 21, no. 4 (2010): 510–39.
Karn, Valerie A. *East Kilbride Housing Survey: A Study of a New Town*. Birmingham: Centre for Urban and Regional Studies, 1970.
Kearns, Ade, Valerie Wright, Lynn Abrams and Barry Hazley. 'Slum Clearance and Relocation: A Reassessment of Social Outcomes Combining Short-term and Long-term Perspectives'. *Housing Studies* 34, no. 2 (2019): 201–25.
Keating, Michael. *The City That Refused to Die: Glasgow: The Politics of Urban Regeneration*. Aberdeen: Aberdeen University Press, 1988.
Kefford, Alistair. 'Housing the Citizen-Consumer in Post-war Britain: The Parker Morris Report, Affluence and the Even Briefer Life of Social Democracy'. *Twentieth Century British History* 29, no. 2 (2018): 225–58.
Kefford, Alistair. *The Life and Death of the Shopping City: Public Planning and Private Redevelopment in Britain since 1945*. Cambridge: Cambridge University Press, 2022.
Kefford, Alistair. 'Global Rise of the British Property Development Sector, 1945–1975'. *Past and Present* 264, no. 1 (2024): 199–235.
Kynaston, David. *Family Britain 1951–57*. London: Bloomsbury, 2009.
Langhamer, Claire. 'The Meanings of Home in Postwar Britain'. *Journal of Contemporary History* 40, no. 2 (2005): 341–62.
Langhamer, Claire. 'Love, Selfhood and Authenticity in Post-war Britain'. *Cultural and Social History* 9, no. 2 (2012): 277–97.
Langhamer, Claire. *The English in Love: The Intimate Story of an Emotional Revolution*. Oxford: Oxford University Press, 2013.
Lawrence, Jon. *Me, Me, Me: The Search for Community in Post-war England*. Oxford: Oxford University Press, 2019.
Levitt, Ian. 'The Origins of the Scottish Development Department, 1943–62'. *Scottish Affairs* 14 (1996): 42–63.
Levitt, Ian. 'New Towns, New Scotland, New Ideology, 1937–57'. *Scottish Historical Review* 76, no. 2 (1997): 222–38.
Levitt, Ian. 'The Creation of the Highlands and Islands Development Board'. *Northern Scotland* 19 (1999): 85–105.
Life Is for Livingston: Our Story. West Lothian Council, undated.
Ling, Arthur. *Runcorn New Town: Master Plan*. Runcorn: Runcorn Development Corporation, 1967.
Livingstone, J. M., and A.J.M. Sykes. *East Kilbride 70: An Economic and Social History*. Glasgow: University of Strathclyde, Department of Sociology, 1971.
Llewellyn, Mark. 'Producing and Experiencing Harlow: Neighbourhood Units and Narratives of New Town Life 1947–53'. *Planning Perspectives* 19, no. 2 (2004): 155–74.
Lock, Katy, and Hugh Ellis. *New Towns: The Rise, Fall and Rebirth*. London: RIBA, 2020.
Mandler, Peter. *The Crisis of the Meritocracy: Britain's Transition to Mass Education since the Second World War*. Cambridge: Cambridge University Press, 2022.
McCabe, Ruth et al. 'Milestone House: The Story of a Hospice for People with HIV/AIDS'. *Journal of the Royal College of Physicians of Edinburgh* 52, no. 1 (2022): 73–9.

McCarthy, Helen. *Double Lives: A History of Working Motherhood*. London: Bloomsbury, 2020.
McCrone, David. *Who Runs Edinburgh?* Edinburgh: Edinburgh University Press, 2022.
McGovern, P.D. 'The New Towns of Scotland'. *Scottish Geographical Magazine* 84, no. 1 (1968): 29–44.
McWilliam, Colin. *Lothian*. Harmondsworth: Penguin, 1977.
Mitchell, Elizabeth. *The Plan That Pleased*. London: Town and Country Planning Association, 1967.
Nicholl, R.E. 'Reviewed Works: Irvine New Town Plan'. *Urban Studies Special Issue: Policy Analysis at the Level of the Individual Metropolitan Area or Region and the Quantification of the Causes of Urbanisation* 9, no. 3 (1972): 389–91.
Opher, Philip, and Clinton Bird. *Cumbernauld, Irvine, East Kilbride: An Illustrated Guide*. Headington: Oxford Polytechnic, 1980.
Ortolano, Guy. 'Planning the Urban Future in 1960s Britain'. *Historical Journal* 54, no. 2 (2011): 477–507.
Ortolano, Guy. *Thatcher's Progress: From Social Democracy to Market Liberalism through an English New Town*. Cambridge: Cambridge University Press, 2019.
Osborn, Frederick J., and Arnold Whittick. *New Towns: Their Origins, Achievements and Progress*. London: Leonard Hill, 1977.
Paterson, Lindsay. *Scottish Education and Society since 1945: Democracy and Intellect*. Edinburgh: Edinburgh University Press, 2023.
Peattie, Emma. *Livingston Lives*. Edinburgh: Luath Press, 2012.
Phillips, Jim. 'Deindustrialization and the Moral Economy of the Scottish Coalfields, 1947 to 1991'. *International Labor and Working Class History* 84 (2013): 99–115.
Phillips, Jim, Valerie Wright and Jim Tomlinson. *Deindustrialisation and the Moral Economy in Scotland since 1955*. Edinburgh: Edinburgh University Press, 2021.
Pierce, Rachel M. 'Marriage in the Fifties'. *The Sociological Review* 11, no. 2 (1963): 215–40.
Pikò, Lauren. *Milton Keynes in British Culture: Imagining England*. Abingdon: Routledge, 2019.
Proctor, Robert. *Building the Modern Church: Roman Catholic Architecture in Britain, 1955 to 1975*. Farnham: Ashgate, 2014.
Ravetz, Alison. *Council Housing and Culture: The History of a Social Experiment*. London: Routledge, 2003.
Reiach, Alan, and Robert Hurd. *Building Scotland: A Cautionary Guide*. Edinburgh: Saltire Society, 1941.
Riden, Philip. *Rebuilding a Valley*. Cwmbran: Cwmbran Development Corporation, 1988.
Robinson, Emily, Camilla Schofield, Florence Sutcliffe-Braithwaite and Natalie Thomlinson. 'Telling Stories about Post-war Britain: Popular Individualism and the "Crisis" of the 1970s'. *Twentieth Century British History* 28, no. 2 (2017): 268–304.
Rodger, Johnny. 'Towards the MacMillan and Metzstein Years'. In *Gillespie, Kidd & Coia: Architecture 1956–1987*, ed. Johnny Rodger, 11–20. Glasgow: Lighthouse, 2007.
Rogaly, Ben, and Becky Taylor. *Moving Histories of Class and Community: Identity, Place and Belonging in Contemporary England*. Basingstoke: Palgrave Macmillan, 2009.
Rosenburg, Lou. *Scotland's Homes Fit for Heroes: Garden City Influences on the Development of Scottish Working-Class Housing, 1900 to 1939*. Edinburgh: Word Bank, 2016.
Ross, Linda M. 'Dounreay: Creating the Nuclear North'. *Scottish Historical Review* 100, no. 1 (2021): 82–108.
Saumarez Smith, Otto. *Boom Cities: Architect-Planners and the Politics of Radical Urban Renewal in 1960s Britain*. Oxford: Oxford University Press, 2019.
Saumarez Smith, Otto. 'The Lost World of the British Leisure Centre'. *History Workshop Journal* 88 (2019): 180–203.
Saumarez Smith, Otto. 'Landscapes of Hope and Crisis: Dereliction, Environment and Leisure in Britain during the Long 1970s'. *Journal of British Studies* 62, no. 4 (2023): 988–1010.
Savage, Mike. 'Elizabeth Bott and the Formation of Modern British Sociology'. *The Sociological Review* 56, no. 4 (2008): 579–605.
Savage, Mike. 'The Politics of Elective Belonging'. *Housing Theory and Society* 27, no. 2 (2010): 115–35.
Schaffer, Frank. *The New Towns Story*. London: Paladin, 1972.
Sharp, Thomas. *Oxford Replanned*. London: Architectural Press, 1948.
Smith, Roger. *East Kilbride: The Biography of a Scottish New Town, 1947–73*. London: HMSO, 1979.

BIBLIOGRAPHY OF PUBLISHED SOURCES

Spencer, Liz, and Ray Pahl. *Rethinking Friendship. Hidden Solidarities Today*. Princeton: Princeton University Press, 2004.

Steedman, Carolyn. *Landscape for a Good Woman*. London: Virago, 1986.

Sugg Ryan, Deborah. *Ideal Homes, 1918–39: Domestic Design and Suburban Modernism*. Manchester: Manchester University Press, 2018.

Summerfield, Penny. 'Culture and Composure: Creating Narratives of the Gendered Self in Oral History Interviews'. *Cultural and Social History* 1, no. 1 (2004): 65–93.

Sykes, Andrew J.M. et al. *Cumbernauld: A Household Survey and Report*. University of Strathclyde, Department of Sociology, 1967.

Szydlowski, Thomas. 'Skelmersdale: Design and Implementation of a British New Town, 1961–1985'. *Planning Perspectives* 37, no. 2 (2022): 341–68.

Tisdall, Laura. *Progressive Education? How Childhood Changed in Mid-twentieth-century English and Welsh Schools*. Manchester: Manchester University Press, 2019.

Tomlinson, Jim, and Ewan Gibbs. 'Planning the New Industrial Nation: Scotland 1931 to 1979'. *Contemporary British History* 30, no. 4 (2016): 584–606.

Tripp, Alker. *Town Planning and Road Traffic*. London: Edward Arnold and Co., 1942.

Wakeman, Rosemary. *Practicing Utopia: An Intellectual History of the New Town Movement*. Chicago: Chicago University Press, 2016.

Washington Development Corporation. *Washington New Town Master Plan and Report*. Washington, DC: WDC, 1966.

Watters, Diane. 'St Columba's, Glenrothes: A Post-war Design Laboratory for Reformed Worship'. *Architectural Heritage* 12 (2001): 66–87.

Wetherell, Sam. *Foundations: How the Built Environment Made Twentieth Century Britain*. Princeton, NJ: Princeton University Press, 2020.

Welshman, John. 'The Emergence of a Discourse Concerning the Rise of the "Problem Family"'. *Social Policy & Society* 16, no. 1 (2017): 109–17.

Williams Goldhagen, Sarah. 'Something to Talk about: Modernism, Discourse, Style'. *JSAH* 64, no. 2 (2005): 144–67.

Wills, Elspeth. *Livingston: The Making of a Scottish New Town*. Edinburgh: Rutland Press, 1996.

Wilmott, Peter. 'East Kilbride and Stevenage. Some Social Characteristics of a Scottish and an English New Town'. *Town Planning Review* 34, no. 4 (1964): 307–16.

Wilmott, Peter. 'Housing in Cumbernauld: Some Residents' Opinions'. *Town Planning Institute Journal* 50 (1964): 195–200.

Wilson, Hugh, and Lewis Womersley. *Irvine New Town: Final Report on Planning Proposals*. Edinburgh: HMSO, 1967.

Wood, Alistair J.D. *40 Years New Glenrothes*. Glenrothes: Wood, 1989.

Worth, Eve. *The Welfare State Generation: Women, Agency and Class in Britain since 1945*. London: Bloomsbury, 2021.

Wright, Valerie, and Alistair Fair. 'The Opportunity and Desire to Buy: Owner-Occupation in Scotland's New Towns, c. 1950–80'. *Contemporary British History* 39, no. 4 (2024): 219–44.

Young, Michael, and Peter Wilmott. *Family and Kinship in East London*. Harmondsworth: Penguin, 1957.

Zweig, Ferdynand. *The Cumbernauld Study*. London: Urban Research Bureau, 1970.

Official reports

Department of Health for Scotland. *Report of the Scottish Advisory Committee on the Incorporation of Architectural Quality and Amenity in the Lay-out, Planning and External Appearance of Houses for the Working Classes*. Edinburgh: HMSO, 1935.

Department of Health for Scotland. *Working-Class Housing on the Continent*. Edinburgh: HMSO, 1935.

Department of Health for Scotland. *New Town at East Kilbride*. Edinburgh: HMSO, 1947.
Department of Health for Scotland. *Rents of Houses Owned by Local Authorities in Scotland, 1958*. Edinburgh: HMSO, 1958.
Industry Department for Scotland. *The Scottish New Towns: Maintaining the Momentum*. Edinburgh: Scottish Office, 1988.
Industry Department for Scotland. *The Scottish New Towns: The Way ahead*. Edinburgh: HMSO, 1989.
Mears, Frank. *Regional Plan for Central and S.E. Scotland*. Edinburgh: Central and SE Scotland Planning Advisory Committee, 1948.
Ministry of Health. *Design of Dwellings*. London: HMSO, 1944.
Ministry of Housing and Local Government. *The South East Study: 1961–1981*. London: HMSO, 1964.
Scottish Development Department. *Central Scotland: A Programme for Development and Growth*. Edinburgh: HMSO, 1963.
Scottish Development Department. *The Lothians Regional Survey and Plan*, 2 vols. Edinburgh: HMSO, 1966.
Scottish Housing Advisory Committee. *Planning Our New Homes*. Edinburgh: HMSO, 1944.
West Central Scotland Plan Team. *West Central Scotland – A Programme for Action*. Glasgow: WCS Plan Team, 1974.

Newspapers

Cumbernauld News
East Kilbride News
Evening Dispatch
Financial Times
Glasgow Evening Citizen
Glasgow Evening Times
Glenrothes Gazette
Hamilton Advertiser
Herald [Glasgow]
Illustrated London News
Irvine Times
National Guardian
Scots Magazine
Scotsman
Scottish Daily Express
Times

Periodicals

American Institute of Architects Journal
Architects' Journal Architectural Design
Country Life
Official Architecture and Planning
Scottish Geographical Magazine
Scottish Grocer and Provision Trader
Scottish Licensed Trade News
South China Morning Post
Town Planning Review

Digital and online resources

ArtUK. https://artuk.org/discover/stories/a-lesson-from-the-past-scotlands-new-towns-and-their-artists
Dictionary of Scottish Architects. www.scottisharchitects.org.uk
Hansard. https://api.parliament.uk/historic-hansard/index.html
Planning Exchange. *New Towns Record*, 2 CD-ROM set, 1996
Realassets.ipe.com. https://realassets.ipe.com/hsbc-alternative-investments-in-224m-scottish-club-deal/10005760.article
Scottish-Places. https://www.scottish-places.info/features/featurefirst19402.html
SUERC. https://www.gla.ac.uk/research/az/suerc/about/
Town and Country Planning Association. https://tcpa.org.uk/new-town/irvine/
The Young Foundation [Holly Smith, *A Historical Perspective. Michael Young's Legacy and the Work of the Institute for Community Studies*]. https://youngfoundation.b-cdn.net/wp-content/uploads/2023/11/History-of-TYF-and-ICS-A4-draft.pdf?x59628

Films

Scottish Moving Image Archive:
    0949 *Stonehouse: Centre for Success* (1974), dir. Robin Crichton
    1826 *New Towns* (1969) [Educational Films of Scotland]
    2227 *Cumbernauld: Town for Tomorrow* (1970), dir. Robin Crichton
    6376 *New Town Blues* (c. 1963), dir. John L. Paterson
    6844 *Town of Tomorrow* (1954), dir. Stanley Russell
Channel 4 documentary: *Silicon Fever*. https://vimeo.com/585525943/849bec81df

Dissertations

Breen, Kat. 'New Life in an Old Town. Wheeler & Sproson and the Post War Reconstruction of Burntisland and Dysart'. PhD dissertation, University of Edinburgh, 2021.
Foord, Jo. 'Conflicting Lives: Women's Work in Planned Communities'. PhD dissertation, University of Kent, 1990.
Lynch, Charlie. 'Scotland and the Sexual Revolution c. 1957–1975: Religion, Intimacy and Popular Culture'. PhD dissertation, University of Glasgow, 2019.
Paterson, Laura. 'Women and Paid Work in Industrial Britain'. PhD dissertation, University of Dundee, 2014.
Szydlowski, Thomas. 'Skelmersdale: The Design and Implementation of a British New Town, 1961–1985'. MSc dissertation, University College London, 2020.
Taylor, Jessica. 'Cumbernauld: The Conception, Development and Realisation of a Post-war British New Town'. PhD dissertation, University of Edinburgh, 2010.

Index

Abercrombie, Patrick 9, 26, 68
Abrams, Mark 138
Ailsa-Volvo 199
'Alcan' new town projects 115
alcohol abuse 166
Aldridge, Meryl 2
Alison and Hutchison 106
Alloa 7
Apricot Computers 53
Ashdown, D. 94
aspiration 156
Associated Electrical Industries 53
Aviemore 121
Ayr 117
Ayrshire 12

Ballantyne Report 7–8
Barnes, Denis 103, 106
Barrie, James 41
Basil Spence & Partners 125
Bathgate, British Motor Corporation 92, 193
Baxter Clark and Paul 125
Bearsden 15
Beckman Instruments 53, 193
Billingham 121
Billingham, John 119
Bishopton 10
Blackburn houses 28
Blindwells 18
Bonnar, Stan 34, 57
Borthwick, Alistair 86
Bott, Elizabeth 176
Bowman, N.C. 95
Brand Rex 53
Brown, Maurice 26
Brown, W. Newman 94
Browne, Denis Martin 94
Brutalism 68
Buchanan Campbell, Alexander 40
Buchanan Report 33, 75, 95
Bunton, Sam 77
Burroughs Machines 53, 143, 193

business parks 41, 91
Buteux, Harold 94, 206

Cameron Ironworks 107
Central Lancashire New Town 115
Central Scotland: a Programme for Development and Growth 93
childcare 164, 165, 178
churches 179
citizenship 26, 60, 171–2, 176–7
Clapham, P. 94
Clyde Valley Regional Plan 9–10, 26, 68, 93
Cocker, Philip 104
Coghill, John 50, 54
Coia, Jack 32
Collins, Godfrey 8
Colvin, Brenda 27
Commission for New Towns 13, 18
community 141, 170–86
    See also privacy
community centres 32, 161–2, 176
Connell, F.J. 26
Cook, Robin 101
Copcutt, Geoffrey 72, 76–7, 94
council housing 8
Coventry 36
Cowan, Ralph 28
Cowling, David 2, 25, 53, 91
Crichton, Robin 86
Crossman, Richard 73–4
Cullen, Gordon 16, 115
Cullingworth, J.B. 3
Cumbernauld 68–89
    Abronhill 85, 87
    Carbrain 82–3, 146, 147
    Cottage Theatre 162, 176, 180
    Cumbernauld Hit 198
    Cumbernauld House 79–80
    designation 12, 71
    Gregory's Girl 87, 180
    heritage value 69–70, 87
    housing areas 78–85

Kildrum 79–82, 146
masterplan 71–4
Planning of a New Town, The 68
reception 68, 78, 85–7
road layout 75
Seafar 84
Town Centre 76–8, 181
Town for Tomorrow 86
'What's It Called?' 198

Dalgety Bay 16
Daniel, Peter 90, 94
Davies, Gordon I. 94
Dawley
   See Telford
deindustrialization 25, 160–1, 198–200
Department of Health for Scotland 25, 49–50
devolution 206
divorce 164–5
Dollan, Patrick 28, 39, 178
Downs, Ian 117
Doxiadis, Constantinos 95
Doyle, R.S. 52

Eaglesham 7
East Kilbride 25–46
   Calderwood 31
   College Milton 41
   designation 11, 26–7
   Development Corporation role in Stonehouse 16, 34
   Development Corporation wind-up 204
   Dollan Baths 39–40, 181
   Greenhills 34, 172, 174
   Kelvin 34, 41
   Key Centre 40, 181
   Limekilns 30
   masterplan 26–7
   Mechanical Engineering Research Laboratory 40
   Ministry of Overseas Development 41
   Murray, The 28–9, 31, 32, 176–7
   Nerston 28, 41
   Newlandsmuir 34, 35
   nuclear reactor 194
   Olympia 38
   overspill 33
   Peel Park 41
   plaza 37
   population target 32
   Princes Street 36
   Repertory theatre 176
   St Bride's Church 32
   St Leonards 33
   Stewartfield 35
   Thorntonhall 40
   town centre 36–40, 181
   Westwood 28, 32
   Whitehills 34, 35
Edinburgh 7, 205–6
education 189–91
Elliott Automation 53
embourgeoisement thesis 138
employment
   statistics 40–1, 53, 107, 160–1, 189
   structure 191
Enterprise Trust 194
Erskine 16, 206
Esher, Lionel 78
European Economic Community 14
expanded towns
   See town expansion

family 154–69, 173, 177
Ferriby, E.A. 49
Festival of Britain 28, 60
flexibility of plan 95–7

Geddes, Patrick 9
gender roles 161–4
General Instruments 53, 193
Gillespie, William 71, 83
Gillespie Kidd and Coia 30, 32, 62–3, 79
Gilliatt, Mary 85, 87
Glasgow
   Castlemilk 178
   council housing 8
   Hillington 8
   image 14
   interwar housing 27, 50
   Knightswood 28
   National Savings Bank 191
   population 10, 92
   post-1970s revival 205
   slums 7, 10, 11, 140
   Woodside estate 206
Glenrothes 47–67
   Balfarg 57
   Cadham 56
   Caskieberran 55
   Collydean 56
   designation 11, 48–9
   housing 53–7
   leisure 62

Macedonia 55, 62
masterplan 49–50, 52
Newcastle 55
Pitcoudie 146
Pitteuchar 55
population target 52
Rimbleton 55, 62
Rothes Colliery 47–8, 51–2
South Parks 55, 146
St Columba's Church 63
St Paul's Church 62–3
Stenton 56
Tanshall 55, 146
Technical College 194
town centre 58–62
Woodside 54, 58
Goldthorpe, John 138
Gosling, David 16, 111, 115, 121, 125, 127
Grantown-on-Spey 7
Greater London Plan 10
Greenock 11
Gregory's Girl [film]
   See Cumbernauld
Grieve, Robert 4, 10, 26, 71

Haddington 12, 16
Harding, David 57
Hart, Judith 40, 42
Hay, Steel, MacFarlane & Partners 100
Heriot-Watt University 194
Higgs, Leslie 91
HMRC 191
Hollamby, Edward 94
homophobia 180
Hook 68, 95, 111, 117
housing 29–31, 33–5, 53–8, 78–85, 102–6, 124–9, 137–53
   attraction of new town 139–43
   deterioration 147
Housing and Town Development (Scotland) Act 1957 12, 33, 174
housing pathway 139
Howard, Ebenezer 7, 48, 204
Hunter, Roy 71, 83
Hurd, Robert 28–9

ICI 40, 112
Inland Revenue 41–2
   See also HMRC
inner-city regeneration 18
Inveraray 7

Irvine 111–34
   1980s/1990s housing 129
   Beach Park 123, 181
   Bourtreehill and Broomlands 127
   community route 124–5
   conservation 119
   designation 12, 112
   employment 198–9
   housing 124–9
   initial plans 112–15
   leisure 120–2, 198–9
   Magnum 121, 182, 200
   masterplan 115–17
   Microgramma type 126
   Pennyburn 127
   Perceton House 115
   population targets 127–8
   Plan for Irvine New Town 111, 115, 198
   town centre 117–19
   vernacular style 125

Jack Holmes Partnership 34
James Parr and Partners 104
Jespersen housing 55, 104
Johnson, Jim 78
Johnson, Krystyna 78
Johnson-Marshall, Percy 93, 94, 115
Johnston, Tom 4, 9

Kilmarnock 117
Kilwinning 117
Kirby, Dennis 127

Labour Party 8, 18
Latimer, Jim 94
leisure 32, 39–40, 62, 111, 120–4, 181
Leslie-Markinch
   See Glenrothes
Ling, Arthur 115
Livingston 90–110
   Craigshill 103, 172
   designation 12, 92–3
   heritage values 106–7
   housing areas 102–6
   Kirkton Campus 91, 196
   masterplan 94–9
   population 93
   roads 97–9
   shale bings 107
   skatepark 107
   St Andrew's Church 106
   town centre (Almondvale) 99–102

INDEX

Llewelyn-Davies, Richard 97
local government reorganization 16–18
Lochgelly-Cowdenbeath 10, 48
London County Council Architect's Department 80
Lothians Regional Survey and Plan 93
Lyddon, W.D.C (Derek) 71, 94
Lyons, Eric 55

Macmillan, Harold 3
Mactaggart and Mickel 206
Magnusson, Magnus 25, 86
'mainstream modernism' 4, 25
Maintaining the Momentum 205 n. 4
Mann, Jean 10
Marconi 193
marriage 157, 164–5
Maryculter 16
Matthew, Robert 9, 26, 68, 79, 93, 94
McDonald, Matt 40
McGovern, Peter 94
McGuinness, J.H. 4, 10, 25, 26
McNeil, Hector 11
McWilliam, Colin 91, 101
Mears, Frank
    Regional Survey and Plan for Central and South-East Scotland 48, 93
men
    employment 187–8
Metra-Weddle Report 115
Miller, Brian 71
Milton Keynes 1, 87, 90, 97, 115, 121, 183
Mitchell, Elizabeth 28
'mixed development' 25, 28
mobility 95, 115
Monsanto 112
Morrocco, Alberto 63
Motorola 192
Munro, J. 95

National Cash Registers 193
National Coal Board 48, 51
National Planning Framework 4 (NPF4) 18
neighbourhood units 26–7, 35, 50, 72–3, 141, 176–7
neighbourliness 176
New Town
    art 34, 57–8, 71
    attraction of housing 139–43
    'blues' 158, 207
    class distinctions 141–2, 144, 146, 148–9, 174
    conceptual fluidity 207
    cost to government 16, 145
    'dream' 6–7, 155–6, 195, 200, 207
    financial strain 159–60, 192
    gang culture 179
    high rents and arrears 143–4, 147, 159
    image of Scotland 14, 68
    later complexity 13, 90–2, 111, 116
    'Mark 1' 25, 53, 71, 111
    'Mark 2' 12, 68, 71
    marketing 41, 53, 91, 198
    origins 7–10
    recent reception 70, 208
    religious divisions 179
    second generation residents 6, 147, 177–8
    selection of residents 85–6, 141, 174
New Towns Act 1946 1, 10
New Towns Record 3
Newton Mearns 15
Nippon Electrical Company (NEC) 107, 193
Nissan/Datsun 16
North Buckinghamshire New City 115
North Sea oil 205
Northampton 112, 115
Northern Ireland 1
nursery provision
    See childcare

Oceanspan Report 115
Osborn, Frederick 2
overseas investment 188
overspill 10, 12, 33, 47, 92, 112, 141–2, 174
owner-occupation
    See tenure

Palmer, J.R.B. 94
Parker Morris Report 35
Paterson, D.D. 95
Paynter, M.S. 94
Peckham, Pioneer Health Centre 121
Peterleen 90
Planning Our New Homes
    See Westwood Report
Plymouth 36
Pre-School Playgroups Association 178–9
Prestwick Airport 112, 121
privacy 127, 141, 143, 154, 173
'Problem families' 161–2
pubs 39, 176
Purches, Brigadier Arthur 94

race and ethnicity 174
Radburn planning 33, 34, 55, 75, 79, 80
    rejection of 56–7, 124

Ravenseft Properties 100, 101
Read, Roger 117, 124
Reay, D.P. 27
Redditch 112, 115
regional planning 9, 14, 93, 115, 117, 204–5
Reiach, Alan 28–9
rent levels (municipal) 8, 26
    See also new towns – rents
Report on Recreation Planning for the Clyde 115
'Right to Buy' 18, 34–5, 106, 139, 145, 148–50
Riss, Egon 47
Robertson, Malcolm 57
Rolls Royce 40, 176, 192
Ronaldson, Donald 93
Ross, Willie 4
Rosyth 7
Rotterdam, Kiefhoek 82
Runcorn 115, 117, 124
Rutherford, Roan 128–30, 206

Saltire Society 29–30
Samuel, Raphael 138
Schaffer, Frank 2
schools 189–91
Schweppes 40
Scott, Alex 71
Scott, F.C. 39
Scott Long, Janice 158
Scottish Council (Development and Industry) 8–9, 14, 41
Scottish Council on Industry 8
Scottish Development Department 14, 93
Scottish Economic Council 8
Scottish National Development Council 8
Scottish Office 1, 4, 8, 10, 71, 100, 112
Scottish Special Housing Association (SSHA) 8, 16, 104, 112, 124, 206
Sharp, Dame Evelyn 73–4, 112
Shaw, Councillor Geoff 18
SHE (Europe) 195
shopping 39, 181
'Silicon Glen' 47–8, 53, 196–7
Simpson, Ron 80
Sinclair, John 86
Sinclair Macdonald & Son 125
Skefco 112
Skelmersdale 71, 94, 112
social class 141–2, 144, 146, 148–9, 174
social development 12–13, 170–2, 177
social mobility 187
'span' housing 55

Special Areas (Development and Improvement) Act 1934 8
Spence, Basil 32, 36
Standard Telephones and Cables 40
Stevenage 121
Stockholm, Gröndal 82
Stonehouse
    de-designation 5, 16–18, 205
    designation 16
    masterplan 16–17, 94–5
Strathclyde Regional Council 16–18
Sturgeon, Nicola 200
supermarkets 16, 35, 39
swinging 162

Tapiola 68
Tayler, David and Herbert Green 55
Taylor, Wendy 34
teenagers 179–81
Telford 92, 115
tenure 6, 8, 12, 15, 16, 18, 34–5, 55, 57, 79, 106, 124, 137, 139, 145–8
    See also Right to Buy
Thomson, Bill 83
Thurso 16
Tindall, Frank 12
Tinto, Peter 49
Toothill, Sir John 14
    report 14, 16, 41, 91, 93, 160–1
Tornagrain 18
tourism 121, 123–4, 199
tower blocks 34, 55, 82, 83, 87
Town and Country Planning Association 7
town expansion 11, 12
Townscape 54
Traffic in Towns
    See Buchanan Report
Tripp, Alker 26
Tweedbank 16, 206

Ullapool 7
unemployment 193–5
university possibilities 194
urbanity 71–3, 102, 115

Vällingby 68, 117
vernacular style 79, 104, 125, 206

Washington (Tyne and Wear) 97
Way Ahead, The 205 n. 4
Weeks, John 97
Weir houses 28

Welfare State 1, 47, 206
West Central Scotland Plan 22 n. 82, 205
Westerton 7
Westwood, Joseph 4, 26, 48
Westwood Report 9, 26, 28–9, 54
Wheeler, Anthony 58, 63
Wheeler and Sproson 63, 125
Whittick, Arnold 2
Whittle, Jack 94
Willmott, Peter 138
Wilson, Hugh 71, 86, 111, 112
women's experiences 157–9, 176, 178–9
    adult education 195–6
    networks 158, 178
    roles 161–4
    work 179, 188–9, 192, 195–8, 199–200
Womersley, Lewis 111, 112
Woodburn, Arthur 4, 48, 49
Workers' Education Association 158
Wylie, A.B. 26

Young, George 41
Young, Michael 138
Youngman, Peter 71

Zweig, Ferdynand 86, 138, 141, 173, 177